Health Technologies and International Intellectual Property

The global transmission of infectious diseases has fuelled the need for a more developed legal framework in international public health to provide prompt and specific guidance during a large-scale emergency. This book develops a means for States to take advantage of the flexibilities of compulsory licensing in the Agreement on Trade-Related Aspects of Intellectual Property Rights (TRIPS), which promotes access to medicines in a public health emergency. It presents the precautionary approach (PA) and the structure of risk analysis as a means to build a workable reading of TRIPS and to help States embody the flexibilities of intellectual property (IP).

The work investigates the complementary roles of the World Health Organization (WHO) and the World Trade Organization (WTO) in order to promote the harmonization of the precautionary approach in relation to the patenting of crucial pharmaceutical products. By bringing together international trade law and intellectual property law Phoebe Li demonstrates how, through the use of risk analysis and the precautionary approach, States can still comply with their legal obligations in international law, while exercising their sovereignty right in issuing a compulsory licence of a drug patent in an uncertain public health emergency.

This book will be of great interest to students and academics of medical and health care law, intellectual property law, international trade law, and human rights law.

Phoebe Li is a lecturer in Law at the University of Sussex, UK. She researches the interface between world trade, intellectual property, and technology regulation, and the extent to which this can be used to embody human rights claims under globalization.

Routledge Research in Intellectual Property

Available:

Re-thinking Intellectual Property
The political economy of copyright protection in the digital era
YiJun Tian

The Development of Intellectual Property Regimes in the Middle East
David Price

Intellectual Property, Community Rights and Human Rights
The biological and genetic resources of developing countries
Marcelin Tonye Mahop

Intellectual Property in Global Governance
The crisis of equity in the knowledge economy
Chidi Oguamanam

Intellectual Property Overlaps
Theory, strategies, and solutions
Robert Tomkowicz

Digital Private Copying
The scope of user freedom in EU digital copyright
Stavroula Karapapa

The Law and Economics of Intellectual Property in the Digital Age
The limits of analysis
Niva Elkin-Koren and Eli Salzberger

The Politics of Patent Law
Crafting the participatory patent bargain
Kali Murray

Copyright Industries and the Impact of Creative Destruction
Copyright expansion and the publishing industry
Jiabo Liu

Health Technologies and International Intellectual Property
A precautionary principle
Phoebe Li

Intellectual Property, Traditional Knowledge and Cultural Property Protection
Cultural signifiers in the Caribbean and the Americas
Sharon Le Gall

Health Technologies and International Intellectual Property
A precautionary approach

Phoebe Li

LONDON AND NEW YORK

First published 2014
by Routledge
2 Park Square, Milton Park, Abingdon, Oxfordshire OX14 4RN

and by Routledge
711 Third Avenue, New York, NY 10017

First issued in paperback 2015

Routledge is an imprint of the Taylor & Francis Group. an informa business

© 2014 Phoebe Li

The right of Phoebe Li to be identified as author of this work has been
asserted by her in accordance with sections 77 and 78 of the Copyright,
Designs and Patents Act 1988.

All rights reserved. No part of this book may be reprinted or reproduced or
utilised in any form or by any electronic, mechanical, or other means, now
known or hereafter invented, including photocopying and recording, or in
any information storage or retrieval system, without permission in writing
from the publishers.

Trademark notice: Product or corporate names may be trademarks or registered
trademarks, and are used only for identification and explanation without
intent to infringe.

British Library Cataloguing in Publication Data
A catalogue record for this book is available from the British Library

Library of Congress Cataloging-in-Publication Data
Li, Phoebe.
Health technologies and international intellectual property law : a precautionary
approach / Phoebe Li.
   pages cm. – (Routledge research in intellectual property)
   Based on thesis (doctoral) – University of Edinburgh, 2012, under title:
   Revisiting public health emergency in international law : a precautionary
   approach.
   Includes bibliographical references and index.
   ISBN 978-0-415-82361-6 (hardback) – ISBN 978-0-203-55066-3 (ebk)
   1. Public health laws, International 2. Intellectual property. 3. Foreign
   trade regulation. 4. Agreement on Trade-Related Aspects of Intellectual
   Property Rights (1994) I. Title.
   K3570.L5 2014
   346.04'86–dc23   2013026655

ISBN 13: 978-1-138-93758-1 (pbk)
ISBN 13: 978-0-415-82361-6 (hbk)

Typeset in Garamond
by Cenveo Publisher Services

Contents

List of figures and tables	ix
Foreword	xi
Acknowledgements	xiii
List of abbreviations	xv

PART I
Introduction: setting the scene   1

1 Introduction: the need for a holistic approach   3

  1.1 Introduction 3
     1.1.1 Overview 3
     1.1.2 Research methodology 3
     1.1.3 Contributions 5
  1.2 The problem: the clash between IP and the right to health 6
     1.2.1 IP and the right to health 6
     1.2.2 Institutional clash between the WHO and the WTO 9
     1.2.3 Compulsory licensing, the Doha Declaration
         and the TRIPS Amendment 12
     1.2.4 Bilateral FTA, TRIPS-plus and data exclusivity 20
     1.2.5 Medicines beyond IP: the Health Impact Fund 22
     1.2.6 The fragmentation of risk regulation in international law 23

2 The solution   32

  2.1 Ethical differentiation of health technologies in world trade 32
     2.1.1 The legitimacy of differential treatment:
         the 'like-product' analysis 32
     2.1.2 Different implications of health technologies 37
  2.2 A holistic approach: risk regulation and the precautionary
     approach in three worlds – fostering an organic, sustainable
     and sophisticated approach to IP 41

vi *Contents*

PART II
Current landscape   45

3 The development of the precautionary approach   47

3.1 Formulations of the PA 47

3.2 The origin and applications: from environmental
protection to the protection of health and food safety 49

    3.2.1 *The precautionary approach from the perspective
of 'State responsibility'* 52

    3.2.2 *United Nations* 53

    3.2.3 *European Union* 56

3.3 Philosophical elements of the PA 61

    3.3.1 *Argumentative versus prescriptive* 64

    3.3.2 *Prohibitory versus information disclosure* 71

    3.3.3 *Strong or weak* 74

3.4 Legal status and terminology – precautionary approach
or precautionary principle? 78

3.5 Conclusion 81

4 The precautionary approach in international law   88

4.1 The PA in the WHO 88

    4.1.1 *The PA in virus surveillance – the International Health
Regulations (IHRs)* 89

    4.1.2 *The PA in food safety – the WHO/FAO
Codex Alimentarius* 96

4.2 The PA in the regulation of biotechnology – the
Cartagena Protocol on Biosafety 100

    4.2.1 *The Advanced Informed Agreement (AIA) procedure* 101

    4.2.2 *Elements of the PA in the Cartagena Protocol on
Biosafety* 101

4.3 The PA in the WTO 103

    4.3.1 *The PA in the General Agreement on Tariffs and Trade* 108

    4.3.2 *The PA in the Agreement on the Application
of Sanitary and Phytosanitary Measures* 118

    4.3.3 *The PA in the Agreement on Technical Barriers to Trade* 127

    4.3.4 *Interim conclusion: the legal hierarchy of exemptions
from WTO obligations* 130

4.4 Conclusion 134

    4.4.1 *Trade supremacy in the regulation of uncertain risk* 135

    4.4.2 *Regimes conflict and the precautionary approaches* 136

    4.4.3 *Elements of the precautionary approach in the
international health regime* 138

    4.4.4 *Redefinition of the precautionary approach* 139

Contents vii

5　**The different faces of the precautionary approach in intellectual property** 146

  5.1 Precautionary entitlements in TRIPS 146
  5.2 Health exceptions in TRIPS 147
      5.2.1 *Exceptions to rights conferred 147*
      5.2.2 *Security exception 148*
  5.3 Health exclusions in TRIPS 149
      5.3.1 *Pre-grant measure 150*
      5.3.2 *Post-grant measure 154*
  5.4 Conclusion 165

PART III
Recommendations 169

6　**The precautionary approach in compulsory licensing** 171

  6.1 Redefinition of compulsory licensing through the precautionary approach 171
  6.2 Differential treatment of adopting the PA in compulsory licensing of pharmaceutical patents 173
  6.3 Precautionary compulsory licensing in a public health emergency 174
      6.3.1 *Trigger threshold 174*
      6.3.2 *The action 177*
      6.3.3 *Duty to review 179*
      6.3.4 *Other non-scientific factors 181*
  6.4 Conclusion 185

7　**Conclusion: the precautionary approach as a means to differentiate health technologies in intellectual property** 190

  7.1 Overview 190
  7.2 Problem and solution 190
  7.3 Approach adopted 191
  7.4 Proposals and arguments developed 192
  7.5 Some challenges and responses 193
      7.5.1 *A better approach than the Doha Declaration? 193*
      7.5.2 *Non-scientific factors? 193*
      7.5.3 *Data exclusivity? 194*
  7.6 Beyond this book 195
  7.7 Closing thought 196

Bibliography 198
Index 222

Figures and tables

Figures

1.1.2	Research parameter: Precaution lens	4
3.3.1	Levels of risk and the precautionary approach	68
4.1.2	Risk analysis	97
4.3	Exemption from WTO obligations	104
4.3.1	Legal hierarchy of exemptions from WTO obligations	105
4.3.4	Precautionary actions in the WTO	131
4.3.4.1	Legal hierarchy of the precautionary approach in the WTO	132
4.4.4	PA formula	140
4.4.4.1	Redefinition of the PA in international health law	140
5.3.2	Exemptions from WTO patent rights	158
5.3.2.1	Legal hierarchy of the precautionary approach in TRIPS	159
6.1	Redefinition of compulsory licensing through the lens of states' precautionary entitlements	173
6.2	The precautionary approach in compulsory licensing and exemptions from patent rights	173
6.3.3	Review of a precautionary compulsory licence	181

Tables

3.3.1	The domain of the precautionary approach	70
3.3.3	Views of precaution within different views of regulation	77
4.1.1	Two tracks of implementing public health measures in the IHRs	94
4.3.4	Precautionary approaches in the WTO	134
6.3.1	Trigger threshold of the PA in phase of pandemic alert	175

Foreword

I recall attending an intellectual property conference in Japan in the early 2000s at which Francis Gurry, then Deputy Director of the World Intellectual Property Organization (WIPO), was speaking. He gave a fascinating account of the history of the international patent system, characterizing it as a largely unreflective and insular animal which had only recently begun to raise its eyes from its own midriff to consider its place in the wider world. What struck me most about his talk – and what I took as a call to arms for lawyers and policy-makers – was his worrying claim that we have 'no methodology whatsoever' for considering how intellectual property regimes relate to other international systems such as human rights, health or the environment.

Much has happened since then, but the shadowy spaces betwixt and between international legal worlds involving IP, trade, human rights and public health remain largely unexplored and poorly understood as interconnected systems. I am delighted, then, to welcome this volume by Phoebe Li. I had the privilege of working with Phoebe while she was conducting research for this book, both as her doctoral supervisor and as Director of the AHRC Research Centre for Studies in Intellectual Property and Technology Law at the University of Edinburgh. We had a specific mandate to examine law's role in the spaces in between, assisted – although some might say hindered – by a strong interest in the ethical dimension. This book is a product of that environment and it is a testament to the dedication of its author, who has skilfully brought together insights that cut across regimes in the name of one of our most fundamental values: human health.

Dr Li's book provides a robust legal account of flexibilities within law when considering how to protect both public health *and* property rights, but it also goes beyond those spaces. It takes up Dr Gurry's challenge in providing us with a frame of analysis – the precautionary approach – that is shown to have a place in each of the regimes that is considered. In doing so, it offers worthy material for the Director General of WIPO to consider in any future account of *integrated* intellectual property regimes.

Graeme Laurie
School of Law
University of Edinburgh

Acknowledgements

This book originates from a doctoral thesis accomplished at the AHRC Research Centre for Studies in Intellectual Property and Technology Law (AHRC/SCRIPT), University of Edinburgh.

To undertake a PhD was never something that was on my 'to do' list until an emergency occurred in my life. On 31 March 2004, when I was in the third trimester of pregnancy, awaiting the birth of my second child, my two-year-old fell into a deep coma after an unknown disease attacked her brain cells. It was an unwritten history during the notorious SARS and bird flu pandemics in East Asia. The doctors failed to spot the culprit as it could have been any possible evolving flu virus strain during a seasonal change. Abbie remained in a persistent vegetative state for ten months before passing away the following winter.

At this time I experienced surreal confusion at the interface between busy birth and muted goodbyes. Therefore, doing a four-year project abroad appeared to offer a perfect sanctuary. This work has proven to be an effective therapy as I have been able to relate to the stories that lie behind the ethical debates over pharmaceutical patents, especially in a public health emergency.

I would like to express my gratitude to Professor Graeme Laurie for helping me shape the framework as well as breathing life into this project. My thanks go to Professor Charlotte Waelde (University of Exeter) and Dr Abbe Brown (University of Aberdeen) for your trust and guidance as always. Thank you to colleagues at the SCRIPT Centre and the University of Edinburgh, in particular Professor Burkhard Schafer, Professor Niamh Nic Shuibhne, Gerard Porter, Dr Kathryn Hunter and Dr James Harrison. It has been a privilege working closely with you all.

Many sincere thanks are also owed to my PhD examiners, Mr Antony Taubman (Director of the IP Division, WTO) and Dr Elisa Morgera, as well as three anonymous examiners for the book, for the perspectives and enlightenment you have brought. I am also grateful to colleagues at the Sussex Law School for supporting this work, particularly professor Heather Keating, Professor Craig Barker, Dr Jingchen Zhao, and Dr Elizabeth Craig. A special thank you to Pheh Hoon Lim (AUT Law School, Auckland, New Zealand) for

xiv *Acknowledgements*

our collaborative project on data exclusivity. Thanks to my friends for all their support, in particular Susanne Beitan, Dr Yu Hong-Lin, Dr Liu Ching-Ping, Prof Beychi Lin, Attorney Vivian Yu, Prof Chris CC Huang, Prof William Shyu, Daniel Tsao, Debi Noel, and Justice Wen-Shyue Hsiao. I am extremely fortunate to have a supportive extended family. For this I would like to express my gratitude to uncle Attorney Hong Quey-San for guiding me into the realm of legal studies, and to auntie Hsieh Hsiu-Rong and uncle Hsieh Kuo-Hsiung for their constant support and care. Finally, I would also like to thank Routledge and its staff – Mark Sapwell, Michelle Antrobus, and Katie Carpenter – for their kind attention and for the opportunity to have this work published.

This book is dedicated to my sweet little angel in heaven and all those who have been held captive by disease in speechless suffering, humbly expecting a dim light to break through the endless tunnel of heartbreaks. This book is also dedicated to my family, who have never ceased in their love and support while passing through the valley of death, and now are celebrating a new life from the completion of this book. Thank you to David, Papa, Mama, Grace, Frank, and Weikai. Thank you also to Candice and Vernice for tolerating those countless hours spent working on this project.

Abbreviations

ADI	Acceptable daily intake
AIA	Advance Informed Agreement
AIDS	Acquired Immunodeficiency Syndrome
ALOP	Appropriate/acceptable level of protection
ANVISA	National Health Vigilance Agency
BSE	Bovine spongiform encephalopathy
CBD	Convention on Biological Diversity
CESCR	Committee on Economic, Social and Cultural Rights
CIPIH	Commission on Intellectual Property Rights, Innovation and Public Health
CFI	Court of First Instance
Codex	Codex Alimentarius
CPB	Cartagena Protocol on Biosafety
DSB	Dispute Settlement Body
DSS	Dispute Settlement System
DoH	Department of Health
EC	European Community
ECJ	European Court of Justice
ECtHR	European Court of Human Rights
EEA	European Environment Agency
EIA	Environmental Impact Assessment
EMP	Essential Medicines and Pharmaceutical Policies
EPC	European Patent Convention
EPO	European Patent Office
ERMH	Emergency Risk Management for Health
EU	European Union
FAO	Food and Agriculture Organization of the United Nations
GATT	General Agreement on Tariffs and Trade 1947
GMOs	Genetically modified organisms
GOARN	Global Outbreak Alert and Response Network
GPO	Government Pharmaceutical Organization
HIF	Health Impact Fund
HIV/AIDS	Human Immunodeficiency Virus/Acquired Immunodeficiency Syndrome

xvi *Abbreviations*

ICCPR	International Covenant on Civil and Political Rights 1966
ICESCR	International Covenant on Economic, Social and Cultural Rights 1966
ICJ	International Court of Justice
IDPA	Information Disclosure Precautionary Approach
IHRs	International Health Regulations
INPI	Instituto Nacional da Propriedade Industrial (National Institute of Industrial Property)
IP	Intellectual Property
IPL	Intellectual Property Law
IPRs	Intellectual Property Rights
ITLOS	International Tribunal for the Law of the Sea
JECFA	Joint Expert Committee on Food Additives
LMOs	Living modified organisms
LRM	Least restrictive measure
MDGs	Millennium Development Goals
MEA	Multilateral Environmental Agreement
MFN	Most-favoured-nation treatment
NGO	Non-governmental organization
NICE	UK National Institute for Health and Care Excellence
NT	National treatment
PA	Precautionary approach
PHEIC	Public health emergency of international concern
PP	Precautionary principle
PPA	Prohibitory Precautionary Approach
QRA	Quantitative risk assessment
SPC	Supplementary Protection Certificate
SPS	Agreement on the Application of Sanitary and Phytosanitary Measures
TBT	Agreement on Technical Barriers to Trade
TIPO	Taiwan Intellectual Property Office
TFEU	Treaty on the Functioning of the European Union
TRIPS	Agreement on Trade-Related Aspects of Intellectual Property Rights
UDHR	Universal Declaration of Human Rights
UN	United Nations
UNCLOS	United Nations Convention on the Law of the Sea
UNCTAD-ICTSD	The joint project by the United Nations Conference on Trade and Development and the International Centre for Trade and Sustainable Development on Intellectual Property Rights and Sustainable Development
VCLT	Vienna Convention on the Law of Treaties 1969
VTR	Varietal Testing Requirements
WHA	World Health Assembly
WHO	World Health Organization
WIPO	World Intellectual Property Organization
WTO	World Trade Organization

Part I

Introduction

Setting the scene

1 Introduction
The need for a holistic approach

1.1. Introduction

1.1.1. Overview

The focus of this book is to suggest a *precautionary approach* (PA) taken in the intellectual property (IP) regime in order to enhance access to medicines in a public health emergency. This book further seeks to promote the harmonization of the PA in the IP and health worlds by fine-tuning the complementary roles of the World Health Organization (WHO) and the World Trade Organization (WTO), with a view to crystallizing the right to health under globalization.

1.1.2. Research methodology

(1) Parameters

Based on the existing human-rights arguments to enhance access to medicines (section 1.2.1), this book examines the PA in the context of international trade and international health, particularly in the WTO Agreement on Trade-Related Aspects of Intellectual Property Rights (TRIPS),[1] the Agreement on the Application of Sanitary and Phytosanitary Measures (SPS Agreement),[2] and the Agreement on Technical Barriers to Trade (TBT Agreement) regimes,[3] and suggests that a safety factor based on the PA can be accommodated into the TRIPS Agreement, particularly in the compulsory licensing provision, to promote access to health technologies and redress the access to medicines dilemma in a public health emergency. (See Figure 1.1.2, Research parameter: Precaution lens.)

(2) Limitation

On the one hand, this book aims to promote access to products/technologies which are associated with the reduction or elimination of risks to human health, specifically in the context of access to medicines; on the other hand, this book could also arguably serve as grounds to restrict products/technologies

4 *Introduction*

Figure 1.1.2 Research parameter: Precaution lens

which increase risks to human health and safety. Due to the limitation of research, I will focus on the above first scenario and set the scene on the promotion of access to medicines in a broadly defined public health emergency, which includes global acute pandemics and chronic diseases. The objective of this book is to pioneer an innovative approach to the existing IP/health dilemma by means of adopting a PA and the scientific rationale of risk analysis into the WTO/TRIPS regime. Existing arguments for promoting the right to health serve as a foundation for this book with regard to a broader use of compulsory licensing.

It is argued that health technologies associated with the reduction and elimination of significant risks to human life or health should receive differential treatment by adopting the PA in the compulsory licensing clause in TRIPS. Differential treatment in order to promote access to medicines could be justified by the harmonization of the rationale of PAs in WTO law.

(3) Structure

In order to legitimize the differential treatment of health technologies in IP, Chapter 1 will discuss the tension between IP and the right to health, a broad overview of compulsory licensing, and the implications of other mechanisms for innovation, such as data exclusivity, and the Health Impact Fund (HIF). Chapter 2 will propose a solution of ethical differentiation of health technologies in IP on the ground of the 'like-product' analysis deriving from the General Agreement on Tariffs and Trade (GATT 1947).[4] Chapter 3 will draw into discussion the current implementation of the PA and the structure of

Introduction: the need for a holistic approach 5

risk analysis from international environmental protection. A template for the PA in the international health framework will consequently be developed by means of the philosophical and legal review of the literature on the approach and the examination of relevant international instruments. Chapter 4 will conduct a comprehensive study on the PA applied in existing international legal instruments in the context of health and environment, specifically the International Health Regulations (IHRs),[5] the Codex Alimentarius,[6] and the Cartagena Protocol on Biosafety (CPB).[7] It is concluded that the implementation of the PA in international law is pervasive, but somehow fragmented and is desperately in need of a clear redefinition in the international public health law regime. In addition to the research of the PA in the health sector, Chapter 4 will also scrutinize its current application in the international trade world, namely the WTO framework. By means of comparative studies on the PA applied in the GATT 1947, the SPS Agreement and the TBT Agreement, this work finds that the current implementation of the PA in the IP regime has been seriously restricted by international political setting. Based on the above analysis, Chapter 5 will suggest that the PA developed in this book be accommodated into the IP regime to promote access to essential medicines. We will then employ the precautionary template developed in Chapter 3 to redefine the compulsory licensing mechanism, and also to assess whether this differentiation of pharmaceutical technologies in compulsory licensing will be in compliance with WTO Members' (Members') obligations in WTO law. We will also examine the legal status of the compulsory licensing provision in the WTO framework, and reaffirm states' precautionary entitlements to grant a compulsory licence in a public health emergency. It is further suggested that the flexibilities in the compulsory licensing clause can be embodied by means of adopting a margin of safety to provide protection in a situation of scientific uncertainty. This leads to a suggestion in Chapter 6 for the introduction of an expedient track to trigger compulsory licensing of pharmaceutical technologies that are strongly associated with the reduction/elimination of risks to human life or health.

1.1.3. *Contributions*

TRIPS flexibilities that can be used to address public health concerns include provisions relating to objectives and principles, transitional periods for implementation of TRIPS, exhaustion of rights, exceptions to patent rights, and compulsory licences (Matthews 2011: 17). There is existing literature exploring the PA incorporated into domestic patent law prior to the issue of a patent (pre-grant), explicitly through exclusions to patentable subject matter based on five criteria: morality, public policy (or public order), legality, public health and environmental harm (Kolitch 2006: 246; Murphy 2009: 657–8).[8] Yet little has been addressed on the PA adopted on issues after a patent is issued (post-grant), specifically related to compulsory licensing.[9]

6 *Introduction*

The contribution of this book would be to develop a workable procedure to take advantage of applying the PA as the flexibilities in TRIPS that would specifically boost states' confidence in compulsory licensing, and to safeguard access to medicines in a public health emergency. This rationale developed in this book could also serve as a basis for the moderation of data exclusivity,[10] as well as the application to other technologies associated with the reduction of risks to the environment and human health, for example, the patenting strategy for climate change technologies.

1.2. The problem: the clash between IP and the right to health

After the WTO TRIPS entered into force in 1995, when exclusive patent protection for all fields of technology without discrimination became mandatory, debates over the legitimacy of patents for essential medicines and whether it threatens access have reached a climax. Attentions have been drawn to the discussions on the nature of and the limitations on IP. The tension between these two rights has been further evidenced by the extension of the terms and scope of IP and the increasing occurrence of global pandemics, especially in developing and underdeveloped countries, where a security net of a well-established national health system is absent or insufficient.

1.2.1. *IP and the right to health*

(1) *IP as a human right*

The right to health and the right to intellectual property are recognized as two distinct human rights enshrined in international human rights instruments. Article 27 of the Universal Declaration of Human Rights provides that everyone has the right to the protection of the moral and material interests resulting from any scientific, literary or artistic production of which he is the author. The International Covenant on Economic, Social and Cultural Rights (ICESCR) also recognizes such a right in Article 15.1(c). In comparing intellectual property rights (IPRs) against the right to health, the United Nations (UN) Committee on Economic, Social and Cultural Rights (CESCR) distinguishes IPRs from other fundamental, inalienable and universal human rights, including the right to health. It is stated in the General Comment 17 that IPRs are generally of a temporary nature, and may be allocated, limited in time and scope, traded, amended and even forfeited, and can be revoked, licensed or assigned to someone else. The UN CESCR further adopted a statement on human rights and intellectual property which emphasizes that human rights are fundamental as they derive from the human person, whereas IPRs derived from IP systems are instrumental, in that they are a means by which states seek to provide incentives for inventiveness. It is also stressed that traditionally IPRs provide protection to individual authors and inventors; however, they are increasingly focused on protecting business and corporate interests and investments.[11] The UN Commission on Human Rights further recognizes that IPRs can provide incentives to stimulate innovation; they can also conflict with, or have adverse implications for, the right to health.[12]

(2) The right to health

The United Nations Charter states that, based on the principle of equal rights of peoples, the UN should promote 'higher standards of living' and 'solutions of international economic, social, health, and related problems' (Article 55(a), (b) United Nations Charter 1945). The Universal Declaration of Human Rights (UDHR) provides that 'Everyone has the right to a standard of living adequate for the health and well-being of himself and of his family, including food, clothing, housing and medical care and necessary social services' (Article 25(1) Universal Declaration of Human Rights, UDHR 1948). Further, the ICESCR states that States Parties should achieve the full realization of everyone's right to enjoy the highest attainable standard of health by taking steps necessary for the prevention, treatment and control of epidemic (Article 12(1) ICESCR).[13] It enumerates a number of steps to be taken by States Parties to achieve the full realization of this right, which includes the right to prevention, treatment and control of disease, and the right to health facilities, goods and services (Article 12.2 ICESCR). The right to prevention, treatment and control of disease includes the creation of a system of urgent medical care in emergency situations (Article 12.2(c) ICESCR). The right to health facilities, goods and services includes appropriate treatment of prevalent diseases, and the provision of essential drugs (Article 12.2(d) ICESCR).[14]

The implementation of the ICESCR is monitored by the CESCR. The Committee specifies 'Availability, Accessibility, Acceptability, Quality' as essential components for the fulfilment of the right to health.[15] General Comment No. 14 is the official interpretations by the CESCR surrounding the issue of the right to health, which acknowledges a collective right to public health through the modernization of state obligations under Article 12 of the ICESCR.[16] It imposes three types of obligations on States Parties with respect to the right to health which includes 'the obligation to respect, protect and fulfil'.[17] Moreover, States Parties also bear international obligations to ensure municipal public health laws comply with their international obligations in relation to Article 12.[18] It spells out the core obligations of States Parties including 'to provide essential drugs, as from time to time defined under the WHO Action Programme on Essential Drugs' and 'to adopt and implement a national public health strategy and plan of action, on the basis of epidemiological evidence, addressing the health concerns of the whole population; the strategy and plan of action shall be devised, and periodically reviewed, on the basis of a participatory and transparent process ...'.[19]

8   *Introduction*

The United Nations Millennium Project sets out that improving health and reversing the spread of HIV/AIDS and other major diseases is one of the primary targets of the Millennium Development Goals (MDGs). Providing access to essential drugs in developing countries in cooperation with pharmaceutical companies is specifically within the ambit of developing a global partnership for development.[20]

(3) Domestic constitutional rights

Following from the universal right to health provisions enshrined in the above international legal instruments, several nations accordingly spell out the right to health in their constitutions. For example, the Constitution of South Africa provides that everyone has the right to have access to a health care service and that the state must take reasonable legislative and other measures to achieve the progressive realization of these rights (Sections 27(1) (a) and 27(2) Constitution of the Republic of South Africa, No. 108 of 1996). It further states that every child has the right to basic nutrition, shelter, health care services and social services (Section 28(1) (b)). Similarly, the right to health is also enshrined in the Constitution of the Federal Republic of Brazil (*Constituição da República Federativa do Brasil*), which states that '[H]ealth is a right of all and a duty of the State and shall be guaranteed by means of social and economic policies aimed at reducing the risk of illness' (Article 196). It explicitly articulates that the nature of health actions and services is of public importance. It is acknowledged that the right to access to medicines is derived from domestic implementing legislations (Article 197). For example, it provides that the Brazilian national health system 'must be responsible for promoting full medical assistance, which includes pharmaceutical assistance' (Article 6 (I) (d) of Law 8.080/90). The Brazilian Federal Government consequently began free delivery of antiretroviral drugs (ARVs) to HIV/AIDS patients from 1990 by negotiating price reduction for ARVs (Correa and Matthews 2011: 13).

Further, the Constitution of India provides that no person shall be deprived of his life or personal liberty except according to procedure established by law (Article 21). In order to protect the right to life enshrined in the Constitution, the Committee on the Revision of the Patents Laws (1957–59) recommended the granting of patents in areas such as food and medicines be curtailed for fear that the high price of patented products could deny access to essential resources and violate the right to life (Matthews 2011: 164). The Committee further recommended that patented inventions were worked locally to facilitate industrial development and that compulsory licensing was to be adopted where foreign patent owners failed to work the invention locally (Matthews 2011: 164).

In view of this, this book is based upon the above right to health claims widely promulgated in international and domestic instruments, and argues that the adoption of a precautionary approach in the IP regime would

Introduction: the need for a holistic approach 9

enhance the right to health under the existing legal framework, with a view to harmonizing the practice of risk regulation in international law, specifically through reconciling the tension between international trade and international health.

1.2.2. Institutional clash between the WHO and the WTO

The rise of non-state actors, including the WHO and the WTO, and their increasing impact on the global public health system demonstrate the need for global governance. In some situations, non-state actors are directly involved in formulating rules that affect public health nationally and globally (Fidler 2002: 150). In an era of globalization, states can survive in a public health emergency only through global collaboration (Sell 2004: 363; Fidler 2002: 151).[21] We will focus our discussion on the linkage of the WHO and the WTO where the institutional clash between the two demonstrates the typical tension between international trade and international health, particularly in a public health emergency.

The goal of the WHO is to ensure the right of everyone to the enjoyment of the highest attainable standard of physical and mental health (the right to health).[22] The protection of human health and safety is regarded as the first priority in the WHO regime (von Tigerstrom 2005: 46). Yet the principles of the WTO are free trade and non-discrimination, which stress the value of free movement of goods and IP protection. On the one hand, the promotion of free trade in order to promote public health is currently stressed by India and Brazil in their recent complaints against the EU and the Netherlands where the complainants argue that the seizure of generic medicines in transit creates unnecessary barriers to free trade.[23] On the other hand, the rule-based character of the WTO, in certain circumstances, would nevertheless create institutional conflict with the role of the WHO as the world leader for promoting health. For example, Lin laments the marginalized role of the WHO as opposed to the WTO in trade responses to the recent H1N1 influenza outbreak in 2009 (Lin 2010: 515). It is observed that the role of the WHO has been overshadowed by the WTO's more effective Dispute Settlement System (DSS) (Kelly 2006: 79). Member States of these two institutions would prefer the WTO procedure in order to resolve health-related disputes. However, Bloche and Jungman express the concern that the dependence on the WTO DSS in resolving health disputes would significantly limit national regulatory authority in health policy-making (Bloche and Jungman 2003: 529). Moreover, the WTO DSS is not obliged to use guidance or advice from the WHO as the basis in determining health-related disputes. The WHO's influence on resolving health disputes in international fora therefore remains relatively weak.

The WTO TRIPS Agreement is the first international agreement that provides minimum-standard protection for pharmaceutical patents. Members of the WTO are obliged to comply with these standards by modifying their

10 *Introduction*

domestic legislation. After the TRIPS Agreement came into force, the UN Commissions on Human Rights Resolution called upon states to refrain from taking measures which would deny or limit equal access for all persons to pharmaceutical products used to treat pandemics such as HIV/AIDS, tuberculosis, malaria or other common infections.[24] The Resolution also urges states to safeguard access to pharmaceutical products by adapting national legislation in order to make full use of the flexibilities in the TRIPS Agreement.[25]

(1) The WHO

With the emergence of the HIV/AIDS pandemic in the 1980s and the discovery of effective treatments in the mid-1990s, the future of patients' treatment appeared to be dominated by the pricing and IP protection of drugs. Hence the WHO proposed the use of TRIPS safeguards to ensure access to essential drugs.[26] The WHO also issued the 'Globalization and Access to Drugs' report to address the repercussions in the pharmaceutical field from the impact of globalization on access to drugs and the TRIPS Agreement.[27] It was argued that 'public health concerns should be highly considered when implementing the TRIPS Agreement', and the report also identified how much freedom was left for Member States to enact legislation that complied with TRIPS and was consistent with domestic health policy.

In order to address the need, in 2002 the World Health Assembly (WHA) adopted a resolution on ensuring accessibility of essential medicines which called upon the WHO 'to pursue all diplomatic and political opportunities aimed at overcoming barriers to access to essential medicines, collaborating with Member States in order to make these medicines accessible and affordable to the people who need them'.[28] Several resolutions passed by WHO Member States have stressed the importance of using the flexibilities in the TRIPS Agreement. For example, a resolution of the WHA urges Members 'to encourage that bilateral trade agreement take into account the flexibilities contained in the WTO TRIPS Agreement'.[29]

Further to several WHA resolutions,[30] the Commission on Intellectual Property Rights, Innovation and Public Health (CIPIH) later issued a report of 'Public Health, Innovation and Intellectual Property Rights' (CIPIH Report) to address the needs of a growing burden of diseases that disproportionately affect developing countries.[31] It examines the role of IP in developing new vaccines, diagnostics and pharmaceuticals in developed, developing and underdeveloped countries. It recognizes that IP rights are an important incentive for the development of new health care products; however, this incentive alone fails to meet the need for the development of new products where the potential paying market is small. Thus it encourages trade agreements to take into account the flexibilities, such as compulsory licensing (CIPIH Report, pp. 117–21) and parallel imports (CIPIH Report, pp. 123–4) contained in TRIPS recognized by the Doha Declaration on the TRIPS Agreement and Public Health (Doha Declaration).[32]

ESSENTIAL MEDICINES AND PHARMACEUTICAL POLICIES (EMP)

The WHO has been working from a human-rights approach to realize the right to health in a public health emergency. The CIPIH report demonstrates that IP should be interpreted and understood through the lens of global health. It reflects the malfunction of IP in resource-poor countries, and urges states to take full advantage of the flexibilities in TRIPS.

Access to essential medicines is regarded as part of the progressive fulfilment of the fundamental right to health in WHO's medicine policy.[33] WHO's Model Essential Drugs List provides a template for countries seeking to establish their own national lists of priority medicines.[34]

However, back to the WTO regime, where 'free trade' is regarded as principal, health is deemed as a factor of exemptions to trade/IP, and conflicts often arise between contending values of international trade and international health. The pursuit of free trade inevitably increases the probability of virus transmission across borders. The collision of these two worlds also magnifies the significant role of the WTO in public health concerns.

(2) The WTO principles and exemptions – the legal hierarchy of WTO provisions

The WTO is the most effective institution in international law which introduces minimum standards for patent protection on pharmaceuticals in its TRIPS Agreement. With its effective DSS in international law, the WTO could also work to promote Members' compliance with health measures between the WTO and the IHRs in the WHO (von Tigerstrom 2005: 73). Public health has increasingly become a trade concern. Therefore it is necessary to understand international public health from the WTO perspective. The basic rules of the WTO are the principle of non-discrimination: Most-Favoured-Nation (MFN) Treatment and National Treatment (NT) for promoting free trade. It is also equipped with a number of key institutional and procedural rules relating to decision-making and dispute settlement.

The obligation of MFN Treatment prohibits discrimination between like products originating in or destined for different countries (Article I:1 GATT 1947). The non-discrimination obligations require that like products should be treated equally, irrespective of their origin.[35] Any differentiation in tariff or non-tariff barriers between imported and domestic like products will be regarded as inconsistent with the obligation of MFN treatment.

The obligation of National Treatment is to avoid protectionism in international trade (Article III GATT 1947). Its aim is to ensure that internal measures 'not be applied to imported or domestic products so as to afford protection to domestic products' (Appellate Body Report, *Japan – Alcoholic Beverages II*, para. 109).[36] Members are obliged to offer equal competitive conditions for imported and domestic like products. It prohibits Members from treating imported products less favourably than like domestic products once the imported product has entered the domestic market.

12 Introduction

The most distinctive feature of WTO law is its enforcement mechanism. In other words, WTO law is binding and enforceable. The WTO is equipped with the Dispute Settlement Body (DSB) to settle disputes among Members. A WTO Member can file a complaint to the DSB when he considers one or more fellow Members to be incompliant with the obligations of the WTO Agreements. Commentators often describe the mechanism of DSB as the 'teeth' of the WTO. It grants Members the right to retaliate if the actions of another party are found to be inconsistent with his obligations in the WTO Agreements. Hence, the WTO appears to be the most effective international trade organization.

The principles of the WTO create a rigid framework to enforce free trade; however, Members' autonomy to protect public health could be substantially restrained under the scrutiny of these principles. Especially under the shadow of 'trade retaliations' or other adverse economic consequences from countries that are home to the major originator companies, developing countries could easily be restrained from asserting their autonomy in domestic public health affairs and exercising their legitimate discretion in the flexibilities of TRIPS (Abbott 2011: 10).

Apart from the basic rules and principles, the WTO also provides a number of rules that address the conflicts between trade liberalization and other economic and non-economic societal values. The non-economic values and interests include the protection of the environment, public health, public morals, national treasures and national security (Articles XX, XXI GATT 1947). When trade barriers are eliminated, health risks inevitably spread without borders; the side effects of free trade inevitably result in increasing unknown risks to human society, thus risk regulation, as a means to modulating health and other non-economic societal values, has consequently arisen as one of the primary tasks in WTO law, predominately in the SPS Agreement and the TBT Agreement, from which the precautionary approach will be transplanted to the IP regime in later sections.[37]

1.2.3. Compulsory licensing, the Doha Declaration and the TRIPS Amendment

The TRIPS Agreement is the most comprehensive multilateral agreement on IP protection. It sets minimum standards of protection of patents, copyrights, trademarks and other forms of IP based on three core commitments of the WTO: minimum standards, national treatment, and most-favoured-nation treatment. Members are left free to determine the appropriate method of implementing the provisions of the Agreement within their own legal system and practice. Adherence to TRIPS is a prerequisite for membership of the WTO, and provisions of the agreement can be enforced through the WTO's Dispute Settlement Understanding Mechanism.

As patent protection on pharmaceutical products was not mandatory prior to the TRIPS regime, the inclusion of pharmaceutical patents is one of the

Introduction: the need for a holistic approach 13

most controversial topics in the TRIPS Agreement. The overprotection of pharmaceutical patents would significantly obstruct access to medicines. Consequently, after the TRIPS Agreement entered into force, the WHO called upon Member States to ensure access to essential drugs and to explore the flexibilities in the TRIPS Agreement.[38]

OBJECTIVES AND PRINCIPLES OF TRIPS

Compulsory licensing, which could moderate the scope of IPRs by curtailing excessive protections in some extreme situations, is an exemption from TRIPS obligations. According to the Vienna Convention on the Law of Treaties (VCLT), a treaty needs to be interpreted first with a textual approach to search for its natural and ordinary meaning; if it still leaves the meaning ambiguous or obscure, then its context, subsequent practice, practice of organizations, preparatory work, can be considered to be a supplementary means of interpretation while applying the principles of restrictive interpretation, effective interpretation, and a teleological approach (Article 31 VCLT; Crawford 2008: 378–84). Thus the interpretation of compulsory licensing needs to be read along with the objectives and purposes of the TRIPS Agreement.

Article 7 of the TRIPS Agreement spells out the objectives of IP by stating that the protection and enforcement of IP should contribute to the mutual advantage of producers and users of technological knowledge and should be conducive to a balance of rights and obligations. Article 8 of the TRIPS Agreement provides the purposes of IP by stressing that Members may adopt measures necessary to protect public health, and to promote *public interest* in sectors of vital importance to their socio-economic and technological development.

While the TRIPS Agreement aims at the protection of IP in order to promote technological innovation, it also recognizes the flexibilities of the standard of protection in order to balance the rights and obligations of patent holders. Notably, in recent years, scholars have adopted a view from human rights and competition to promote a balance in public and private interests in IP (Maskus and Reichman 2004: 279; MacQueen 2008; Brown 2012); the role of 'public interest' in the public domain in the IP regime has also been discussed (Waelde and MacQueen 2007).

Indeed, the role and function of IP is not only restricted to trade purposes. It is indicated in the objectives and principles of TRIPS that the role of *public interest* could serve as grounds for the legitimate differentiation of IP (Articles 7, 8 TRIPS). For example, if a given product or technology is strongly associated with the reduction or elimination of a certain public health risk, it then could receive differential treatment in IP. IP should be able to reflect different dimensions/characteristics of products and technologies in accordance with their implications for society. Particularly, Abbott notes that the WTO Appellate Body adopts a cautious approach against 'expansive interpretation

14   *Introduction*

of TRIPS obligation'. He argues for a broader perspective on IP by stating that 'IPRs are not only trade-related. They are also education-related, health-related, nutrition-related, defence-related, environment-related, energy-related and so on' (Abbott 2005: 85).

In addition, Carvalho notes that '[o]nly public interest justifies the taking of private rights by governments' (Carvalho 2005: 151). Gervais also argues that the public interest is considered greater with regard to the cases of 'life-saving pharmaceutical products in crisis situations' (Gervais 2003: para. 2.79). He contends that Articles 7 and 8 serve as a basis for the interpretation of the TRIPS provisions. Moreover, he argues that Articles 7 and 8 TRIPS have 'higher legal status not only for the negotiations but in interpreting the Agreement in the context of, e.g., dispute settlement procedures' (Gervais 2003: para. 2.85). Hence, the interpretation of compulsory licensing would need to take into account the objectives and principles of TRIPS. Compulsory licensing should be examined through the lens of public health, and be able to reflect the different implications of pharmaceutical products for society.

(1) Compulsory licensing

In order to balance different social agendas besides individual private rights, TRIPS introduces exemptions from IP protection. Specifically, the scheme of 'compulsory licensing' is considered an exemption from IP which enables states to grant permission to suspend the 'exclusiveness' of patent protection under certain circumstances. Compulsory licensing could be deemed as a means of equity to redress the imbalance of IP protection. Confronted by emergent global public health emergencies in recent years, compulsory licensing has received attention in international societies in relation to drug access. For example, the UK Gowers Review of Intellectual Property (Gowers Review) identified that patent rights are territorial and that a single one-size-fits-all approach is inappropriate. It suggested that different IP regimes are more appropriate at different stages of development.[39] It also expressed concerns that TRIPS may be too restrictive to meet the needs of developing countries in relation to access to pharmaceutical products. The Gowers Review further identified the conditions of compulsory licensing in TRIPS as a hindrance to the effectiveness of compulsory licensing. It concluded that proposals to amend TRIPS may be necessary to address public health crises in developing countries (paras. 4.64–4.66).

TRIPS spells out several conditions for granting a compulsory licence including anti-competitive practice, national emergency or other circumstance of extreme urgency, and public non-commercial use (Correa 2007: 305).

(a) Anti-competitiveness   The first condition for compulsory licensing is 'anti-competitive' practice, which is the primary application of compulsory licensing in the US (Love 2007a: 679).[40] The provision of compulsory

licensing in the US is mainly applied for anti-competition concerns. In other fields of compulsory licensing, the Bayh-Dole Act provides the primary legal ground for compulsory licensing while the so-called 'march-in rights' can intervene where public funding of an invention is involved.[41]

The 'march-in rights' are covered in the Bayh-Dole Act for government to redress the malfunction of patent protection through compulsory licensing; however, in practice, the US takes a relatively hard-line position of patent protection on medicines. Empirical studies show that the US Government avoids granting a compulsory licence of pharmaceuticals within its march-in rights.[42]

(b) National emergency or other circumstances of extreme urgency The condition of 'national emergency or other circumstances of extreme urgency' is another legitimate route to issue a compulsory licence in TRIPS. The pandemic outbreak of HIV/AIDS in South Africa, Brazil and Thailand is considered typical of the said condition.

South Africa had faced the pressure of AIDS prevalence in its population and it decided to adopt a law to give the Minister of Health the authority to limit patent rights through compulsory licensing in 1997. Nevertheless, the said South African Medicines and Related Substances Control Amendment Act soon faced pressure from the international pharmaceutical industry, especially from the US government and EU officials.[43] In 1998, many multinational pharmaceutical companies, in a huge number of 42 applicants, filed suit against the South African government.[44] The pharmaceutical industry argued that many provisions of the Amendment Act violated its constitutionally protected property right, especially Section 15(c) which vests the Minister of Health the power to limit patent rights by granting compulsory licences.

After the debates on the Medicine Amendment Act, the South African government decided to tackle the bottleneck of the access to medicines issue with an *anti-competitive* approach, and seemed to successfully bypass the controversies of 'national emergency' in compulsory licensing in TRIPS. The approach of examining the exclusive market power of drug firms may provide another window for states to negotiate with the drug firms and to seek to enhance access to medicines.[45]

Interestingly, in recent years, evidence shows that states tend to deviate from the 'national emergency' track and to adopt the third track of 'public use' to issue a compulsory licence.

(c) Government non-commercial use The third condition to issue a compulsory licence is 'public non-commercial use'. Despite the AIDS outbreak being a legitimate trigger of compulsory licensing, in recent years, Brazil and Thailand both opted for the condition of 'public non-commercial use' for granting

16   *Introduction*

a compulsory licence on AIDS drugs in order to avoid the implementation of the licence on the ambiguous criterion of 'national emergency or other circumstances of extreme urgency' in TRIPS.

Notably in the UK Patents Act, the production or supply of specific drugs or medicines is regarded as 'Service of the Crown' and as such as deemed necessary or expedient by the Secretary of State (MacQueen *et al.* 2010: 475).[46] In the history of British patent law, a special provision of compulsory licences on food and drug patents was maintained during 1919 to 1977 (Cornish and Llewelyn 2007: 295). This regime was ended by a Monopolies Commission Report which granted the Secretary of State power to order price reduction on the two leading patented tranquillisers.[47] The order by the Secretary of State led to the introduction of a specific procedure for compulsory licensing which was later incorporated into the Patents Act 1977.[48] In the Patents Act 1977, the Comptroller has the power to grant compulsory licences on certain conditions once the patent has been granted for three years (Section 48).

It is noteworthy that Crown use is a legitimate ground to grant compulsory licences for civil responsibility and is regarded as overriding the private interest of a patentee (Section 55(1)). Hence, the Crown's powers in domestic administration become very wide due to the vague definition of 'national security' (Cornish and Llewelyn 2007: 294; Section 59 PA 1977).[49]

The above examples in the developed world show that compulsory licensing has been established as an instrument to promote the balance of public and private interests; regrettably, in the UK, the distinct feature of food and medicines which relate to national security has become blurred in the current patent law framework. It is also observed that in the developing world, states tend to adopt the 'public interest' track instead of the 'public health emergency' track in compulsory licensing in order to avoid the controversial interpretation of 'emergency' in international law.

For example, the severe HIV/AIDS pandemic is overwhelming to the national public health system in Brazil. Notably, Brazil has the capacity to manufacture generic versions of AIDS drugs through reverse engineering, and thus the Brazilian government has achieved remarkable success in its AIDS programme by providing free HIV/AIDS drugs to any patients who were registered with the public health system from the mid-1990s (Hestermeyer 2007: 10).[50]

Nevertheless, Brazil is a Member of the WTO, and is subject to its obligations in TRIPS. In January 2001, the US officially filed a complaint to the WTO Dispute Settlement Body against Brazil's Intellectual Property Law (IPL) Article 68, which allows compulsory licences to be issued in situations where the patent holder does not locally manufacture the patented product (known as a 'local working' provision).[51] The US argued that this provision was a breach of Articles 27 and 28 of TRIPS because it discriminated against locally made and imported products.[52] However, the US received much criticism and was forced to withdraw the case in June. The two WTO Members later resolved their disputes through a bilateral 'Consultative Mechanism'.[53]

In April 2007, the Brazilian Minister of Health declared the AIDS drug Efavirenz to be in the 'public interest' domain.[54] The Brazilian government consequently issued a compulsory licence of Efavirenz to ensure the supply of the drug for its national AIDS programme after a series of negotiations with the patent holder, Merck, broke down in 2010.[55]

Like South Africa's recent preference for the anti-competitive approach, Brazil's approach also avoided the controversial 'national emergency' track in compulsory licensing. Both attempts were followed by Thailand's compulsory licensing of HIV/AIDS and heart disease drugs on the grounds of public non-commercial use in 2007 (Krikorian 2009: 29). Five years after Thailand's compulsory licences, India finally granted its first compulsory licences of cancer disease drugs on the ground of failure to work locally.[56]

When resolving the disputes arising from compulsory licensing, a fundamental question arises as to the legal status of compulsory licensing: Is compulsory licensing a *positive right* or merely an *affirmative defence* in the legal hierarchy of TRIPS? The legal status of this provision entails a direct impact on the definition of WTO Members' entitlements to exercise their sovereignty right in issues relating to compulsory licensing in a public health emergency. We will analyse the legal status of the compulsory licensing mechanism in later sections.[57]

The tension between IP and access to medicines is also exemplified in a pandemic preparedness plan. Specifically, The WHA resolution requests an international stockpile of vaccines for H5N1 for use in countries in need in a timely manner.[58] Research suggests that states should stockpile sufficient medications for an upcoming pandemic when sustained human-to-human transmission of an H5N1 virus is identified and is considered to have the potential to initiate an influenza pandemic,[59] yet questions arise as to the legitimacy of compulsory licensing: Can it be used prior to the actual outbreak of the pandemic to secure medication stockpiling for pandemic preparedness? Further, the trigger for compulsory licensing depends on the identification of a 'public health emergency', yet this phrase appears to be self-defining. Even after the interpretation of the Doha Declaration on the TRIPS Agreement and Public Health (Doha Declaration) in 2001,[60] scholars have observed that the number of countries taking advantage of compulsory licensing has been minimal due to political limitations (Krikorian 2009: 30); only a few developing countries have granted such licences to address public health needs. Correa and Matthews thus conclude that the Doha Declaration does not seem to have triggered a widespread incorporation and use of TRIPS flexibilities to promote access to medicines (Correa and Matthews 2011: 20).

(2) Doha Declaration: the promise and its limitations

In the review of the Doha Declaration, Correa and Matthews note that it has contributed significantly to providing legal clarity on the flexibilities contained in the TRIPS Agreement; however, as other factors such as TRIPS-plus

18   *Introduction*

demands have evolved, much remains to be done to give full force to the Declaration and to develop other policies that ensure that access to medicines becomes a reality (Correa and Matthews 2011: 30).

POLITICAL REALITY AND POWER ASYMMETRY IN 'ACCESS TO MEDICINES'

Taubman notes that compulsory licensing of patents was effectively dormant in many countries and had not been listed for domestic legislative review or for the tighter procedural safeguards of TRIPS (Taubman 2011: 206). Hence, the compulsory licensing provision has barely been used to redress the access to medicines dilemma, as it is often used as a threatening tool to force drug price reductions instead of being a satisfactory and systematic channel to address the 'access to medicines' problem.[61] When confronted with a firm pro-IP stance from developed countries which often use trade retaliation in response to a compulsory licensing grant, developing countries are inevitably forced to use compulsory licensing as a defensive bargaining tool (Cameron 2004: 541). Yet, in John Jackson's analysis of 'power-oriented' diplomacy versus 'rule-oriented' diplomacy, he argues that the move to a rule-oriented approach was normal evolution in human affairs as well as democratically justified in the economic sphere. A rule-based system which would bring 'stability and predictability of government activity' requires that behaviour be based on prescribed principles – that it should not be based on discretionary decision-making or simply on the exercise of power (Jackson 1978: 93, 1979: 3–4; Gervais 2007: 5–6). Thus, developing a workable and systematic reading for the implementation of compulsory licensing is desirable, with a view to increasing stability and predictability in a rule-based institution.

FAILURE TO DECLARE A PUBLIC HEALTH EMERGENCY OF INTERNATIONAL CONCERN

It can be observed from the above cases that international work to embody the flexibilities in TRIPS has been less than satisfying, especially in relation to a public health emergency. Taubman states that TRIPS only establishes general principles, and detailed elaboration under national law is required. This would include the definitions of and limitations on rights and the substantive grounds for compulsory licences (Taubman 2011: 212–13). This book therefore attempts to analyse the nature and legal status of exceptions of and limitations on IP, and to explore the specific grounds to grant a compulsory licence. As discussed above, in recent years, states have shown preference for the 'anti-competitive' and 'public non-commercial use' tracks instead of resorting to the condition of 'national emergency or other circumstances of extreme urgency' in compulsory licensing in order to avoid the undefined and ambiguous characteristics of 'national emergency' in WTO law. Their deliberation reflects the controversies of the existing mechanism for fear that conflicts may arise over the interpretation of 'national emergency'.

Introduction: the need for a holistic approach 19

At the domestic level, the declaration of a public health emergency is a prerequisite to empower a state with emergency powers which can invoke relative responses to an emergency. It can then enable government to allocate appropriate resources to combat the epidemic. However, in the TRIPS context, the term 'national emergency' appears to be vague and self-defining in WTO law (Article XXI GATT 1947), thus the question arises as to how to define 'national emergency' in TRIPS. To what extent can a WTO Member exercise a margin of appreciation in compulsory licensing under the state of 'emergency'? Taubman states that: 'A calm reading of the plain black-letter text of TRIPS would have mostly settled these questions, but the intensity of the debates created a need for political solution to reinforce the legal reality' (Taubman 2011: 48). In Taubman's words, the Doha Declaration consequently articulated what had been implicit in TRIPS and provided a political gloss on TRIPS (Taubman 2011: 48–9). Nevertheless, even after the interpretation of the Doha Declaration, it is still observed that Members appear to have been deliberately bypassing compulsory licensing on the grounds of 'national emergency or other circumstances of extreme urgency'. The grant of a compulsory licence aimed to relieve national burden of disease has been minimal, and the repercussions often unsatisfactory. This book hence aims to bolster the political and moral basis for using this measure by providing a workable reading of the text.

According to the 'Paris Minimum Standards of Human Rights Norms in a State of Emergency' (Article 1),[62] 'public emergency' means an exceptional situation of crisis or public danger, actual or imminent, and an official proclamation of a public emergency will justify the declaration of a state of emergency (Chowdhury 1989: 11). Nevertheless, empirical studies suggest that states tend to avoid the declaration of a public health emergency for fear of possible adverse effects. For example, during the HIV/AIDS pandemic in Africa, states hesitated to declare a state of public health emergency despite being urged to do so by NGOs and the WHO.[63] Notably, the outbreak of SARS (severe acute respiratory syndrome) in Asia-Pacific countries including Canada, Hong Kong, China, Vietnam, Malaysia, Australia, Thailand, and Indonesia resulted in huge economic loss for these countries from the adverse effects on tourism.[64] Hence the identification of a public health emergency is frequently made behind closed doors: the granting of a compulsory licence, however, appears to be less transparent and convincing. Thus a compulsory licence granted for pharmaceuticals in an emergency situation has been controversial mainly due to the unclear trigger threshold, as the WHO CIPIH Report indicates that 'the most significant barrier to the use of compulsory licensing is the absence of simple, straightforward legislative and administrative procedures to put the system into effect'. It also suggests that the possible grounds for the issue of such licences should be specified and urges the establishment of clear decision-making processes in order to avoid ambiguity and uncertainty (CIPIH Report, p. 19). It is thus desirable that a clear and workable framework for the invocation of compulsory

20 Introduction

licensing in a public health emergency is developed within the flexibilities in TRIPS.

(3) TRIPS Amendment

The Doha Declaration reaffirmed a range of flexibilities built into the TRIPS Agreement; it also instructed the amplifying of existing flexibilities by establishing legal mechanisms to enable countries with insufficient or no manufacturing capacities in the pharmaceutical sector to obtain imports from abroad. The Decision of 30 August 2003, also known as the 2003 Waiver,[65] would contribute to a permanent Amendment to the TRIPS Agreement by inserting an Article 31 *bis* and Annex,[66] which would provide an expeditious solution to the difficulties that Members lacking manufacturing capacities in the pharmaceutical sector face in taking advantage of compulsory licensing. The Amendment would in certain circumstances exempt Members' obligations under Article 31(f) and (h) of the existing Agreement.

Given that the Amendment would alter the rights and obligations of Members, Article X: 3 of the WTO Agreement provides that amendments 'shall take effect for the Members that have accepted them upon acceptance by two thirds of the Members and thereafter for each other Member upon acceptance by it'. Regrettably, despite the sense of urgency that preceded the adoption of the Protocol on Amendment, the number of WTO Members that have accepted the Protocol is far fewer than the requirement for the Amendment to enter into force (Kennedy 2010: 459).[67] In addition, there has been very limited application to the Waiver Decision – Rwanda is so far the only Member to trigger the said mechanism to import patented drugs from Canada (Amollo 2009: 240).[68] As the Decision requires both the importing and the exporting Members to submit a notification to the TRIPS Council on details of the licence, it has been criticized as imposing restrictive requirements which make the use of compulsory licensing onerous (Wakely 2011a: 303).

It is therefore observed that though the Doha Declaration sought to embody the right to grant compulsory licences of Members lacking manufacturing capacities in the pharmaceutical sector, in practice, the Waiver has been used by only one country, and the number of Members ratifying the Amendment has been far lower than required. The unsatisfactory outcomes of the Doha Declaration are further compounded by regional Free Trade Agreements (FTAs), which seek to strengthen IPR protection by incorporating the so-called TRIPS-plus provisions, which require additional IPR protection such as data exclusivity.

1.2.4. Bilateral FTA, TRIPS-plus and data exclusivity

After receiving considerable limitations on patents from the Doha Round negotiation, developed countries, particularly the United States, have increasingly introduced stronger IPR provisions for pharmaceutical patents, which

Introduction: the need for a holistic approach 21

demand protections beyond the minimum requirements of the TRIPS Agreement, in bilateral or regional FTAs. Commentators note that such FTAs are now part of 'a ratcheting process that is seeing intellectual property norms globalize at a remarkable rate' beyond that required by the TRIPS Agreement (Drahos 2001). The so-called 'TRIPS-plus' provisions often limit the use of TRIPS flexibilities in the context of pharmaceutical products. These restrictions include: (1) limiting flexibilities to introduce new grounds of exclusion from patentability; (2) extending the patent term; (3) 'evergreening' the patent: renewing patents after they have expired by applying for new patents for new uses of the same products (Khor 2009: 21); (4) narrowing the parallel import regime; and (5) restricting the grounds for compulsory licensing and government use. Apart from the patent-related provisions, other provisions in FTAs that may impact on access to generic pharmaceutical products include the regulation of the granting of marketing approval and clinical data exclusivity (Ng 2010; Article 39.3 TRIPS).

Specifically, as the data exclusivity regime provides independent parallel protection with the patent regime, the data exclusivity provisions could limit the use of compulsory licensing by preventing generic pharmaceutical companies from relying on the originator's clinical data when applying to register a generic version during the period of data exclusivity (Wakely 2011b: 758). It significantly delays the market entry of generic products, even when a compulsory licence has been issued, data exclusivity provisions can still restrict the abilities of generic manufacturers to register generic drugs.

There are debates over whether clinical data should be deemed as IP, as Correa notes that the data exclusivity regime is a reward for the investment in data production, rather than for the creativity or inventiveness involved in generating the data, and that the inclusion of test data in TRIPS does not necessarily indicate that such data should be protected through the grant of exclusive rights (Correa 2002a: 14). In differentiating various forms of data protection in the IP regime, Taubman categorizes three forms of data protection as: (1) Data exclusivity or propriety rights, which entails at a minimum a fixed period of exclusive rights over the data, so that the originator can prevent competitors from using their data when seeking regulatory approval for their competing products; (2) Compensatory regime: the originator cannot prevent others from using or referring to the data, but is entitled to receive from competitors a share of the costs of its production; and (3) Direct data protection only: data are to be protected from unauthorized disclosure and only limited to data acquired by dishonest means, and no exclusivity or compensation is provided (Taubman 2008a: 595).

Article 39.3 of the TRIPS Agreement provides that WTO Members protect undisclosed data from *unfair commercial use* when considerable effort was involved in obtaining that data, and where that data was used to register new chemical entities. Article 39.3 does not oblige Members to observe data exclusivity, but Members are required to prevent leakage

22 *Introduction*

to competitors of data submitted to the regulatory authority for marketing approval (Yamane 2011: 471). In other words, TRIPS requires the protection of the test data under the framework of unfair competition, but data exclusivity provisions in regional or bilateral FTAs demand the grant of exclusive rights under a *sui generis* regime for a period of at least five years (Correa 2009: 370).

It is stressed by the joint project by the United Nations Conference on Trade and Development and the International Centre for Trade and Sustainable Development (UNCTAD-ICTSD) that the reasoning behind clinical data protection is relevant in situations where patent law fails to provide protection of the originator's investment in research in order to acquire such data (UNCTAD-ICTSD 2005: 538). This includes the situation where an active component would soon be out of patent or when the drug is based on a combination of known substances used in a novel manner. It then begs the question as to the necessity of an additional data exclusivity regime when patent protection is already in place for rewarding the originator's investment in research and development. Developing countries should be aware of the recent development of the inclusion of data exclusivity in regional or bilateral FTAs which significantly limits existing TRIPS flexibilities in this respect.

1.2.5. Medicines beyond IP: the Health Impact Fund

In view of the dissatisfactions caused by the imbalance between innovation and access to patent protection in the pharmaceutical sector, Pogge notes that the current globalized patent regime has resulted in the following seven undesirable problems: high prices due to the profit-maximizing monopoly system; neglect of diseases concentrated among the poor as innovation is awarded patent protection; bias (favours) towards maintenance drugs instead of curative or preventive drugs; wastefulness resulting from global patent filing and enforcement against generic companies; increasing counterfeiting; excess marketing; and the last mile problem, which indicates that the patent system only provides incentives for pharmaceutical companies to disregard the medical needs of the poor (Pogge 2010: 139–42). Pogge further notes that despite the reaffirmation in the Doha Declaration, governments daring to issue compulsory licences are resented by pharmaceutical companies and routinely censured and penalized by the rich-country governments (Pogge 2010: 142). Pogge questions the legitimacy of imposing a huge mark-up for IP on poor patients, and effectively excluding them from the medicines they need for survival. He further argues that compulsory licensing would serve to free poor patients from being prevented from buying medicines from willing suppliers at competitive market prices. He then criticizes the injustice and unfairness brought by the current patent monopoly system, and proposes the complementary public 'Health Impact Fund' (HIF) regime as an alternative

Introduction: the need for a holistic approach 23

to fund pharmaceutical innovation,[69] which aims to allow poor patients their freedom of access by reducing the monopoly rents.

Pogge's proposal to reform the current patent system involves six elements: a promise to reward any successful new medicine in proportion to its success; the success of a medicine to be assessed by the reduction in human morbidity; the rewards claimed to be tied to what the medicine actually achieves; a two-track system including the development of the new high-impact medicines for poor patients and the conventional patent track for low-impact medicines; price to be no higher than the lowest feasible cost of production and distribution; and the system to be funded by governments as a public good. He therefore urges that an international agreement should be introduced to reinforce the commitment of countries to the HIF scheme (Pogge 2010: 148–9).

Pogge argues that the HIF scheme has better prospects for success in protecting poor patients' right to access. As the HIF scheme is extremely ambitious in requiring substantial donations from national governments, a question needs to be addressed as to its practicality from the perspective of IP. Such concerns include the unclear relation between the HIF and the patent system – whether it would exacerbate the expansionist trend of IP – and the lack of sufficient empirical evidence to justify public funding for the already very wealthiest pharmaceutical companies (Liddell 2010: 156).

Based on the above considerations, although the HIF seems to provide a complementary alternative to redress the patent system, it is still in its infancy and its cost-effectiveness remains to be seen. Due to the uncertainties about the TRIPS Amendment, TRIPS-Plus provisions, and the future development of the HIF, for the time being, in order to maximize the flexibilities in IP within the current framework, the aim of this book is to foster a workable reading of the existing text. The following section will provide an introduction to the rationale of risk regulation, and the precautionary approach (PA) will be adopted as a lens through which to interpret the current patent system in the following chapters.

1.2.6. *The fragmentation of risk regulation in international law*

From the late twentieth century onwards, several global virus transmissions have challenged the values and rights of states in the international legal framework. A new generation of risks arising from viruses, persistent chemicals, pollution, nuclear disarmament, ocean fisheries, biotechnology, and climate change has posed threats to human life and health in the era of globalization (De Sadeleer 2008: 150–5). The emergence of these newly discovered infectious diseases exposes the lack of a mature legal framework in international public health to provide prompt, concrete and specific guidance during a large-scale emergency.

For example, the rise of the Acquired Immunodeficiency Syndrome (HIV/ AIDS) brought the issue of access to essential drugs to the international forum

24   Introduction

in the late twentieth century.[70] Moreover, the SARS outbreak in 2002 severely damaged society in Canada and Asian countries due to the virus's rapid transmission rate which meant it could not be prevented within current medical and social infrastructure (Kimball 2006: 44–9).[71] More recently, states' preparation of sufficient medicines and vaccines for containing the highly virulent strain of avian influenza H5N1 (popularly known as 'bird flu') and H1N1 (known as 'swine flu') also triggers contention about the conflict between the 'right to health' and the protection of intellectual property rights.[72]

Health risks caused by globalization penetrate every aspect of our daily lives. Economic and technological globalization advances free trade in a world market, yet free movement of people and commodities also increases the prevalence of virus transmission (Fidler 2000: 220). The free movement of people and commercial goods is a global trend of 'trade liberalism'. When the trade barriers are diminished, risks to human health inevitably increase. Globalization accelerates the free movement of people and goods, and thus creates new pathways of transmission. Globalization of trade and travel may be the main reason for infection transmission (Weinberg 2005: 56–9). The movement of vectors of disease is attributed to the large-scale movement of people and traded goods.[73] Nevertheless, in the trade regime, given the importance of free movement of commodities and people, it appears that the WTO is willing to take acceptable risks to human health in order to pursue maximum economic benefit.

Globalization is a double-edged sword for public health. On the one hand, globalization brings about the promise of quality public health infrastructure; on the other hand, economic globalization accelerates the deterioration of environments, from causes such as pollution and global warming, which are relevant to the flourishing of infectious diseases and severely increase the risks to public health. When states compete to gain a comparative advantageous share in the global market, concern for the costs of long-term impact on the environment are inevitably compromised in the pursuit of economic interests. This is particularly common in developing countries which are striving to keep up economically with developed countries (Yuan 2009).[74] For example, Kimball describes the deterioration of the environment in Asia as rendering it the origin of the majority of newly reported human infections worldwide (Kimball 2006).[75]

It is suggested that the recent economic development via globalization comes at the undesirable price of an increasing risk of pandemic outbreaks. Hence, risk management of a public health emergency has increasingly become a priority topic in international law. Particularly, the WHO has identified and applied the principles of all-hazards emergency risk management for health (ERMH) to pandemic influenza risk management.[76] A risk-based approach must therefore be a concern for both international health regimes and international trade/IP regimes.

In view of these conflicts, this book draws the structure of risk analysis and the rationale of the PA as a safety valve into the IP regime to argue for the

Introduction: the need for a holistic approach   25

adoption of a safety factor as a margin of appreciation in contemporary patent protection. The PA could serve as a legitimate ground to redefine IP in a risk society.

Notes

1 Compulsory licensing is a mechanism of limitation on a patent right after it is issued, Article 31 Agreement on Trade-Related Aspects of Intellectual Property Rights, Marrakesh Agreement Establishing the World Trade Organization Annex 1C (TRIPS). See Section 1.2.3.
2 Agreement on the Application of Sanitary and Phytosanitary Measures (SPS Agreement), Marrakesh Agreement Establishing the World Trade Organization, Annex 1A: Multilateral Agreements on Trade in Goods. See Section 4.3.2.
3 Agreement on Technical Barriers to Trade (TBT Agreement), Marrakesh Agreement Establishing the World Trade Organization, Annex 1A: Multilateral Agreements on Trade in Goods. See Section 4.3.3.
4 General Agreement on Tariffs and Trade (GATT 1947). See Section 4.3.1.
5 Revision of the International Health Regulations (IHRs), WHA Res. 58.3, World Health Assembly, 58th Assembly, 23 May 2005.
6 Codex Alimentarius. See Section 4.1.2.
7 Cartagena Protocol on Biosafety (CPB). See Section 4.2.
8 See Section 5.3.1.
9 See Section 5.3.2.
10 See Section 1.2.4.
11 United Nations Economic and Social Council Committee on Economic, Social and Cultural Rights Statement (2001), 'Substantive Issues Arising in the Implementation of the International Covenant on Economic, Social and Cultural Rights: Follow-up to the day of general discussion on article 15.1 (c)', 26 November, Human Rights and Intellectual Property. E/C.12/2001/15.
12 United Nations Commission on Human Rights (2001), *Economic, Social and Cultural Rights: The Impact of the Agreement on Trade-Related Aspects of Intellectual Property Rights on Human Rights: Report of the High Commissioner*, 27 June, E/CN.4/Sub.2/2001/13/, p. 5.
13 International Covenant on Economic, Social and Cultural Rights (New York, 16 December 1966) 993 UNTS 3, 6 ILM 360 (1967), GA Res. 2200A (XXI), UN Doc.A/6316(1996) (entered into force 3 January 1976).
14 WHO Bulletin (2003), 'Access to Essential Medicines as a Human Right', Essential Drugs Monitor, Issue No. 33.
15 Committee on Economic, Social and Cultural Rights (2000), General Comment No. 14: The Right to the Highest Attainable Standard of Health (Art. 12) UN Doc.E/C.12/2000/4.
16 Ibid.
17 UN document E/C. 12/2000/4, 11 August 2000, para. 33.
18 Ibid., para. 39.
19 Ibid., para. 43. See also: United Nations Human Rights Council Resolution (2013), Promotion and Protection of All Human Rights, Civil, Political,

26 Introduction

Economic, Social and Cultural Rights, including the Right to Development, A/HRC/23/L.10/Rev.1, 11 June.

20 Millennium Development Goals (MDGs), see 'Millennium Development Goals Reports' (published by the Statistics Division of the United Nations Department of Economic and Social Affairs), at: http://www.un.org/millenniumgoals/reports.shtml

21 Sell defines 'global governance' in IP and public health as 'devising, implementing, and enforcing policies in a way that accommodates a broad range of stakeholders and policies'. She also identifies the WHO, the WTO, the International Monetary Fund (IMF), and World Bank, and the World Intellectual Property Organization (WIPO) as institutions that involve the 'intersection between public health, trade, and intellectual property, governance in public health'. There are still other non-state actors such as the World Medical Association and Médecins Sans Frontières (MSF) which have helped to shape public health policies in global governance.

22 The Member States of WHO adopted important principles in regard to public health that are enshrined in the preamble to its Constitution. Hence, the Constitution establishes as a fundamental international principle that enjoyment of the highest attainable standard of health is not only a state or condition of the individual, but '… one of the fundamental rights of every human being without distinction of race, religion, political belief, economic or social condition …'.

23 *European Union and a Member State – Seizure of Generic Drugs in Transit*, Request for Consultations by India and Brazil, WT/DS408/1; WT/DS409/1, 19 May 2010.

24 Commission on Human Rights Resolution 2004/26: Access to Medication in the Context of Pandemics: Such as HIV/AIDS, Tuberculosis, and Malaria (2004), Article 7.

25 Ibid., Article 11.

26 For example, with regard to the possible impending avian flu pandemic, the WHO also calls on countries to work out plans to balance the availability of patented pharmaceuticals and ensure adequate protection of populations. In the access to medicines campaign, the WHO's role is to provide advice and technical assistance to countries to help them implement the full flexibilities in the TRIPS Agreement to address the 'health implications of trade and intellectual property devices'. It aims at 'promoting the development and incorporation of TRIPS safeguards within the national policy and legal framework'. See: WHO Bulletin (2003), 'Access to Essential Medicines: a Global Necessity', 32 *Essential Drugs Monitor*; 'Access to Medicines, Intellectual Property Protection: Impact on Public Health', WHO Drug Information Vol. 19, No. 3, 2005. At the same time, WHO also explored the flexibilities within the TRIPS framework by publishing the CIPIH Report. See also: Tsang, K.W.T. (2005) 'H5N1 Influenza Pandemic: Contingency Plans', 366 *Lancet* 553–4.

27 WHO, *Globalization and Access to Drugs* (2nd edition) January 1999.

28 WHA Resolution (2002) 55.14, 'Ensuring Accessibility of Essential Medicines', in: Fifty-fifth World Health Assembly, Geneva, 18 May. Ninth plenary meeting, Geneva, World Health Organization (A55/VR/9).

29 Resolution WHA 57.14. 'Scaling up treatment and care within a coordinated and comprehensive response to HIV/AIDS', in: Fifty-seventh World Health Assembly, Geneva, 22 May 2004. Eighth Plenary Meeting, Geneva, World Health Organization, 2004.

Introduction: the need for a holistic approach   27

30 WHA52.19, WHA53.14, WHA54.10, and WHA57.14.

31 For more discussions, see: WHO (2006), 'Elements of a Global Strategy and Plan of Action: Progress to Date in the Intergovernmental Working Group', Intergovernmental Working Group on Public Health, Innovation and Intellectual Property, Agenda item 2.3, A/PHI/IGWG/1/5, 8 December.

32 World Health Assembly (2006) Fifty-ninth World Health Assembly, 'Public Health, Innovation, Essential Health Research and Intellectual Property Rights: Towards a Global Strategy and Plan of Action', WHA59.24, 27 May. Doha Declaration on the TRIPs Agreement and Public Health (Doha Declaration), adopted by the fourth Ministerial Conference of the World Trade Organization in Doha, Qatar, on 14 November 2001. WT/MIN(01)/DEC/2 of 20 November 2001.

33 WHO Bulletin (2003), 'Access to Essential Medicines: A Global Necessity', *Essential Drugs Monitor*, Issue No. 32.

34 WHO (2008) 'Medicines Strategy 2008–2013', Draft 8, http://www.who.int/ medicines/publications/Medicines_Strategy_draft08-13.pdf, p. 16.

35 In *European Communities – Report for the Importation, Sale and Distribution of Bananas* (*EC – Bananas III*), the issue was whether the EC treated bananas imported from Latin America less favourably than bananas from EC countries. WT/DS27/ AB/R, adopted 25 September 1997. Under the requirement of MFN treatment, imported products should be subject to the same commercial criteria as domestic like products. For example, in *Spain – Unroasted Coffee*, the Panel considered: the characteristics of the products; their end-use; and the tariff regimes of other Members to determine whether the various types of unroasted coffee were 'like products'. Appellate Body Report, *EC – Bananas III*, para. 190; GATT Panel Report, *Spain – Tariff Treatment of Unroasted Coffee* L/5135, adopted 11 June 1981, BISD 28S/102, paras. 4.6–4.9.

36 Appellate Body Report, *Japan – Taxes on Alcoholic Beverages* (*Japan – Alcoholic Beverages II*), WT/DS8/AB/R, WT/DS10/AB/R, WT/DS11/AB/R, adopted 1 November 1996, para. 109.

37 Sections 4.3.2, 4.3.3, 6.3.

38 World Health Assembly (1999), Resolution 52.19, 'Revised Drug Strategy', 24 May.

39 UK Gowers Review of Intellectual Property (2006) HMSO, paras. 4.56 and 4.57 (Gowers Review).

40 For example, James Love contends that a compulsory licence can be granted for anti-competitiveness if the drug price is unreasonably unaffordable for most people; if the patent impedes the transfer and dissemination of technology, or constitutes an abuse of IP rights.

41 35 US Code § 200. On 25 October 2005, the US Congress introduced the 'Public Health Medicine Act' to provide compulsory licensing of certain patented inventions relating to health care emergency and to ensure that applications under Section 505 of the Federal Food, Drug, and Cosmetics Act that are submitted pursuant to such licences may be approved. This Bill gives the Secretary of Health and Human Service discretion to grant compulsory licences to address public health crises. The patent holder should be paid a reasonable amount of royalty as compensation. The Secretary may also issue compulsory licences without the consent of the patentee to exercise the importation of patented pharmaceuticals to address global public health emergencies. The Secretary also has the discretion to adopt measures which fulfil the purpose

28 *Introduction*

of Section 505 under the obligations of the TRIPS Agreement. This Bill was proposed in a previous congress session; however, it did not pass to become law (the Proposed Act of 35 US Code Sec. 158).

42 For example, on 29 January 2004, the non-profit corporation Essential Inventions (EI) petitioned the US Department of Health and Human Services for compulsory licences of generic versions of latanoprost (Xalatan) and ritonavir (Norvir), which were both developed with federal funding. Essential Inventions asserted that the government has the 'march-in right' under the Bayh-Dole Act, and the patent should be licensed to another producer. Yet empirical studies show the government shuns issuing a compulsory licence with its march-in right.

43 South African Medicines and Related Substances Control Amendment Act 1997, Republic of South Africa Government Gazette No. 18505, Act No. 90, 1997, 12 December 1997.

44 High Court of South Africa, *Pharmaceutical Manufacturers' Association of South Africa et al.* v. *President of the Republic of South Africa*, Case No. 4183/98, 1998.

45 In 2002, the Treatment Action Campaign gathered 11 complainants and lodged a collective complaint with South Africa's Competition Commission against two pharmaceutical companies, GlaxoSmithKline (GSK) and Boehringer Ingelheim (BI). The complaint also accused the two companies of dominating the market by an exclusionary act. GSK and BI were found to have contravened the Competition Act of 1998. http://www.cptech.org/ip/health/cl/recent-examples.html#South; 'Competition Commission Finds Pharmaceutical Firms in Contravention of the Competition Act', 16 October 2003, http://www.cptech.org/ip/health/sa/cc10162003.html; 'Competition Commission Concludes an Agreement with Pharmaceutical Firms', 10 December 2003, http://www.cptech.org/ip/health/sa/cc12102003.html

46 UK Patents Act, s 56(2). This includes supply of anything for foreign defence purposes, production or supply of specific drugs or medicines, and such purposes relating to the production or use of atomic energy or research.

47 Tranquillisers Report, HC 197, 1973.

48 See Patents Act 1977 ss 48(4), 51, 55–9; Articles 8, 31(k), 40 TRIPS. The Patents Act 1977 differentiates four situations where compulsory licenses can be granted. First is the various grounds set out in section 48 and further divides 'the relevant grounds' into two categories by whether the patentee is a WTO proprietor or not. Second follows a report of the Competition Commission; third is for Crown use; and fourth is in relation to biotechnology inventions. Following Directive 98/44/EC, the Legal protection of Biotechnological Inventions, the UK amended its patent law to provide for mandatory compulsory cross-licensing of certain biotechnology inventions used for agriculture. The licence is available to plant breeders who demonstrate a technical advance. However, the UK Growers Review on 6 December 2006 noted that the provision is ineffective in the UK, and called for an expanded research exception, to permit broader use of the compulsory licence.

49 For example, the House of Lords held that the Ministry of Health might authorize an importer to bring in drugs not made by the patents for use in the NHS hospital service.

50 The price of AIDS drugs fell by 82 per cent over a five-year period as a result of generic competition. The AIDS programme reduced AIDS-related mortality by more than 50 per cent between 1995 and 1999. The rate of new infection has been controlled since then.

Introduction: the need for a holistic approach 29

51 WTO (2001) Request for the Establishment of a Panel by the United States, Brazil – Measures Affecting Patent Protection, WT/DS199/3, 9 January.

52 *Brazil – Measures Affecting Patent Protection.* Request for the Establishment of a Panel by the United States, WT/DS199/1(2001).

53 Brazil agreed to notify the US in advance if the compulsory licence is being issued under Article 68. 'Examples of Health-Related Compulsory Licenses', http://www.cptech.org/ip/health/cl/recent-examples.html#Brazil

54 'Brazilian Government Declares Efavirenz To Be of Public Interest', Essentialdrug. Org, 26 April 2007, http://www.essentialdrugs.org/edrug/archive/200704/msg00085.php

55 'Compulsory Licensing of Efavirenz in Brazil', Access to Pharmaceuticals, 23 February 2010, http://www.accesstopharmaceuticals.org/case-studies-in-global-health/efavirenz-brazil/

56 India Compulsory License Application No. 1 of 2011. See Section 5.3.2.

57 Ibid.

58 WHA 60.28, 'Pandemic Influenza Preparedness: Sharing of Influenza Viruses and Access to Vaccines and Other Benefits', Sixtieth World Health Assembly, 23 May 2007.

59 Bill and Melinda Gates Foundation (2009) 'Options for the Design and Financing of an H5N1 Vaccine Stockpile: Key Findings and Study Methodology'. The WHO has also advised states to 'promote vaccination' and 'review vaccine use strategies' from phase 3 of 'pandemic alert period' onwards. However, phase 3 of the pandemic alert period is only the preparatory period of a public health emergency; it would be difficult to legitimize the grant of a compulsory licence on the grounds of 'national emergency or other circumstances of extreme urgency' during such time. See: WHO (2005) 'WHO Global Influenza Preparedness Plan: the Role of WHO and Recommendations for National Measures before and during Pandemics', WHO Influenza Preparedness, WHO/CDS/CSR/GIP/2005.5.

60 *Doha Declaration on the TRIPS Agreement and Public Health* (Doha Declaration), adopted by the fourth Ministerial Conference of the World Trade Organization in Doha, Qatar, on 14 November 2001. WT/MIN(01)/DEC/2 of 20 November 2001.

61 For example, Brazil and South Africa have threatened granting such licences in order to obtain substantial price reductions on HIV/AIDS drugs. See: 'Public Health, Innovation and Intellectual Property Rights', WHO Report of the Commission on Intellectual Property Rights, Innovation and Public Health, p. 117.

62 Article 1, The Paris Minimum Standards of Human Rights Norms in a State of Emergency. See Report of the 61st Conference (Paris 1984) of the ILA Committee of the Enforcement of Human Rights Law.

63 'African Countries Urged to Declare HIV/AIDS A National Emergency', WHO/AFRO Press Releases, 24 June 1999; 'Mbeki Refuses to Declare Emergency Over Aids', Panafrican News Agency (Dakar), 14 March 2001, available at: http://www.aegis.com/news/pana/2001/PA010316.html

64 Krauss, C. (2003) 'The SARS Epidemic: Canada; Toronto Is Stricken from Warning List Issued by WHO', *The New York Times*, 15 March, available at: http://www.nytimes.com/2003/05/15/world/the-sars-epidemic-canada-toronto-is-stricken-from-warning-list-issued-by-who.html; 'Economic Impact of SARS on Tourism in Seven Selected APEC Member Economies' (2003), Asia-Pacific Economic Cooperation (APEC), 22nd Tourism Working Group Meeting, 2003/TWG22/016.

30   *Introduction*

65 WTO General Council Decision of 30 August 2003, Implementation of Paragraph 6 of the Doha Declaration on the TRIPS Agreement and Public Health, Doc. WT/L/540 and Corr.1, 1 September 2003.

66 WTO General Council Decision of 6 December 2005, Amendment of the TRIPS Agreement, WT/L/641, 8 December 2005, with attachment 'Protocol Amending the TRIPS Agreement' (with Annex setting out Article 31 *bis*).

67 'Members Accepting Amendment of the TRIPS Agreement', at: http://www.wto.org/english/tratop_e/trips_e/amendment_e.htm

68 Rwanda, Notification Under Paragraph 2(a) of the Decision of 30 August 2003 on the Implementation of Paragraph 6 of the Doha Declaration on the TRIPS Agreement and Public Health, circulated 17 July 2007, WTO Council for TRIPS, IP/N/9/RWA/1, 19 July 2007.

69 Health Impact Fund: A Proposal of Incentives for Global Health (HIF), at: http://www.healthimpactfund.org/

70 AIDS was first diagnosed just over two decades ago in the affluent western world, but within a few years it had begun to have the severest impacts in Africa and other resource-poor places such as Thailand. Notably, the HIV therapy initiated international debate on 'access to medicines'. The cocktail therapy, also known as highly active antiretroviral therapy (HAART) has been developed to manage the condition of AIDS patients, but the therapy incurs huge costs which are far beyond those that resource-poor countries can afford due to drug patent protection policy. A global outcry for equitable access to essential medicines for the treatment of HIV/AIDS has resulted in the controversies over the legitimacy of pharmaceutical patent protection in the TRIPS Agreement.

71 The spread of the SARS virus was attributed to 'on board transmission' on an aeroplane, and the crisis developed quickly in a matter of weeks to reach two continents including Asia and North America. Other significant features of SARS are its novelty and the lack of effective treatment. It was not until SARS broke out that researchers set out to identify it. The SARS virus evolved and adapted globally before humans took steps to recognize it. Even though the pathogen, a coronavirus, was identified in one month, after the collaboration of scientists, there was still no arsenal of medical treatments for this new coronavirus.

72 Since the first H5N1 outbreak in 2003, the WHO has been coordinating the global response to human cases of avian influenza and monitoring the corresponding threat of an influenza pandemic. The World Bank has suggested that millions of people would die and the global economy would shrink by some $800 billion per year should avian influenza become pandemic in humans. The next bird flu outbreak has increasingly become the world's primary focus in infectious disease surveillance systems in many international institutions such as the WHO and the World Bank. World Bank, 'Evaluating the Economic Consequences of Avian Influenza', available at: http://siteresources.worldbank.org/INTTOPAVIFLU/Resources/EvaluatingAIeconomics.pdf; WHO, http://www.who.int/csr/disease/avian_influenza/en/index.html;theWorldBank:http://web.worldbank.org/WBSITE/EXTERNAL/TOPICS/EXTHEALTHNUTRITIONANDPOPULATION/EXTTOPAVIFLU/0,,menuPK:1793605~pagePK:64168427~piPK:64168435~theSitePK:1793593,00.html

73 From the late twentieth century, several significant infectious disease outbreaks have occurred globally. Various types of infectious diseases have emerged and spread across borders since the outbreak of Spanish flu in the early twentieth

Introduction: the need for a holistic approach   31

century. The transmission of Spanish flu was facilitated by the ending of the First World War when soldiers on the European Continent were discharged to their home towns. Spanish flu resulted in three waves of disease, and is estimated to have infected one billion people in the world, with a death toll of 228,000 in the UK. Agence France-Presse (2007). 'Mystery of the Spanish Flu Solved', *COSMOS*, 18 January, available at: http://www.cosmosmagazine.com/node/978; '1918 Killer Flu Secrets Revealed', BBC News, 5 February 2004.

74 Kwok-yuan Yuan observes that the economic growth of many developing countries, including China and Mexico, known as the world factories, face the problem of inadequate improvement in biosecurity and regulatory measures in public health protection. Therefore people experience bird flu, SARS and many food-borne infections, antibiotic-resistant bacteria and swine flu in the shadow of globalization.

75 In addition to the SARS virus, the H5N1 outbreak in 1997 in Hong Kong also originated from the Guangdong province. The south-eastern part of China has become one of the most developed areas in China's economy, but it has also been identified as the origin of most emerging diseases in recent years. It shows that the nexus between economic development and environmental degradation has positive relevance, and that environment degradation directly results in the flourishing and evolution of viruses.

76 WHO (2013) 'Pandemic Influenza Risk Management WHO Interim Guidance', WHO/HSE/HEA/HSP/2013.3

2 The solution

2.1. Ethical differentiation of health technologies in world trade

This book proposes the precautionary approach (PA) as ethical grounds to legitimize differential treatment of pharmaceutical technologies in the World Trade Organization (WTO) Agreement on Trade-Related Aspects of Intellectual Property Rights (TRIPS).[1] The PA has been widely adopted in international environmental protection as well as in the public health sector, yet its application has been sporadic and fragmented in the WTO regime due to the ambiguity in definition and legal status.

As discussed in the previous chapter, compulsory licensing could be viewed as an equity basis to redress the imbalance of IP and health. However, developing countries have been deterred from resorting to this instrument for political reasons, specifically on the grounds of 'national emergency'. In view of the increasing role of the PA in risk regulation in international law, this book proposes that the PA be accommodated into the identification of 'national emergency' in TRIPS, and with a view to serving as a tool to embodying the trigger threshold of 'national emergency' in compulsory licensing. In so doing, we would also reconcile the World Health Organization (WHO) and the WTO agendas in relation to pandemic preparedness in order to take advantage of the TRIPS flexibilities.[2]

2.1.1. The legitimacy of differential treatment: the 'like-product' analysis

'Free trade' is the primary goal of economic globalization within the development of the General Agreement on Tariffs and Trade (GATT 1947) from 1948 to 1994. The WTO is currently the principal advocate of a global market-based economic system after its succession to the GATT in 1995. The WTO aims at the utilization of world resources and promoting the economic fulfilment of humankind. The philosophy of the GATT/WTO is the belief that, through global free trade, employment and living standards will be raised; it thus promises a large and steadily

The solution 33

growing volume of income and demand by developing the full use of the resources of the world and expanding the production and exchanging of goods.[3] Trade liberalism, global market access and the elimination of tariffs as barriers and non-tariff barriers to global trade are the primary concerns of the WTO.

Non-discrimination in free trade is a key concept in WTO law and policy. There are two main principles of non-discrimination in WTO law: the most-favoured-nation (MFN) treatment obligation and the national treatment (NT) obligation. The MFN treatment obligation requires Members to treat all other Members in a non-discriminatory way to the same 'most-favoured' standard when dealing with the sale of 'like products',[4] and the NT obligation requires Members to apply to imported 'like products' from other Members the same criteria as are applied in its domestic market (Van den Bossche 2008: 329–31; Bernasconi-Osterwalder *et al.* 2006: 7–17). In other words, if two products are classified as 'like products', then they should enjoy the same treatment in tariffs and in market access.

'Discrimination' is illustrated in the context of 'like-product' analysis in the WTO/GATT system as follows:

> The products of the territory of any contracting party imported into the territory of any other contracting party shall be accorded treatment *no less favourable than* that accorded to *like products* of national origin in respect of all laws, regulation and requirements affecting their internal sale, offering for sale, purchase, transportation, distribution or use.
> (Article III: 4 GATT 1947, italics added)

Under the non-discrimination principle, if two products are treated as 'like products', then the foreign like product should not receive less advantageous treatment than the domestic product. Any 'differential treatment' to market will only be legitimate if the two products concerned are categorized as 'unlike' products.

In the TRIPS context, Howse notes that the non-discrimination provision in article 27.1 is nevertheless very different from those typically found in other WTO treaties (Howse 2000: 505–6). Article 27.1 TRIPS bans the discrimination with regard to the 'field of technology' which indicates that intellectual property (IP) protection should be applied to all fields of technology, while typical non-discrimination provisions in other WTO treaties are with respect to the prohibition of discrimination between domestic and foreign products. He states that:

> [B]ased on legitimate social and economic objectives, a Member may well wish to limit intellectual property rights in one particular industrial sector – generic medicines is of course a classic example. The importance of *health concerns* in this sector might well argue in favour of

34 *Introduction*

limits that it would be inappropriate to impose across the board on all sectors.

(Howse 2000: 505, italics added)

Hence, Howse argues that a WTO Member may enjoy regulatory autonomy in the limitation to IP with regard to issues of health concerns. Similarly, it is also noted on the Transatlantic Consumer Dialogue that:

Article 27.1 should not be interpreted as requiring a 'one size fits all' patent law. The language in Article 27.1 ... should not be interpreted as preventing countries from addressing public interest concerns in patents, when provisions to address those public interest concerns are consistent with the TRIPs framework. Article 30 of the TRIPs regarding exceptions to patent rights should be interpreted to permit countries to address public interest concerns, including those specifically related to fields of technology.

(Transatlantic Consumer Dialogue 2000)

Further, the Appellate Body in *Canada–Patent Protection of Pharmaceutical Products* (*Canada – Pharmaceutical Patents*[5]) suggested that 'differential treatment' needs to be discerned from 'discrimination' by stating that:

The primary TRIPS provisions that deal with discrimination, such as the national treatment and most-favoured-nation provisions of Articles 3 and 4, do not use the term 'discrimination'. They speak in more precise terms. The ordinary meaning of the word 'discriminate' is potentially broader than these more specific definitions. It certainly extends beyond the concept of differential treatment. It is a normative term, pejorative in connotation, referring to results of *the unjustified imposition of differentially disadvantageous treatment. . . . The standards by which the justification for differential treatment is measured are a subject of infinite complexity.* 'Discrimination' is a term to be avoided whenever more precise standards are available, and, when employed, it is a term to be interpreted with caution, and with care to add no more precision than the concept contains.

(WTO Panel Report, *Canada – Pharmaceutical Patents*, para. 7.94, italics added)

It was also noted that 'Article 27 [TRIPS] prohibits only discrimination as to the place of invention, the field of technology, and whether products are imported or produced locally. Article 27 does not prohibit *bona fide* exceptions to deal with problems that may exist only in certain product areas'.[6] The Appellate Body articulated that the standards to distinguish 'differential treatment' and 'discrimination' are a matter of complexity, which may suggest that multiple factors are involved in the determination of the boundaries between these two concepts. It was also stressed that the term 'discrimination' needs to be avoided if the 'differential treatment' of a particular technology is justified with a precise and legitimate factor.

In order to establish the legitimacy of differential treatment of technologies referred to in *Canada – Pharmaceutical Patents*,[7] the WTO Appellate Body's examination of the 'like-product' analysis in *European Communities – Measures Affecting Asbestos and Asbestos-Containing Products* (*EC – Asbestos*) can shed some light on the standards of the distinction between the two concepts of 'differential treatment' and 'discrimination'.[8]

The Appellate Body in the *Asbestos* case interpreted 'like products' as 'products [that] share a number of identical or similar characteristics or qualities'.[9] It also suggested 'similar' or 'identical' as a synonym of 'like'. The Appellate Body described the determination of 'likeness' as 'a determination about the nature and extent of *a competitive relationship* between and among products' (italics added).[10] Specifically, the Appellate Body identified the following four criteria to analyse the 'likeness' of products:

- the properties, nature and quality of the products;
- the end-uses;
- consumers' tastes and habits – more comprehensively termed 'consumers' *perception and behaviour* – in respect of the products'; and
- the tariff classification of the products.[11]

Particularly, the Appellate Body took into account 'health risk' factors relating to the product while considering the 'physical properties' and 'consumers' perception and behaviour' of the product. It stated that '[w]e are very much of the view that evidence relating to the *health risks associated with a product* may be pertinent in an examination of 'likeness' under Article III: 4 of the GATT 1994' (emphasis added).[12] It is obvious that the Appellate Body took carcinogenicity or toxicity as a highly significant physical difference in examining the physical properties of a product.[13] It was stressed that the product associated with risks to human life and health was deemed 'physically very different' from other products which have no such health implications.[14] Products which are associated with risks to human health thus are regarded as 'unlike' other products which are not associated with such risks. The carcinogenicity or toxicity of a product thus serves as a legitimate ground to differentiate products in the trade world.

Further, in the recent *Philippines – Taxes on Distilled Spirits* (*Philippines – Spirits*) case,[15] the Appellate Body reaffirmed that competitiveness is the key to the 'likeness' analysis:

> We understand that products that have very similar physical characteristics may not be 'like', within the meaning of Article III: 2, if their

36 *Introduction*

competitiveness or substitutability is low, while products that present certain physical differences may still be considered 'like' if such physical differences have a limited impact on the competitive relationship and among the products.

(Philippines – Spirits, para. 120)

Using this analogy, it could well be suggested that if the competitiveness or substitutability between two technologies is low, even if they have very similar physical characteristics, they may not be deemed 'like' in WTO/GATT jurisprudence.

In the context of health protection, for example, the health impact on society of a health technology may serve as a legitimate factor for the differentiation of technologies. It is recognized that patent laws in many countries allow for de facto differentiation based on the field of technology, as demonstrated by the extension of protection conferred to pharmaceutical patents as in the Supplementary Protection Certificate (SPC) system in order to compensate for the period required to obtain the marketing approval of a new drug (Bentley and Sherman 2008: 349).[16] On the flip side, a product or a technology which is associated with significant health risks in terms of either introducing or eliminating health risks could be granted differential treatment in international trade.

With regard to pre-grant issues, the 'like-product' analysis developed from WTO/GATT jurisprudence may enable a new reading of the discrimination/ differential treatment distinction in TRIPS Article 27.1. Differential treatment of health technology which is strongly associated with risk will not amount to discrimination against the field of technology when these technologies have low competitiveness or substitutability. In order to improve clarity, it is suggested that the text of Article 27.1 TRIPS be revised as follows to afford a sophisticated distinction between discrimination and differential treatment:

> ... patents shall be available and patent rights enjoyable without *UNJUSTIFIABLE* discrimination as to the place of invention, the field of technology and whether products are imported or locally produced.

In other words, though patents are to be granted to all fields of technology, Members still enjoy their regulatory sovereignty to differentiate between technologies on legitimate grounds in accordance with the social implications of technologies and their particular needs. By the same token, in post-grant exemptions, specifically in compulsory licensing, it may be suggested that medical technologies could also receive *justifiable* differential treatment and that the exclusiveness of pharmaceutical patents would be temporarily

The solution 37

limited on the legitimate grounds of eliminating health risks to the public. Thus the policy-making of IP and the determination of fields of technology is within Members' regulatory autonomy.

2.1.2. *Different implications of health technologies*

(1) Appropriate level of health protection

In a contemporary society confronted by various risks arising from new technologies or mutation of infectious diseases, states have the responsibility to pursue a *high* level of health protection in their risk regulatory frameworks in order to cope with uncertain threats to human life and health (Du 2010: 1078). The protection of human health is given the *highest* priority in certain international legal instruments. For example, the United Nations (UN) International Covenant on Economic, Social and Cultural Rights (ICESCR) articulates that states need to 'recognize the right of everyone to the enjoyment of the *highest* attainable standard of physical and mental health' (italics added).[17] More specifically, European Union (EU) institutions are required to seek to achieve a *high* level of security,[18] public health protection and consumer protection,[19] and the WTO recognizes Members' policy to pursue 'zero risk' health protection.[20] States are free to achieve their appropriate level of protection (ALOP) in international law (Du 2010: 1107).

Regarding domestic risk regulations, the highest French administrative court also took a PA concerning AIDS-contaminated blood. It was concluded by *Commissaire du Gouvernement Légal* that: '[i]n a situation of risk, a hypothesis that has not been invalidated should provisionally be considered valid, even if it has not been formally demonstrated' (De Sadeleer 2008: 131). In other words, in order to minimize potential threats to public health, when risks to human life or health are involved, a government may be legitimate in taking *extra caution* before a full scientific assessment of the risks has been carried out.

(2) Health risks as a legitimate factor of the 'like-product' analysis

Health technologies, which are strongly associated with risk to human life and health, would contribute to legitimate social and economic objectives. For example, in *Canada – Pharmaceutical Patents*,[21] Cuba as a third party presented arguments in favour of differential treatment of pharmaceutical product inventions by noting that: 'The subject of patent protection for pharmaceutical products had always warranted special attention from the legislative and doctrinal point of view, a fact easily attributed to the nature of the products involved and their social impact.'[22] It also restated the Panel's observation of the complex issues concerning the scope of patent protection of pharmaceutical products in *India – Patent Protection for Pharmaceutical and Agricultural Chemical Products*.[23] Moreover, Cuba identified the '*particularity*'

38   *Introduction*

of the pharmaceutical sector by recognizing its fundamental role for research; the 'vulnerability' to imitation; the unique market and competition model; and its subjection to strict control by the public authorities.[24]

Thus, based on the above arguments and the 'like-product' analysis in the *Asbestos* case, a health/risk factor could as well legitimately distinguish fields of technology. Regrettably, the Panel in *Canada – Pharmaceutical Patents* did not consider whether measures limited to a particular area of technology are 'discriminatory', or whether 'under certain circumstances they may be justified as special measures needed to restore equality of treatment to the area of technology in question'.[25] There appears to be a certain scope for distinction between discrimination and justifiable differential treatment. Therefore, I propose to adopt the 'like-product' analysis as an objective threshold device to differentiate the 'unlikeness' of health technologies from other technologies in order to explore the extent to which health technologies could be granted legitimate differential treatment in compulsory licensing.

When *health risk* is regarded as a legitimate factor in the 'like-product' analysis in the Appellate Body's ruling, it can further be argued that health technologies strongly associated with the elimination of risks to human life or health can be distinguished from other technologies by the same 'likeness' test. Following on from the likeness analysis, if two products are deemed 'unlike', differential treatment of these products is subsequently legitimate. Likewise, if two technologies are identified 'unlike' under the likeness analysis, differential treatment of these technologies would be legitimate. For example, if a certain pharmaceutical technology, which acts as a vital instrument to control or eliminate the spread of an acute infectious disease, could be categorized as 'unlike' a beauty-treatment technology; the differential treatment of the given pharmaceutical technology in the context of IP and compulsory licensing would then not amount to discrimination.

In view of this, the likeness analysis can demonstrate the 'unlikeness' characteristic of health technologies associated with the elimination of significant risks to human life and other technologies which are not directly relevant to the preservation of public interests of health and security. Given its immense impacts on human life or health, it can therefore be argued that the PA granted on the said former health technologies could constitute legitimate differential treatment rather than discrimination in international trade.

Based on the above argument, different technologies indeed have various implications for society. For example, Abbott contends that inventions are not neutral with respect to the field of technology; he contends that technologies associated with public interests and security, including education, health, nutrition, defence, environment and energy, play an important role in IP which is not restricted to trade purposes (Abbott 2005: 85). Brown specifically suggests the treatment of 'essential technologies', such as pharmaceutical drugs, computer software, and renewable energy, particularly merits considerations from human rights and competition perspectives (Brown

2012: 1). Therefore, inventions which have fundamentally different implications for public health may be distinguished from other inventions based on the legitimate differentiation of field of technologies.

Hence, in order to protect public interests of health, technologies which have a direct impact on reducing significant risks to human life or health can be argued to merit differential treatment based on the rationale of the PA and risk regulation in the trade context. Precaution and risk management can serve as legitimate grounds for the differentiation of health technologies in the IP regime. This is to say that by adopting the PA in the health-related trade measure, human life or health can still be safeguarded under the threat of *unknown risks* to human life or health. After all, health is an indispensable and vital element to the sustainability of a human being; the value of human health and security is too profound to be overshadowed by uncertain risks in free trade. By adopting the PA as a safety factor in the trade regime, we will be able to integrate social and economic implications of a public health emergency, and ultimately redefine the trade rules in the contemporary IP system, in order to accommodate diverse values in a risk society.

(3) Different implications of health technologies associated with risks to human life or health

The principle of national treatment (NT) requires that imported like products should receive no less favourable market treatment than domestic products (Article III: 4 GATT 1947). However, if a particular technology cannot be treated as 'alike' other technologies based on certain legitimate factors, for example, public health, then differential treatment of the said technology will not amount to discrimination.

It is therefore contended in this book that when health technologies are associated with risks of *significant* impact on the maintenance of human life or health, the unique association of the health risks and the said technology then consists of very different physical properties from those of other technologies. We can thus consider the Appellant Body's *'like-product'* analysis as a threshold device to distinguish health technologies which are strongly associated with the elimination of significant risks to human health from other technologies.

It is also noteworthy that, historically speaking, Section 41 of the UK Patents Act 1949 distinguished foods, medicines and surgical devices from other patented products to ensure a favourable use of compulsory licensing (Cornish and Llewelyn 2007: 295; Scherer and Watal 2002: 918). It was articulated that those patents concerning foods, medicines and surgical devices should be 'available to the public at the lowest prices consistent with the patentees' deriving a reasonable advantage from their patent rights' (Scherer and Watal 2002: 918). However, after accession to the WTO, the UK Patents Act was amended to abolish those provisions which singled out foods, medicines and surgical devices patents for a strong presumption in favour of compulsory licensing (Scherer and Watal 2002: 918). Yet, by contrast, the

40 *Introduction*

French patent law still differentiates in the treatment of pharmaceutical products for the purpose of granting compulsory licences.[26]

Following on from the Doha consensus where the Ministers explicitly stated that no country should be prevented from taking measures for the protection of health at the levels it considers appropriate;[27] the Doha Declaration on the TRIPS Agreement and Public Health (Doha Declaration) again articulated that TRIPS should be interpreted and implemented in a manner supportive of Members' rights to protect public health.[28] Members retain the right to determine the appropriate level of health protection; matters of public health concerns are legitimately within the domain of Members' regulatory authority.[29] The fact that public health, in particular pharmaceuticals, has been singled out in paragraphs 6 and 7 of the Doha Declaration as an issue requiring special attention in the implementation of TRIPS, suggests that public-health-related patents may deserve to be treated differently from other patents.[30] Regrettably, the unique properties of those products have been overshadowed by the 'non-discrimination' umbrella after accession to the WTO, and their relevance to public policy has been made indistinct.

Paradoxically, under the free trade blanket, human beings are even more vulnerable to health risks arising from globalization, including increasing international disease transmission, bioterrorism, and unknown risks accompanying emergent technologies,[31] for the new arising risks are constantly evolving and difficult to predict or track down (Petersen *et al.* 2007: 117–24; Mehta 2001: 205).

Further, though public health exclusions are not explicitly reflected in the compulsory licensing provision, the health exclusions in the patentability clauses nevertheless indicate the unique properties of health technologies in the IP regime. Public health exclusions from patent protection are still articulated in the patentability clauses in TRIPS. It can still be observed that in Articles 27(2) and 27(3) TRIPS the distinct values of 'foods, medicines, and surgical patents' are differentiated from other patents as such products are highly associated with public and national security interests, which are directly concerned with a population's health and are essential interests of a nation. Further, WTO Members may exclude from patentability inventions which are deemed 'necessary to protect *ordre public* or morality, including protecting human, animal or plant life or health' and 'diagnostic, therapeutic and surgical methods for the treatment of humans or animals' (Articles 27.2 and 27.3(a) TRIPS). Accordingly, in reaching a harmonious interpretation of TRIPS, a corollary would suggest that health technologies associated with the elimination of significant risks to human health could also be distinguished from other technologies in compulsory licensing.

It is therefore appropriate to restore the incommensurable value of human life and health in the global trade net – more specifically in the IP regime, the employment of the PA to adopt a safety factor would facilitate the balance of public and private interests.

2.2. A holistic approach: risk regulation and the PA in three worlds – fostering an organic, sustainable and sophisticated approach to IP

I argue that when a particular technology is associated with the elimination of significant risks to human health, differential treatment can be justified considering its unique physical properties and consumers' perceptions and behaviour. As discussed in Chapter 1, we learn that the current practice of compulsory licensing in redressing access to medicines has been deemed less than satisfactory, and that the provision has been acting as a bargaining tool in states' power play rather than as a clear structure for invocation of IP limitation in the WTO TRIPS regime.[32] The compulsory licensing mechanism is well placed to be a tool for redressing the imbalance of IP and health and delineating the boundary of rights holders' rights and obligations in international trade. The Doha Declaration has reaffirmed the rights of states to compulsory licensing;[33] however, empirical studies show that developing countries still hesitate to use this instrument to relieve their disease burden for fear of trade retaliation. Regrettably, this instrument has been mainly used as a threatening tool to negotiate drug price reduction instead of being a fair mechanism to redress the imbalance of health and IP. It would be even more controversial to grant a compulsory licence of a patented drug in preparedness for a pending pandemic which has not yet taken place. It then begs the question, is it legitimate for states to take official information and suggestions from the WHO as 'scientific evidence or other relevant information' to grant a compulsory licence on the grounds of a public health emergency as detailed in the TRIPS Agreement?

A workable and practical interpretation to trigger the process of compulsory licensing is thus desired to facilitate states' institution of a precautionary measure in a public health emergency. Accordingly, through the lens of precaution, it is worth examining whether the rationale of risk management for a public health emergency can be harmonized in the context of WHO and WTO laws.[34] This book therefore aims to bring harmonization to the legal infrastructures of risk management in the two regimes with a view to promoting access to essential medicines. Furthermore, a PA analysis would bolster the political and moral basis for compulsory licensing, which will bring congruence of risk management in WTO law.

The first precautionary grant of compulsory licensing was granted by the Taiwanese government for a preparedness plan of a pending bird flu pandemic in November 2005, following the WHO's recommendation of stockpiling sufficient antivirals for at least 10 per cent of its population.[35] It was noted that this grant appeared to trigger announcements by other countries of plans to issue compulsory licences (Abbott and Reichman 2007: 948). The legitimacy of a precautionary compulsory licence then attracted international debates.[36] Legally speaking, if compulsory licensing could not be given a PA reading, governments would not be able to legitimately resort to this

42 Introduction

measure until the actual outbreak of a pandemic, after a certain number of deaths had been reported. As stockpiling of medicines for pandemic preparedness could take months to years from the point of the identification of the pandemic strain to produce enough pandemic vaccine to satisfy global need,[37] by then it could be too late to contain the disease. It then begs the question, is the loss of human life the only trigger for compulsory licensing? Or could compulsory licensing act as a trigger to prevent any death at all? It was under these circumstances that the legitimacy of a precautionary compulsory licence started to attract my interest in deliberating the optimal application of PA as a tool for tempering IP and health in post-grant situations (Hung 2010: 74). Further, as the PA has been an important underpinning in risk regulation with regard to environmental protection, it is as well anticipated that the PA would act as a legitimate factor to moderate public and private interests in IP.

In order to reflect the unique properties of health technologies for enhancing access to medicines, as well as to have a coherent interpretation and application of the PA in international law, it is suggested that the PA should be incorporated into the framework of compulsory licensing. I propose to redefine compulsory licensing through the lens of precaution and also to create the legal status of the PA in compulsory licensing in Chapter 6. It is argued in this book that the PA can serve as a tool for reconciling the discrepancies between the WHO and the WTO agendas, and for harmonizing the domestic policy-making of legal preparedness in a public health emergency.

Notes

1 Compulsory licensing is a mechanism of limitation on a patent right after it is issued, Article 31 of the Agreement on Trade-Related Aspects of Intellectual Property Rights, Marrakesh Agreement Establishing the World Trade Organization Annex 1C (TRIPS).
2 See Chapter 6.
3 Preamble of the General Agreement on Tariffs and Trade (GATT 1947), para. 2.
4 The classification of 'like product' is addressed in the *Spain – Unroasted Coffee* case and the *Asbestos* case. GATT Panel Report, *Spain – Tariff Treatment of Unroasted Coffee (Spain Unroasted Coffee)* L/5135, adopted 11 June 1981, BISD 28S/102; WTO Appellate Body Report, *European Communities – Measures Affecting Asbestos and Asbestos-Containing Products (EC – Asbestos)*, WT/DS135/AB/R, paras.130 and 145.
5 *Canada – Patent Protection of Pharmaceutical Products (Canada – Pharmaceutical Patents)* WT/DS114/5, WT/DS114/R, 12 March 2000.
6 Ibid., para. 7.92.
7 See above, note 5.
8 *EC – Asbestos*, above, note 4.
9 *EC – Asbestos*, above, note 4, para. 91.
10 *EC – Asbestos*, above, note 4, para. 99.

The solution 43

11 *Spain – Tariff Treatment of Unroasted Coffee*, above, note 4; *EC – Asbestos*, paras. 85, 130 and 145, above, note 4.

12 WTO Appellate Body Report, *EC – Asbestos*, para. 113, above, note 4.

13 WTO Appellate Body Report, *EC – Asbestos*, para. 114, above, note 4.

14 WTO Appellate Body Report, *EC – Asbestos*, paras. 121–2, above, note 4.

15 *Philippines – Taxes on Distilled Spirits (Philippines – Spirits)*, WT/DS396/AB/R, WT/DS403/AB/R, adopted 21 December 2011.

16 For example, EU Supplementary Protection Certificate can extend 'the effect of the basic patent' for up to five years through this supplementary right. See also Australian Patents Act 1990 ss 70–79A; Japanese Patent Act article 67(2), and US Patents Act s 156.

17 Article 12 *International Covenant on Economic, Social and Cultural Rights*, adopted and opened for signature by the United Nations General Assembly Resolution 2200A (XXI) on 16 December 1966, entered into force 3 January 1976 (ICESCR).

18 Article 67.3 *Consolidated Versions of the Treaty on European Union and the Treaty on the Functioning of the European Union* (TFEU).

19 Articles 114.3, 168.1 and 169.1 TFEU.

20 WTO Appellate Body Report, *Australia – Measures Affecting the Importation of Salmon (Australia – Salmon)*, WT/DS18/AB/R, adopted 20 October 1998, para. 125; *EC – Asbestos*, paras. 168 and 174, above, note 4.

21 See above, note 5.

22 *Canada – Pharmaceutical Patents*, para. 5.18, above, note 5.

23 *India – Patent Protection for Pharmaceutical and Agricultural Chemical Products (India – Pharmaceutical Patents)*, WT/DS50/R, adopted 5 September 1997, para. 8.29.

24 *Canada – Pharmaceutical Patents*, para. 5.18, above, note 5.

25 *Canada – Pharmaceutical Patents*, footnote 439, above, note 5.

26 UNCTAD-ICTSD (2005), *Resource Book on TRIPS and Development*, Cambridge University Press, p. 374

27 Doha Ministerial Declaration, WT/MIN(01)/DEC/1, 20 November 2001, para. 6.

28 *Doha Declaration on the TRIPS Agreement and Public Health* (Doha Declaration), adopted by the fourth Ministerial Conference of the World Trade Organization in Doha, Qatar, on 14 November 2001. WT/MIN(01)/DEC/2 of 20 November 2001, para. 4. See Chapter 1, Section 1.2.3.

29 Above, note 26.

30 Ibid.

31 For example, a wide range of fears and uncertainties about the potential consequences of novel technologies, including those caused by nuclear accident, genetically modified foods, BSE, and nanotechnologies have been the subject of academic debates.

32 See Chapter 1, Section 1.2.3.

33 See above, note 28.

34 'Risk management' is defined in the Codex Alimentarius Procedural Manual as: 'The process, distinct from risk assessment, of weighing policy alternatives, in consultation with all interested parties, considering risk assessment and other factors relevant for the health protection of consumers and for the promotion of fair trade practices, and, if needed, selecting appropriated prevention and control options'. Codex Alimentarius Commission 21st Procedural Manual (Codex Manual), 'Definitions for the Purposes of the Codex Alimentarius'.

44 *Introduction*

35 Hille, K. (2005) 'Taiwan Employs Compulsory Licensing for Tamiflu', FT.com, 25 November, available at: http://www.ft.com/cms/s/0/cebeb882-5dcb-11da-be9c-0000779e2340.html

36 For example, the patent holder of Tamiflu, Roche, expressed the view that compulsory licensing was unnecessary. See: 'Tamiflu Compulsory License not Necessary, Roche Tells Three Asian Nations', Thepharmaletter, 5 December 2005. Available at: http://www.thepharmaletter.com/file/37733/tamiflu-compulsory-license-not-necessary-roche-tells-three-asian-nations.html

37 In order to build a global monitor network, the WHO has also recommended that countries should stockpile appropriate antiviral medication sufficient for 10 per cent of the population or more to contain the virus spread from phase 3 of pandemic alert period. The stockpiling of antivirus medication often requires six months to one year, therefore governments need to prepare for sufficient dosage of drugs before the virus outbreak. See: WHO (2005) 'WHO Global Influenza Preparedness Plan: the Role of WHO and Recommendations for National Measures before and during Pandemics', WHO Influenza Preparedness, WHO/CDS/CSR/GIP/2005.5, p. 23; Bill and Melinda Gates Foundation (2009) 'Options for the Design and Financing of an H5N1 Vaccine Stockpile: Key Findings and Study Methodology', p. 3.

Part II

Current landscape

3 The development of the precautionary approach

The precautionary approach (PA) has been developed from international environmental protection policy in the past few decades. Its main premise is that where the threat of a particular harm is serious and the damage is irreversible, the notion of precaution should take priority over scientific justification. A purely evidence-based approach has been central to environmental and public health policy-making; however, it has been identified as outdated and unable to cope with emerging risks in contemporary society. The PA is therefore proposed to supplement the inadequacy of the traditional evidence-based approach.

Notably, the Nuffield Council on Bioethics in the UK has highlighted the importance of precaution when dealing with threats to public health.[1] It points out that 'an evidence-based approach to public health policy can be fraught with difficulties'. It also states that even when every step has been taken to ensure the validity of the evidence, 'in practice it is often incomplete or ambiguous, and usually will be contested'.[2] Public health guidance from the UK National Institute for Health and Clinical Excellence (NICE) (renamed in 2013 the National Institute for Health and Care Excellence) also states that: '[a]ll evidence requires interpretation as evidence alone cannot determine the content of a recommendation'.[3] It has been argued that policy-making dependent only on scientific evidence is no longer fit for modern society. This is where the PA comes into play as an important role in contemporary public health protection.

3.1. Formulations of the PA

There exist numerous formulations of the PA related to risk management of the environment and health protection in international law. I will first introduce typical versions from international declarations, treaties, and legislations in order to grasp the initial impression of precaution. The PA is found to have a pervasive influence on risk regulation in international law; however, its application is fraught with fragmentations in different legal regimes.

Among all definitions, Principle 15 of the Rio Declaration on Environment and Development appears to be the most well-known version of the PA. It reads:

48 *Current landscape*

> In order to protect the environment, the *precautionary approach* shall be widely applied by States according to their capacities. Where there are threats of *serious or irreversible* damage, lack of full scientific certainty shall not be used as a reason for postponing cost-effective measures to prevent environmental degradation.
>
> (Rio Declaration 1992, emphasis added)

The Rio Declaration involves a 'triple-negative' connotation, which may leave ambiguity in its interpretation. In view of this, the European Environment Agency (EEA) proposes a more proactive and assertive definition as follows:

> The PP provides justification for public policy actions in situations of scientific complexity, uncertainty and ignorance, where there may be a need to act in order to avoid, or reduce, *potentially serious or irreversible threats* to health or the environment, using an appropriate level of scientific evidence, and taking into account the likely pros and cons of action and inaction.
>
> (WHO Dealing with Uncertainty Report, p. 3, italics added)

Another frequently cited version of the approach, which was developed from the Wingspread Conference in the United States, known as the Wingspread Statement, reads:

> When an activity raises threats of harm to human health or the environment, *precautionary measures* should be taken even if some cause and effect relationships are not fully established scientifically.[4]
>
> (Wingspread Statement on the Precautionary Principle 1998, emphasis added)

With regard to environmental protection in domestic legislations, the Australian Government defines the PA as follows:

> Where there are threats of serious irreversible environmental damage, lack of full scientific certainty should not be used as a reason for postponing measures to prevent environmental degradation.[5]
>
> (The Intergovernmental Agreement on the Environment 1992)

It was described that the version in the Wingspread Statement is generally adopted by non-governmental organizations aiming at a more stringent approach to environmental and health protection (Salmon 2005: 138–49, n. 70). These formulations lead to different conclusions in their interpretations and applications. Some may be justification for doing nothing while others might be justification for intervening to action. This distinction will be further

The development of the precautionary approach   49

discussed when we categorize the PA into the 'Argumentative version' or the 'Prescriptive version'.[6]

The PA is perceived by the European Court of Justice (ECJ) as constituting 'an integral part of the decision-making process leading to the adoption of any measure for the protection of human health'.[7] In addition, Kriebel and Tickner note that the PA seeks to shift health and environmental policy from a strategy of 'reaction' to one of 'precaution' (Kriebel and Tickner 2001: 1351), which would more aggressively cause significant change to the linkage of science and policy (Kriebel *et al.* 2001: 871).

From the view of regulation, Somsen further argues for 'enabling precaution' to be a 'morally and legally acceptable principle', which substantively enables regulators to 'channel regulatory tilt towards constraints on new technologies' (Somsen 2008: 223). He maintains that '[W]hen under such circumstances uncertainty about the impact of a technology persists, enabling precaution posits that regulators should *temporarily prohibit or constrain that technology* until there is new evidence suggesting no risk or acceptable risk' (Somsen 2008: 230, emphasis added).

Moreover, Somsen argues from the perspective of future generations that the costs of 'irreversible harm' to the environment are to be borne by future generations who are not represented in current political and legal process. Therefore, precaution arises to give future generations a voice in legal and political processes (Somsen 2008: 225). This is argued from the angle of intergenerational equity. Somsen further concludes that precaution is used for environmental regulations to help 'redress some very clear and serious imbalances that ultimately undermine mankind's chance of survival' (Somsen 2008: 225). Indeed, Somsen's argument focuses on the adoption of a 'margin of safety' in environmental and health policy-making which would provide a buffer zone in the situation of scientific ignorance or uncertainty. An ample margin of safety in policy-making will still be able to provide sufficient protection to human health in extreme or emergency situations, and to ensure that scientific advancement would not come at the cost of human health. In order to avoid unpredictable or irreversible damage to humankind and future generations, the role of PA serves as a safety valve in the regulation of risk posed by modern technologies under globalization.

3.2. The origin and applications: from environmental protection to the protection of health and food safety

The PA first emerged from international environmental protection prior to its application in the protection of human health and food safety. Freestone and Hey have commented on it as 'intrinsic to international environmental policy' (Freestone and Hey 1995: 3–15). Freestone further notes the rise of the approach as 'one of the most remarkable developments of the last decade,

50   *Current landscape*

and arguably one of the most significant in the emergence of the new discipline of international environmental law itself' (Freestone 1999: 135–64). It has arisen as an applied ethic to complement the blind spot of scientific uncertainty or ignorance in the shadow of economic progression (Stirling 1999; Gee and Stirling 2003),[8] and is often applied to redress the vacuum in circumstances of insufficient scientific evidence.

More specifically within the health sector, precaution has been argued to be one of the fundamentals of public health ethics (Weed 2004: 313–32; Martuzzi 2007; Kopelman *et al.* 2004: 255–8), it has been characterized as being 'at the heart of medical and public health theory and practice and is an underpinning to many of our current environmental and public health policies' (Tickner and Kriebel 2006; Pearce 2004). An Australian judge also states that: 'the precautionary principle is a statement of commonsense and has already been applied by decision-makers in appropriate circumstances prior to the principle being spelled out' (Trouwborst 2002: 8).[9]

On the one hand, the PA has been incorporated widely in environmental protection policy in international law and has also been recognized as a fundamental value in the health regime. On the other hand, it has been criticized as incoherent and leading to paradox (Harris and Holm 2002: 355–68). Yet existing formulations of precaution represent a wide range of implications which appear to be confusing and even contradictory. There is no current consensus on using the term 'precautionary approach' (PA) or 'precautionary principle' (PP) in international law. The debates over the function and application of precaution without a focused target inevitably result in even more myths, and adversely undermine the grounds for communication among different stakeholders.

As a WHO Report points out: 'the problem with the PP definition is not in their accuracy, but that the definitions, possibly any synthetic definition, miss the values and role of the PP as an overarching, inspiring principle in environment and health' (WHO Dealing with Uncertainty 2005: 3). The significance of the role of the PA has been blurred after contradictory debates. Therefore, developing a tailor-made definition in the context of my research is necessary to facilitate further discussion and implementation. Thus, this chapter aims at shaping the contour of the PA in this book by literature review and comparative studies of previous works of philosophers and lawyers.

'Precaution' is distinguished from 'prevention' in terms of risk regulation. Prior to the emergence of the PA, the 'preventive principle' was documented in the literature (Sands 2003: 267). Whereas the preventive principle can be traced back to international environmental treaties since the 1930s (Sands 2003: 267), the PA emerged in the context of marine pollution legislation in international law, and 'cleaner production' in Europe (De Sadeleer 2008: 61–90). 'Precaution' is relevant in situations of scientific uncertainty, while 'prevention' relates to situations in which the risk of potential damage can be

The development of the precautionary approach   51

determined or identified on the basis of a scientific assessment (Perrez 2008: 257). The PA thus is only involved in the condition that there is *scientific uncertainty* concerning the existence or seriousness of a risk. In other words, when a risk can be managed with a quantitative risk assessment (QRA), it is included in the exercise of prevention rather than precaution (Cameron 1999: 34–5); on the contrary, if the risk involves scientific uncertainty which cannot be measured by QRA, or the causal relationship has not been established under current pertinent scientific justification, the PA may be introduced to address the need to prevent further damage to human health and safety (Cameron 1999: 34–5).

The PA originated from air pollution legislation in Germany in the phrase 'Vorsorgeprinzip' (Harding and Fisher 1999). Tickner and Kriebel argue for an alternative translation of this word as the 'foresight principle' or 'forecaring principle', which emphasizes an anticipatory action: 'a proactive idea rather than precaution, which may sounds reactive and even negative' (Tickner and Kriebel 2006). Birnie *et al.* state that its purpose is 'to make greater allowance for uncertainty in the regulation of environmental risks and the sustainable use of natural resources' (Birnie *et al.* 2009).

The PA is becoming increasingly relevant as an international legal measure to guide decision-making in the face of scientific uncertainty. It is reflected in a growing body of legal instruments which form part of developing international customary and treaty regimes (Trouwborst 2002). It has been applied in relation to the adoption of measures to address ozone depletion; to protect the marine environment of the North Sea (Third North Sea Conference 1990); to prevent the causes of climate change (Rio Declaration 1992; Framework Convention on Climate Change 1992); to regulate handling and use of living modified organisms (Cartagena Protocol on Biosafety 2000); and for the protection of human health and food safety (Maastricht Treaty 1992; Stockholm Convention on Persistent Organic Pollutants 2001). It is observed that after the Rio Declaration, the PA soon appeared in many dimensions in different legal instruments to meet the demands of various risks under scientific uncertainty. For example, the WTO *Agreement on the Application of Sanitary and Phytosanitary Measures* (SPS Agreement), the *Cartagena Protocol on Biosafety* ('Cartagena Protocol' or 'CPB'), the WHO *International Health Regulations* (IHRs), and the *Codex Alimentarius* have further expanded the application of precaution from specific environmental protection to the protection of human health (Article 5.7 SPS Agreement; Article 10.6 Cartagena Protocol; Article 43 IHRs; Codex Alimentarius Procedural Manual). This will be further addressed in Chapter 4.

We will now revisit its development within the United Nations (UN) and the European Union (EU) respectively in order to identify recent trends in the protection of the international environment with a special regard to the protection of human health and food safety.

52 Current landscape

3.2.1. The precautionary approach from the perspective of 'State responsibility'

The precautionary approach emphasizes that when there is a possibility of serious or irreversible harm to the environment, protective action should be taken in advance of scientific proof of harm. From the perspective of *State responsibility* in international law, governments may be obliged to act to avoid irreversible damage even under the circumstances of scientific uncertainty (Brownlie 2003: 419; Tinker 1996a; Gathii 2006: 943; Crawford 1999: 436). In view of this, Trouwborst contends that the PA taken by states is embodied as *'a right or duty of states'* in international law when the threat of a particular harm crosses the 'significant harm' threshold (Trouwborst 2006). Trouwborst divides states' precautionary actions into a 'right' or a 'duty' in accordance with the degree of risk. I adapt Trouwborst's concept of 'precautionary rights and duties', but as this book will not follow his sophisticated distinction of a 'right' or a 'duty' of a precautionary action, the terminology of states' *'precautionary entitlements'* is proposed for later discussions.

Similarly to the above argument in international law, Brownsword proposes a *State stewardship* model in domestic public health regulation, which suggests that a state has a responsibility to protect and to promote the conditions of public health, and further requires the state to keep its citizens informed about risks to their health and the channel of democratic participation to improve the conditions of public health (Brownsword 2008: 46). Furthering this argument, the UK Nuffield Council on Bioethics also highlights that the state stewardship model imposes on states responsibilities 'to look after important needs of people both individually and collectively' (Nuffield Council on Bioethics 2007). This Report distinguishes paternalism from a stewardship model by its emphasis on 'seeking the least intrusive way of achieving policy goals, taking into account also the criteria of effectiveness and proportionality'. It also identifies five main elements of the PA: scientific assessment of risk; fairness and consistency; consideration of costs and benefits; transparency; and proportionality (Nuffield Council on Bioethics 2007: 35).

Further, this Nuffield proposal has been picked up by NICE in the UK with respect to public health (NICE 2009; Killoran *et al.* 2009: 451–2). It acknowledges that NICE's advisory committees are encouraged to take 'non-scientific values' into consideration in 'bridging the gaps between the evidence and producing a recommendation' (NICE 2009: 118–19). Another NICE report stresses the significance of 'individual choice and of respecting individual values, cultural attitudes and religious views', but nevertheless also mentions that sometimes individual choice may need to be limited for public interests (NICE 2008: 19).

From the above observation, it can also be understood that 'precaution' has emerged to provide a safety net or a buffer zone between the boundary of risk and safety in the domain of scientific uncertainty. Either from the rule of

The development of the precautionary approach   53

'State responsibility' or the perspective of future generations, the PA appears to have a vital role to play in risk management in modern society. However, the terms 'precautionary principle' or 'precautionary approach' have appeared in the literature in a rather random order. The words 'approach' and 'principle' will be distinguished in our discussion below (see section 3.4).

3.2.2. United Nations

The precautionary approach has been adopted in international law to put states under a duty to prevent or mitigate transboundary environmental harm caused by activities in territory under their jurisdiction or control. The PA imposes regulations on polluters or on those introducing new technologies to force them to accept responsibility for managing unknown risks associated with their activities.

Many threatening environmental issues such as ozone depletion, climate change and transboundary waste dumping all require international cooperation. The UN has played an important role in the proliferation of the PA to prevent international environmental deterioration. Though some of the resolutions of the General Assembly may not be legally binding as treaties, they are recommended to be taken into consideration by the International Court of Justice (ICJ) as a manner in which 'the development of international law may be reflected' when disputes arise (UN Resolution 29/332, 1974).

In 1982 the UN General Assembly adopted the *World Charter for Nature* (*World Charter*) within the framework of the World Conservation Union, which is also known as 'the Magna Carta of ecological environmental policy'. Despite the absence of the term 'precautionary principle' or 'precautionary approach', the Charter reflects the basic elements of the PA by stating that:

> Activities which might have an impact on nature shall be controlled and the best available technologies that minimize *significant risks* to nature or other effects shall be used, in particular:
>
> (a) Activities which are likely to cause *irreversible damage* to nature shall be avoided;
> (b) Activities which are likely to pose a significant risk to nature shall be preceded by an *exhaustive examination*; their proponents shall demonstrate that expected benefits outweigh potential damage to nature, and where potential adverse effects are not fully understood, the activities should not proceed;
> (c) Activities which may disturb nature shall be preceded by *assessment of their consequence*s, and environmental impact studies of development projects shall be conducted sufficiently in advance, and if they are to be undertaken such activities shall be planned and carried out so as to minimize potential adverse effects.
>
> (Principle 11 of the World Charter for Nature, emphasis added)

54 Current landscape

Principle 11 identifies some major factors in the implementation of the PA: significant risks; irreversible damage; cost-effectiveness; and environmental impact assessment (EIA). The European Commission (EC) thus referred to the *World Charter for Nature* as the first legal instrument to recognize the PA at the international level (Communication from the European Commission on the Precautionary Principle, p. 11), and it is described as 'one of the most important UN documents in which the precautionary principle has been recognized as the central principle of environmental policy' (Trouwborst 2002: 152). Trouwborst further comments that the precautionary thinking on the international plane has proliferated since the adoption of the *World Charter*.[10]

Further to the completion of the *World Charter*, the UN General Assembly later approved *Goals and Principles of Environmental Impact Assessment* in 1987 and extended the application of the PA into the problems of global climate change (UN Resolution 43/53); marine resource and large-scale driftnet fishing (UN Decision 15/27; UN Resolution 44/225; UN Resolution 46/215; UN Resolution 59/25); sustainable development (UN Resolution S/19-2); hazardous waste and persistent organic pollutants (UN Decision SS II/4; UN Decision 18/32; UN Decision 19/13C). Relevant cases before the ICJ and the International Tribunal of the Law of the Sea (ITLOS) will be introduced briefly to highlight the fundamental ingredients of the PA.

(1) Gabcikovo–Nagymaros Case

The International Court of Justice (ICJ) is the principal judicial organ of the United Nations. It was established by the Charter of the United Nations in 1949 to settle legal disputes submitted by states and to give advisory opinions on legal questions. The *Gabcikovo–Nagymaros* case was heard in the ICJ when in 1989 Hungary invoked the PA to suspend work on the two barrages for the sake of its natural environment in the region affected by the project in consideration of 'ecological necessity'.[11] Gabcikovo–Nagymaros was a Slovakia–Hungary hydrological project. Having received an ad hoc expert committee's report on the environmental, ecological and water quality impacts of the project, the Hungarian Government relied upon the precautionary principle in concluding that it did not have adequate knowledge of the consequences of environmental risks and proposing suspension of the project. The formal proposed suspension was rejected by Czechoslovakia. Hungary thus complained to the Court of Czechoslovakia's unilateral continuation of the project (Trouwborst 2002: 162).

Nevertheless, the ICJ found that Hungary did not prove a 'real, "grave", and "imminent" "peril" existed in 1989, and the measures taken by Hungary were the only possible response to it' (ICJ Report 7, paras. 50–2, 54).[12] It was also alleged that an adequate Environmental Impact Assessment (EIA) had not been carried out before the project, but the court did not address the need for a prior EIA. EIA is 'a procedure for evaluating the likely impact of a proposed activity on the environment'.[13] In particular, the Court required the parties to 'look afresh' at the environmental impact of the project, and treated prior EIA and subsequent monitoring of the ongoing risks as a continuing obligation throughout the whole project (Birnie *et al.* 2009: 164–8). Birnie *et al.* note that: 'If EIA is a necessary precondition for effective notification and consultation with other states, then monitoring may equally be regarded as a necessary element of an effective EIA' (Birnie *et al.* 2009: 164–8). It can therefore be suggested that monitoring may also be part of the obligation of due diligence, and needs to be incorporated in a complete EIA through the life of the project.

The *Gabcikovo–Nagymaros* case may indicate that the triggering threshold of the PA needs to prove a 'real, "grave", and "imminent" "peril"' exists (ICJ Report 7, pp. 50–2, 54), and the one who carries out the project associated with the risk may be obliged to carry out a prior EIA and subsequent monitoring of the ongoing risks. The ongoing risks need to be constantly evaluated and updated to ensure the adopting measure is proportionate and effective.

(2) Southern Bluefin Tuna Case

The United Nations Convention on the Law of the Sea (UNCLOS) establishes a comprehensive legal framework to regulate ocean space, its uses and resources. It provides for the protection and preservation of the marine environment in particular. The Convention is equipped with several channels for the settlement of disputes: the International Tribunal for the Law of the Sea (ITLOS), the International Court of Justice, an arbitral tribunal constituted in the Convention.

In the *Southern Bluefin Tuna* case,[14] Australia and New Zealand requested the ITLOS to order 'that the parties *act consistently with the precautionary principle* in fishing for Southern Bluefin Tuna pending a final settlement of the dispute' (Sands 2003: 275, emphasis added). The Tribunal relied on scientific uncertainty of the conservation of tuna stock to justify the grant of *provisional measures* to prevent the stock from further depletion. It stated that 'the parties should in the circumstances act with *prudence and caution* to ensure that effective conservation measures are taken to prevent serious harm to the stock of southern bluefin tuna' (ITLOS Nos. 3 and 4, para. 77, emphasis added).

'Scientific uncertainty' regarding provisional measures to be taken to conserve the stock of bluefin tuna is acknowledged in the case (ITLOS Nos. 3 and 4, para. 79). The *Southern Bluefin Tuna* case thus recognized that the measure to grant a provisional measure can be considered as a legitimate precautionary action in international law (ITLOS Nos. 3 and 4, para. 17).

In conclusion, the above two cases identify three basic elements of PA which are features formed in other operations of the approach: the triggering threshold of the approach, the duty of scientific assessment and monitoring,

56 Current landscape

and the adoption of provisional measures. Furthermore, in the legislation of the WTO SPS Agreement, the adoption of provisional SPS measures is also considered typical application of the PA. Yet the said provisional measure is subject to the accompaniment of procedural requirements, which will be elaborated in Chapter 4 (Section 4.3.2).

3.2.3. European Union

The European Union (EU) or the previous European Community (EC) is the main endorser of the precautionary principle (Tait 2001: 175–89; Christoforou 2003; Nucara 2003: 47–53; Coleman 2002: 609). The word 'principle' instead of 'approach' is preferred in order to suggest that the employment of 'precaution' enjoys a stronger assertion in the EU domain than in other areas. We will thus follow the EU's preference for the term 'precautionary principle' (PP) in this section.

The precautionary principle was first developed from environmental protection in *Action Programmes on the Environment* from 1973 to 1992 (Trouwborst 2002, n. 687), and following the regulations of new chemicals such as pesticides and antibiotics (Directive 67/548; Directive 79/831; Decision 80/372; Directive 80/778; Regulation 98/2821), wildlife (Directive 79/409; Directive 92/43), pollution (Directive 91/271; Directive 96/91), growth hormones in cattle (Directive 81/602; Directive 88/146; Directive 88/299), and GMOs (Directive 90/219; Directive 90/220). The precautionary principle also received recognition in international treaties in environmental protection by the EU (Trouwborst 2004: 147). The EC *Communication on the Precautionary Principle* (*EC Communication*) and the Court of First Instance (CFI) of the European Court of Justice (ECJ) have suggested that precaution applies to all EU policies as a 'central plank' of Union policy (EC Communication 2000: 12; *Alpharma Inc.* v. *Council of the EU*, para. 135).

More recently, since the presentation of the Green Paper on the *General Principles of Food Law in the European Union* in 1997 and the bovine spongiform encephalopathy (BSE) crisis, the EU comprehensively adopts the precautionary principle from the perspective of consumer health in the regulation of food safety (Streinz 1998: 413). Specifically, the *Codex Committee* on General Principles of the Codex Alimentarius Commission states that the precautionary principle might be extended to food safety aspects. Streinz thus comments that the precautionary principle has been extended from the law of public security and environmental law to national and European food law (Streinz 2009: 54–5). In particular, the precautionary principle has been established as one of the basic principles in food law in the European Parliament and of the Council (Basic Regulation). Article 7 stipulates that:

> In specific circumstances where, following an assessment of available information, the possibility of harmful effects on health is identified but scientific uncertainty persists, provisional risk management measures

necessary to ensure the high level of health protection chosen in the Community may be adopted, pending further scientific information for a more comprehensive risk assessment.

(Article 7 of the *Regulation No. 178/2002*)

It further identifies some basic factors in determining the application of the precautionary principle by stating:

Measures adopted on the basis of paragraph 1 shall be proportionate and no more restrictive of trade than is required to achieve the high level of health protection chosen in the Community, regard being had to technical and economic feasibility and other factors regarded as legitimate in the matter under consideration. The measures shall be reviewed within a reasonable period of time, depending on the nature of the risk to life or health identified and the type of scientific information needed to clarify the scientific uncertainty and to conduct a more comprehensive risk assessment.

(Paragraph 2 of Article 7 of the *Regulation No. 178/2002*)

The features of this Article include the following: Members' right to adopt a higher level of health protection than the international standard is respected; Member States enjoy discretion in determining the appropriate level of health protection in customary international law. It suggests that the precautionary principle should be based on available information; it needs to be adopted on a provisional basis and reviewed within a reasonable period of time; it needs to be no more restrictive to trade than is required to achieve an appropriate level of health protection, and the adopting state is obliged to conduct a 'more comprehensive risk assessment' after invocation. Particularly, the Article further identifies the element of 'proportionality', 'technical and economic feasibility' and other factors regarded as legitimate. Other legitimate factors are generally referred to as non-scientific factors which include different cultural contexts and civilians' preferences.

We now examine the current practice of the precautionary principle in the EU and relevant cases in order to get a better grasp of the more active application in the protection of human health and food safety.

(1) Appropriate levels of health protection

The EU acknowledges that the Union has the right to establish the appropriate level of environmental protection. Specifically, the Consolidated Versions of the Treaty on European Union and the Treaty on the Functioning of the European Union (Treaty on the Functioning of the European Union, TFEU) incorporate the precautionary principle into a high level of safety and consumer protection in order to safeguard human health and environment

58   *Current landscape*

under the eclipse of scientific progression. For example, the TFEU consists of provisions introduced by the Maastricht Treaty which states:

> Union policy on the environment shall aim at a high level of protection taking into account the diversity of situations in the various regions of the Union. It shall be based on *the precautionary principle* and on the principles that preventive action should be taken, that environmental damage should as a priority be rectified at source and that the polluter should pay ... In preparing its policy on the environment, the Union shall take account of available scientific and technical data, ... the potential benefits and costs of action or lack of action.
>
> (Article 191 TFEU)

Moreover, with regard to the level of protection, the TFEU provides that:

> The Commission, in its proposals envisaged in paragraph 1 concerning *health, safety, environmental protection and consumer protection*, will take as a base *a high level of protection*, taking into account in particular of any new development based on scientific facts.
>
> (Article 114 TFEU, emphasis added)

The TFEU acknowledges that 'human health' is included in the context of environmental protection which shall be based on the precautionary principle and that preventive action should be taken to avoid environmental damage (Article 191 TFEU). Member States of the EU are allowed to take *provisional environmental measures* for non-economic environmental reasons.

Scholars have argued for consistency in the regulations of human health and the environment in WTO laws (Green and Epps 2007: 285). 'Human health' has been included as a policy objective in environmental protection in the EU legal system. For example, in EC Directive 2001/18, the Commission stipulates that the regulations on genetically modified organisms following the precautionary principle should protect 'human health and the environment'. 'Environment' in international environmental law is broadly referred to as including 'air, water, land, flora and fauna, natural ecosystem and sites, human health and safety, and climate' (Trouwborst 2006). Human health is central to the concerns of environmental protection, thus 'human health' is intertwined with 'environment' and the two cannot be separated. It is thus self-evident that the application factors of the precautionary principle in the protection of the environment can also be applied in the context of human health.

(2) EC Communication on the Precautionary Principle

The EC issued the *Communication on the Precautionary Principle* (EC Communication) in 2000 to assert its implementation but, as with many

The development of the precautionary approach   59

other legal instruments, avoided defining it (McNelis 2000: 545–51). The *EC Communication* only describes the precautionary principle as having a role 'to protect the environment' and it proposes several guidelines for applying the precautionary principle, which consist of the principles of:

- proportionality;
- non-discrimination;
- consistency;
- cost-benefit analysis;
- examination of scientific developments; and
- burden of proof.

The *Council Resolution on the Precautionary Principle* was later adopted in Nice, December 2000. The *Resolution* calls on the Commission to 'incorporate the precautionary principle, where necessary, in drawing up its legislation proposals and in all its actions', and asks Member States to 'ensure the precautionary principle is fully recognized in the relevant *international health*, environment and *world trade fora*' (paras. 24–5, emphasis added). The *Resolution* stresses that the precautionary principle should be fully implemented specifically in areas of international health and world trade.

Attention will now be turned to two typical EU cases which recognize Member States' precautionary entitlements regarding the regulation on food safety and human health.

(3) Case studies

PFIZER ANIMAL HEALTH V. COUNCIL OF THE EU

Antibiotics added to animal feed have been used as growth promoters to improve weight gain and prevent certain diseases in animals. However, scientists have claimed that the practice results in a risk of resistance to the antibiotics in humans through the food chain. Thus some antibiotics cannot be used effectively in human medicine for certain diseases.[15] The WHO has also recommended the immediate or gradual discontinuance of the practice.[16]

Yet there was no scientific proof of the link between the antibiotics concerned and resistance to those antibiotics in humans when the ban was implemented. As producers of the said antibiotics, Pfizer Animal Health and Alpharma Inc. brought actions for annulment of the regulation before the Court of First Instance (CFI);[17] they claimed that the ban was based on political expediency instead of objective scientific analysis, and the Council had taken an unrealistic approach to pursue 'zero risk'. They further argued that the link between the use of certain antibiotics as feed additives and an increase in resistance to those antibiotics in humans remains uncertain.[18]

The Court stated that in cases relating to food safety (in particular the BSE crisis), based on the precautionary principle, Community institutions may

60 *Current landscape*

take protective measures without having to wait until the reality and seriousness of the risks perceived become fully apparent (para. 139). The Court viewed that the ban was designed to prevent the risks from the probability of the negative effects of the practice. In relation to the procedural requirements, it explained that the adoption of the preventive measure should be triggered by a risk assessment, which consists of a scientific component and a political component. A scientific component is to carry out a risk assessment, and a political component is regarded as 'risk management' in which the public authority can get involved in determining the appropriate measure in response to the degree of risk.

The Court further noted that the Community institutions are entitled to take a preventive measure regarding the use of antibiotics as an additive in feedstuffs according to the precautionary principle enshrined in the EC Treaty (para. 140). The Court also referred to the provisional communication from the Codex Alimentarius Commission of the Food and Agriculture Organization (FAO) of the United Nations and the WHO in relation to identifying the level of risk that will adversely affect the interests of human health (para. 147).

In relation to the implementation of a risk assessment, it identifies a risk assessment as 'determining what level of risk is deemed unacceptable' and as 'conducting a scientific assessment of the risks' (para. 149). The Court also stated that a Member's right in determining the appropriate level of health protection is provided in the WTO SPS Agreement (para. 150). It further noted that the Community institutions have the 'powers' conferred by the Treaty 'in defining the political objectives to be pursued'. The Community institutions are obliged to determine the level of risk (the critical probability threshold of adverse effect on human health) to ensure a high level of human health protection (paras. 151–2).

It concludes that 'under the precautionary principle the Community institutions are entitled, in the interests of human health to adopt, on the basis of as yet incomplete scientific knowledge, protective measures which may seriously harm legally protected positions, and they enjoy a broad discretion in that regard' (para. 170).

A relevant case will also be discussed below with analysis of elements of the precautionary principle.

ALPHARMA INC. V. COUNCIL OF THE EU

In *Alpharma Inc.* v. *Council of the EU*,[19] the Court again stressed that the PP is one of the principles on which Community policy on the protection of human health and environment is based (para. 152). The Court also reaffirmed that the Community institutions have the 'right and obligation' to adopt protective measures they deem appropriate to prevent the risks to human health. The Court emphasized that under the PP, the Community institutions enjoy a broad discretion in their responsibility for defining public health policy and

The development of the precautionary approach   61

are entitled to adopt protective measures against those activities which may seriously harm the interests of human health (paras. 181, 318).

From the above cases, it can be observed that the European Court of Justice (ECJ) examined the PA from the perspective of Members' powers/rights and obligations. Its rulings reaffirmed that Members enjoy broad discretion in determining appropriate level of health protection, and that Members have the powers/rights and obligations to adopt the PA to safeguard public health. In addition, the Court suggested that the measure should be triggered by a risk assessment, which consists of a scientific component and a political component.

However, there is currently no consensus on whether a political component should be included in a risk assessment in international law (Motaal 2005: 486; Cheyne 2006b: 837–64). Some argue that subjective elements need to be excluded from a scientific assessment, yet such debates are beyond the purpose of this book. Besides this debate, the EU's argument of acting from states' rights and obligations echoes scholars' arguments for examining the PA from 'State responsibility' in international law.

In summary, the above cases show that while the causal relationship of adding antibiotics to animal feed and the risks of resistance of human antibiotics is not yet established, the PA is employed to legitimize the ban on using several antibiotics as additives in animal feed. In addition, the Court also stressed that the Community Institutions have the *powers and duties* to adopt the PA to protect public health. The basic elements of the PA can be synthesized as a cumulative list derived from all of the discussions so far:

- The adoption of the PA in international law should be established from the view of '*State responsibility*'.
- The measure should be *necessary* to protect human life or health.
- The PA is employed within the domain of *scientific uncertainty* or scientific ignorance.
- It should be non-discriminatory to international trade.
- The PA is suggested to be based on a *risk assessment*.
- *Provisional measures* are considered as a means of the PA; however, the adoption of a provisional measure is suggested to be accompanied with a set of procedural requirements which restrains its use from bringing unnecessary interference to free trade and globalization.
- The set of procedural requirements of a provisional measure is suggested to include ongoing duties of *monitoring and review* of the measure.
- Non-scientific factors such as *civilians' social and cultural preferences* and *consumers' tastes and habits* should also be taken into account.

3.3. Philosophical elements of the PA

Despite the PA's merit of providing a margin of safety in public health and environmental protection, its application has been controversial in international

62 *Current landscape*

trade partly due to the ambiguity of its definition. Fragmentation exists among different operations of PAs in international law; therefore, it would be necessary to revisit PAs from philosophical perspectives. We would then be able to delineate the classical contour of PAs, and learn different categories and basic features of PAs in the literature, which will help shape a tailored model of the PA in this book.

Trouwborst notes that at least 16 global and regional environmental treaties and protocols contain reference to the 'precautionary principle', 'precautionary approach', 'precautionary measures' or 'precaution' without defining the terms (Trouwborst 2006: 22). There are various versions of the PA developed by scientists, philosophers, policy-makers, and the lawyers. For example, Sands describes it as: 'to provide guidance in the development and application of international environmental law where there is scientific uncertainty' (Sands 2003: 267). Kriebel *et al.* identify the PA with four central components: 'taking preventive action in the face of uncertainty; shifting the burden of proof to the proponents of an activity; exploring a wide range of alternatives to possibly harmful actions; and increasing public participation decision making' (Kriebel *et al.* 2001: 871). Freestone further illustrates the essence of precaution as the following:

> The precautionary approach then is innovative in that it changes the role of scientific data. It requires that once environmental damage is threatened, action should be taken to control or abate possible environmental interference even though there may still be scientific uncertainty as to the effects of the activities.
>
> (Freestone 1994: 211)

Freestone and Hey further state that 'once a risk is identified the lack of scientific proof of cause and effect shall not be used as a reason for not taking action to protect the environment' (Freestone and Hey 1995: 13). Moreover, Perrez depicts the content of the PA which reflects the recent development in international policy and law as follows:

> If a risk assessment indicates that according to the scientific information available today one cannot exclude the possibility that a certain activity or a certain product may involve unacceptable risk to the environment or, in a certain policy area, to human health, governments may address this potential risk by adopting protecting measures which are intelligible, proportional and coherent with measures adopted in similar situations, and which are not distinguished by protectionist restrictions to trade. Moreover, such precautionary measures should be regularly reviewed, and modified in the light of new scientific findings.
>
> (Perrez 2008: 258)

Further, Perrez identifies several key elements and criteria relevant to the application of precaution: lack of scientific certainty; precaution as part of risk management; scientific assessment; transparency; intelligibility and review; proportionality; no disguised trade restrictions; and, in certain policy areas, application to health (Perrez 2008: 256–8). He also notes that the recent development of the application of precaution has been expanded to the protection of human health, such as policy areas of chemicals and waste policies in particular (Perrez 2003: 17–18). It is found that the PA has a pervasive influence on health and risk regulation, yet the above descriptions and the trigger threshold of the PA still lack a uniform definition.

There are still numerous definitions of PAs in different contexts in a wide variety of perspectives on risk and sources of risk (Wiener and Rogers 2002: 317, 320–21; Morris 2000; Bohanes 2002: 323, 331). Some are simply declaratory while others appear to be more aggressive and demanding of actions. Currently there is no single universal definition of this approach. We will develop a tailored model of this approach[20] after the philosophical and legal analysis in the following sections.

MODELS OF PRECAUTIONARY APPROACHES

In order to examine the PA from philosophical and legal foundations, our discussions will cover the works of both philosophers and lawyers. Particularly, I will base the following discussion on the models developed by Sandin, Sunstein and Trouwborst, and interpret and apply the PA in the real world.

As a philosopher studies the rationale of the PA, Sandin's work of defining the PA has been widely discussed and considered among lawyers (Sunstein 2005: 16; Trouwborst 2006: 317; Peterson 2006: 595). His attempt to generalize the formula of various versions of the approach can serve as a foundation for further interpretation. He believes that 'the core of the precautionary principle is clearly identifiable, and can be used as a starting point for further discussions' (Sandin 2004: 23). Sandin lists 19 versions of the precautionary principle with an applied-ethics approach and then proposes the definition of the PA with a simplified formula (Sandin 1999: 889–907).

From the perspective of international environmental law, Trouwborst further conducts a detailed legal study on the evolution and the definition of the principle which acts to provide complementary underpinning to Sandin's work (Trouwborst 2002, 2006). He attempts to define the PA in the context of '*a state's rights and duties*' and thus proposes a formulation of the 'Precautionary Tripod'. Trouwborst's definition is based on the theme of '*precautionary rights and duties of states*', and he argues that when there are reasonable grounds for concern that significant harm exists, states are deemed to have a customary *right* to act; when the anticipated harm is not only significant but also serious or irreversible, states are considered to have an *obligation* to take action.

64   *Current landscape*

Furthermore, Sunstein scrutinizes the PA from the perspective of economic analysis of law and argues that it should be transformed into an 'Anti-Catastrophe Principle' which emphasizes the full range of risk and other side factors, such as cost-benefit analysis, deliberative democracy, and distributive justice (Sunstein 2005; 2009: 1049). He then provides the definition of the 'Anti-Catastrophe Principle' with a 'four-if formula'. In conjunction with the Anti-Catastrophe Principle, he also proposes the 'Prohibitory Precautionary Approach' (PPA) which favours a flat ban on the product/technology associated with a high probability of a serious harm and the 'Information Disclosure Precautionary Approach' (IDPA) which emphasizes the duty to disclose fresh evidence to the public by the promoter of a new product/technology.

In order to create a common ground for the definition of the PA, it is necessary to accommodate all the relevant factors relating to the PA in international law, which aim to reconcile health, trade, and IP. Trouwborst, Brownsword, and Somsen all contend that the adoption of the PA should be established from the perspective of states' responsibility. In particular, Trouwborst classifies the PA into states' rights and duties considering the impact of the feared threat. If the feared threat is identified as significant, then the state may have the right to adopt the PA; if the threat is identified as not only 'significant' but also 'serious or irreversible', then the state may have the duty to adopt the approach in international law. Sandin's definition is classic and generally applicable; Trouwborst's work formulates the definition from the international public law perspective; and Sunstein's proposal identifies non-scientific factors of the PA in a democratic society. All their models can be complementary to offer new insight into the implementation of the PA in this book.

This book will examine the PA by the following three major categories respectively to illustrate some basic characteristics of this approach: the first is 'argumentative versions versus prescriptive versions', which distinguishes whether different versions require a specific precautionary action to redress a particular risk (Sandin 1999); the second is 'prohibitory versions versus information disclosure versions', which is developed from Sunstein's Anti-Catastrophe Principle (Sunstein 2005: 118); and the third is 'strong versions versus weak versions', which can either refer to the triggering threshold of the approach or the shift of the burden of proof.

3.3.1. Argumentative versus prescriptive

Sandin classifies the PA into two types: one is an argumentative version and the other is a prescriptive version. The argumentative version of the PA is less problematic than the prescriptive type which prescribes that certain actions should be adopted in order to avoid or decrease risk. Principle 15 of the *Rio Declaration* represents the typical argumentative version which does not demand that certain precautionary action should be adopted, and only functions as a declaratory and directive tool.

The development of the precautionary approach   65

On the contrary, the prescriptive versions of the PA focus on the 'actions aiming at the prevention of something that is undesirable but not certain to happen'. This version of the PA prescribes certain actions that would be interpreted as precautionary to the uncertain risk, and can be interpreted with the four-dimensional 'if-clause'. Sandin contends that the PA can be expressed in the following if-clause:

> *If* there is (1) a threat, which is (2) uncertain, then (3) some kind of action (4) is mandatory.
>
> (Sandin 1999: 891)

He proposes that the prescriptive formulations of the PA share four common elements: (1) the threat dimension; (2) the uncertainty dimensions; (3) the action dimension; and (4) the command dimension (Sandin 1999: 891–5).

With the exception of the argumentative version of the PA, which does not require action to respond to a threat, Sandin argues that all the other different versions of the PA can be recast into the 'four-dimensional if-clause' formula, although each element may vary in precision and strength. By 'strength' he means the degree of cautiousness (Sandin 1999: 895).

Like Sandin, Trouwborst also identifies some key elements of the PA. He refers to the three legs of the 'Precautionary Tripod': (1) a threat of harm; (2) uncertainty; and (3) action (Trouwborst 2006: 30). Specifically, Trouwborst defines the precautionary action in the context of *rights and duties of states* in international law. According to his argument, if the threat of harm is designated as 'serious or irreversible', and where the precautionary action is deemed as a duty and right of a state, the precautionary action is thus identical to Sandin's formulation as a mandatory measure. Trouwborst designates the precautionary action to be within the domain of the 'rights and duties of states' when the threat of harm is 'serious or irreversible' to the environment. On the other hand, if the threat only crosses the 'significant' threshold, the precautionary action then only falls within the domain of 'right of states' to adopt measures towards the risk.

Trouwborst's perspective on the definition of the PA suggests that the strength of the precautionary action needs to be adaptive according to the extent and seriousness of the particular risk. Once the risk is identified as *significant*, states are entitled to take precautionary action in order to safeguard the environment and human health. His argument is a more sophisticated tool of the prescriptive version of PA in international law. An argumentative version of the PA, which may only be good for lip service, would not be considered in this book due to efficacy concerns. Therefore, I will adopt Trouwborst's argument to interpret *the entitlements of states to adopt the PA in IP policy-making* in a public health emergency in Chapter 6. Attention will be turned in the following paragraphs to more detailed discussion on the basic

66 Current landscape

elements of the PA, including threat of harm, uncertainty and action, developed from Trouwborst's work.

(1) Threat of harm

Versions of the formulation of the PA exist which do not set out any minimum standard of the anticipated harm, thus giving rise to one of the main critiques: that the PA could be used as a tool for protectionism in international trade. For example, some formulations regarding the degree of harm to health and environment only refer to the vague wording of 'unacceptable risk' or 'unreasonable and otherwise unmanageable risk',[21] which may result in arbitrary use of this approach.

In order to set apart insignificant risks of harm which consist of inapplicable conditions to invoke the PA, Trouwborst seeks to distinguish 'harm that embodies at least some degree of significance and harm that does not' (Trouwborst 2006: 47). It is therefore suggested that the PA cannot be presumed to come into play when the 'projected harm is insignificant' (Trouwborst 2006: 50).

'SIGNIFICANT' HARM AS A THRESHOLD

Trouwborst suggests that the PA is of relevance only when the feared harm is identified as *significant* and that this should then be considered as a minimum threshold (Trouwborst 2006: 50). 'Significant' is defined in the dictionary as 'extensive or important enough to merit attention'.[22] Some commentators explain that the standard of significance is met when harm is neither minor nor trivial. Some locate it in between 'serious' and 'minor trouble to be tolerated' (Trouwborst 2006: 50–51). The International Law Commission (ILC) has noted that the harm must be 'tangible' and 'appreciable' but need not amount to the level of being 'substantial'.[23] The ILC later describes a threshold of significant transboundary harm as 'real' and measurable, but drawn lower than 'substantial' or 'serious' harm.[24] Trouwborst then concludes that *tangible*, *appreciable* and *measurable* harm instead of minor or trivial harm falls within the purview of precaution. This book will also opt for 'significant harm' as the minimum trigger threshold of the PA in IP in order to avoid abuse of this approach.[25]

'SERIOUS OR IRREVERSIBLE' HARM AS A THRESHOLD

One interpretation by the UK government of Principle 15 of the Rio Declaration states that: 'it is not acceptable just to say "we can't be sure that serious damage will happen, so we'll do nothing to prevent it"'.[26] The UK government declares that the PA 'applies particularly where there are good grounds for judging either that action taken promptly at comparatively low

The development of the precautionary approach   67

cost may avoid more costly damage later, or that irreversible effects may follow if damage is delayed' (Trouwborst 2006: 58; Haigh 1994: 229–51).[27] It suggests that precautionary action needs to be taken when there is a threat of irreversible damage.

In the *Gabcikovo-Nagymaros* case,[28] Hungary contended that the impending damage to the Hungarian environment due to the hydrological project was irreparable and enormous.[29] Similarly, in the *Southern Bluefin Tuna* case, Australia and New Zealand claimed that the threat to tuna stocks from the Japanese experimental fishing programme caused 'serious or irreversible damage to the environment'.[30]

It is noteworthy that in addition to 'significant', 'serious' or 'irreversible' harm, the ILC also mentions the term 'grave' as a standard of harm higher than 'serious'.[31] It can be further concluded that '"serious" is located between "significant" and "grave"' (Trouwborst 2006: 64). However, the triggering thresholds most required are either 'significant' harm or 'serious or irreversible' harm; 'grave' harm is not officially referred to in the formulation of the PA.[32]

In summary, the PA should be triggered when the risk from a particular harm is proved to be crossing the 'significant' threshold; any risk that is identified as *de minimis* can be disregarded (Sandin 2005: 191–200). Further, if the risk is objectively identified as 'serious or irreversible harm', then the legitimacy to trigger the PA will increase. In other words, the legitimacy of the precautionary action depends on the extent or the gravity of the potential harm: when the unknown risk is identified as causing 'serious or irreversible' harm to human health or the environment, states are not only entitled but may also be required to take precautionary measures to protect their citizens and the environment under their responsibility in international law. Therefore, this book will recommend 'significant harm' as the trigger threshold of the PA in IP. If the harm is identified as 'serious or irreversible', then the legitimacy of the precautionary action will increase.

A question then arises as to the extent to which a state can determine what is a subjective/objective *unacceptable* degree of risk, and when, if ever, a line can be drawn which can be stated with relative certainty to be an objectively unacceptable degree of risk. The level of unacceptable risk should be established through an objective risk assessment and a subjective element of risk communication, which focuses on the public's right to information. It is embodied in the stimulation of public debates, which will be addressed in the following section. This might arguably also be the point where we draw a line between the right of a state to act and the duty of a state to act.

(2) Uncertainty

In order to trigger the PA, there must be a basic element of scientific uncertainty. It is of vital importance to set the triggering threshold of the PA at an

68 *Current landscape*

appropriate level of risk. De Sadeleer identifies different levels of risk by building a hierarchy of risks (De Sadeleer 2008: 156–61):

- Residual risks: these are hypothetical risks, and can be ignored and do not require regulatory measures;
- Uncertain risks: these are under the domain of the PA;
- Certain risks: these are within the scope of prevention.

The aim of a precautionary measure is to invoke the PA in situations of uncertain risks (see Figure 3.3.1). Residual risks refer to risks that are low in probability, which can be ignored and cannot be applied in the precautionary model (Sandin 2005: 191–200). If the risks are identified as certain, then the prevention principle will play a role in risk management.

The European Commission comments on scientific uncertainty as follows:

> Scientific uncertainty results usually from five characteristics of the scientific method: the variable chosen, the measurements made, the samples drawn, the models used and the causal relationships employed. Scientific uncertainty may also arise from a controversy on existing data or lack of some relevant data. Uncertainty may relate to qualitative or quantitative elements of the analysis.
> (EC Communication on the Precautionary Principle (2000): 14)

Commentators have further distinguished epistemological uncertainty from ontological uncertainty (Trouwborst 2006: 73–9). Epistemological uncertainty refers to uncertainty due to lack of information, while ontological uncertainty is related to uncertainty due to complexity and variability. However, there appears to be no indication in legal instruments of specific

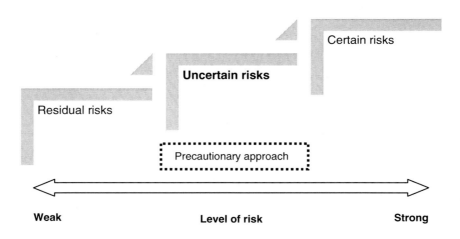

Figure 3.3.1 Levels of risk and the precautionary approach

The development of the precautionary approach   69

classifications of uncertainty. For example: Principle 15 of the Rio Declaration refers to a 'lack of full scientific certainty'. Similarly, the EC Communication on the Precautionary Principle indicates that the precautionary principle is related to situations 'where scientific information is *insufficient, inconclusive,* or *uncertain*' (italics added).

The uncertainty of the cause and effect relationship is one dimension of scientific uncertainty. In *Pfizer Animal Health* v. *EC* and *Alpharma Inc.* v. *EC*,[33] it is noted that there was no scientific proof of any link between the prohibited antibiotics used in animal feedstuffs and resistance to those antibiotics in humans. Under the circumstance of no available scientific assessment on the causal relationship, the European Council adopted the PA and concluded that the ban was not inappropriate.

However, the risk of harm needs to be a real risk and 'more than hypothetical or [a] remote possibility of such harm'.[34] In the *MOX Plant* case,[35] Ireland challenged the legitimacy of the authorization by the British government of a new nuclear fuel processing facility at the Sellafield site on the Irish Sea coast. Ireland claimed that the PA obliged the United Kingdom to 'apply caution, and take preventive measures even where there is no conclusive evidence' of a causal relationship between the operation of the MOX plant and marine environmental hazards. The UK contended that it is 'generally accepted that [the PA] can operate only where there are some reasonable grounds for concern'. It was therefore argued that the Irish allegation did not pass the test, and there were 'no reasonable grounds for believing' that the MOX plant would cause unacceptable changes to the environment of the Irish Sea due to the risks involved being classified as 'infinitesimally small'.

The European Court of Justice (ECJ) in *Alpharma Inc.* v. *EC* also stressed that precautionary measures cannot be adopted on 'purely hypothetical considerations', on 'mere conjecture', or be taken 'solely on the basis of rumors' (paras. 155–6).[36] The ECJ in *Pfizer Animal Health* v. *EC* noted that the Community institutions cannot take a hypothetical approach to risk and cannot make their decision on a 'zero-risk' basis (para. 152).[37] Similarly to the implications from the *MOX Plant* case and the above-mentioned ECJ cases, Motaal states that the precautionary action needs to be based on 'some sort of scientific foundation', and 'cannot be based on completely unsubstantiated or unresearched fears' (Motaal 2005: 488). In the WTO regime, the Appellate Body in *Australia – Salmon* confirmed that evaluation of the risks of harm can either be expressed quantitatively or qualitatively (paras. 123–4),[38] and in *EC – Hormones*, the Appellate Body indicated that the report of risks is based on the right to act on the basis of 'minority' scientific evidence (para. 194).[39]

In summary, the application of the PA is suggested to be within the domain of uncertain but nonetheless real risks. The PA could be triggered in circumstances of scientific uncertainty where the threat of harm has crossed the 'significant' threshold (see Table 3.3.1).

70   *Current landscape*

Table 3.3.1 The domain of the precautionary approach

		Risks		
Harm		*Residual risks*	*Uncertain risks*	*Certain risks*
Hypothetic/Minor/Trivial				
Real;	**Significant**		**Precautionary**	Prevention
Tangible;	Substantial		**Approach**	Principle
Appreciable;	Serious/ irreversible			
Measurable	Grave			

Scientific uncertainty is a significant factor in the precautionary formulation. The adopting state's duty to review is particularly relevant in updating the situation of scientific uncertainty. If the risk is proved positively harmful after discoveries from ongoing monitoring and review, then the PA should be adapted as a permanent ban; if proved otherwise, the approach should be abolished in due course.

In addition to the criteria of threat of harm and uncertainty, the element of 'action' is also highlighted as an elementary feature of a prescriptive PA, which distinguishes itself from an argumentative PA.

(3) Action

In Sandin's formulation, precautionary action is mandatory in prescriptive versions. Likewise, Trouwborst argues that states should have a customary right to act when there are reasonable grounds for concern that significant harm exists, and an obligation to take action when the harm is not only significant but also serious or irreversible. The EU Court of Justice in *Alpharma Inc* v. *EC* also noted that 'a public authority may be *required* to take action even before adverse effects have become apparent' in a situation where the Community institutions make the provisional withdrawal of the authorizations for antibiotics (para. 355, italics added).[40]

In addition, from past precedents in international law, precautionary actions are required to be effective and proportionate. Effectiveness ensures that the relevant purpose is served. In the *Southern Bluefin Tuna* Order, the ITLOS suggested parties 'act with prudence and caution to ensure that *effective* conservation measures are taken to prevent serious harm to the stock of southern bluefin tuna'.[41] *Proportionality* ensures that the means can be well adjusted to fit the purpose. For example, the International Chamber of Commerce states that precautionary action must be 'proportionally responsive' to the environmental concern at issue (Trouwborst 2006: 150).[42]

The European Court of Justice has often emphasized the importance of proportionality in the implementation of the PA by choosing the least restrictive precautionary measure.[43] Under the current trend of globalization, precautionary measures stipulated in international legal instruments are frequently required to be least restrictive to international trade or traffic.

TYPES OF PRECAUTIONARY ACTIONS

There are many forms of precautionary actions. Typical precautionary measures include precautionary bans,[44] the employment of safety margins,[45] carrying out detailed research on the risk and monitoring,[46] reversal of the burden of proof to the one who promotes a new technology, prior information and consultation, liability and compensation rules, the use of economic instruments like subsidies or taxes, and participatory decision-making procedures (Trouwborst 2006: 177–8). The range of measures taken by states in response to the PA is very wide; Trouwborst further contends that 'essentially every type of environmental measure can be a precautionary measure in the scheme of the precautionary principle' (Trouwborst 2006: 179).

3.3.2. Prohibitory versus information disclosure

In addition to the *argumentative* versus *prescriptive* versions of the PA, the PA can also be classified into *prohibitory* versus *information disclosure* versions according to the severity of the damage. This is derived from Sunstein's Anti-Catastrophe Principle.

(1) Anti-Catastrophe Principle

Sunstein criticizes the traditional precautionary principle as having a tendency to lead people to think in terms of the worst-case scenario and also because it tends to lead to the risk of over-regulation (Sunstein 2005: 64–88). As an alternative, he proposes the model of 'Anti-Catastrophe Principle' by which the Prohibitory PA and the Information Disclosure PA (IDPA) are distinguished in accordance with the severity of the anticipated harm (Sunstein 2005: 118). A flat ban on the product/technology in question is recommended when it is associated with a high probability of serious harm; otherwise, when the risk concerns a relatively lower probability of less serious harm, the promoter of the new product/technology is obliged to monitor and disclose information on the ongoing risk (Sunstein 2005: 118).

(2) Trimming exercise

With regard to risk regulation in addition to the Anti-Catastrophe Principle, Sunstein also argues for the concept of 'trimming' (Sunstein 2009: 1049), by which he refers to the seventeenth-century 'Trimmer[s]', 'who tend to reject

72   Current landscape

the extremes and to borrow ideas from both sides in intense social controversies'. It is recorded that 'Trimmers believed it important to steer between the polar positions and to preserve what is deepest and most sensible in competing positions' (Sunstein 2009: 1053). Sunstein notes that trimming might be defended as 'producing the best outcomes' and 'responding to judges' lack of information', and can serve to reduce social exclusion or humiliation. He focuses on the reasons why judges involved in constitutional disputes might choose to trim. He maintains that being 'humble and uncertain about the right result', justices might steer between the poles to minimize possible damages (Sunstein 2009: 1061).

In summary, the core concept of the 'Trimming' and 'Anti-Catastrophe Principle' is to adopt a margin of safety to manage unknown risks. These two concepts are similar to the precautionary measure to adopt a 'safety margin' which provides extra buffer zones to minimize the direct impact of risk to the environment or human health. They provide a safety net in the blind spot of science to safeguard human health and the environment.

A duty of information disclosure is highlighted in the 'Anti-Catastrophe Principle' model. Under the IDPA, the party who introduces a new technology should bear the burden of disclosing the risk and uncertainties of the technology at issue and leave the public to decide the margin of safety of the product. It is suggested that a review of the risks and uncertainties can be conducted within a certain period of time to update the relevant scientific information and evaluate its margin of safety. Ideally, relevant scientific justifications should become clearer in time with the advancement of scientific breakthroughs, and the public will be better informed to decide the appropriate margins of safety.

Sunstein's Anti-Catastrophe Principle consists of four factors: uncertainty; magnitude of harm; tool; and margin of safety. Particularly, the element of 'public engagement' plays a vital role in the determination of an appropriate level of protection and a margin of safety.

(3) Public engagement

In the Anti-Catastrophe Principle model, Sunstein highlights the significance of public engagement in a democratic society, which is of particular relevance in risk communication in the structure of risk analysis (Sunstein 2005: 158). It appears to incorporate the subjective element of risk perception into risk management. In this regard, he suggests citizens should get involved in the decision-making process of risk management by deliberating their preferences and values (Sunstein 2005: 158).[47]

'Public engagement' is deemed a fundamental feature of a democratic society. It is mentioned in some international instruments regarding the implementation of the PA. The first official legal instrument to recognize public engagement is the Rio Declaration. The Rio Declaration notes that environmental issues are best handled with public participation, and individuals' access to

The development of the precautionary approach 73

information, access to decision-making and access to justice are endorsed (Principle 10). The detailed action plan for the Rio Declaration, Agenda 21, also addresses the importance of access to information. It highlights that the United System should involve the participation of 'Major Groups' which include the expertise and views of non-governmental organizations (Section III, *Agenda 21*).

Further, public participation is developed as the objective of specific international obligations binding upon the EU and its Member States as a result of the Aarhus Convention (Jans 2003).[48] The Aarhus Convention developed a three-pillar structure in its agenda: public access to environmental information; public participation in decision-making; and public access to justice in environmental matters.

Public participation in the Aarhus Convention involves the following three dimensions: public participation in decisions on specific activities; public participation concerning plans, programmes and policies; and public participation during the preparation of executive regulations and generally applicable legally binding normative instruments (Articles 6, 7 and 8). It is stressed that Member States are obliged to 'promote environmental education and environmental awareness among the public, especially on how to obtain access to information, to participate in decision-making and to obtain access to justice in environmental matter[s]' (Article 3.3). The public should be allowed to submit any 'comments, information, analyses or opinions that it considers relevant' during the process of communication (Article 6.8). The public is also engaged during the preparation of regulations and other legally binding rules that may have a significant effect on the environment (Articles 6 and 8).

Specifically, it is identified in the Aarhus Convention that 'the state of human health and safety' and 'conditions of human life' are affected by the environment (Article 2.3(c)). It is fair to say that Member States bear the duty to promote health education and health awareness among the public, particularly on how to obtain access to information, to participate in decision-making and to obtain access to justice in health and safety matters.

Further, the TFEU stipulates that citizens 'have the right to participate in the democratic life of the Union' (Article 10.3 TFEU); the EU institutions need to 'maintain an open, transparent and regular dialogue' with civil society; and citizens' initiatives of submission of proposals need to be recognized (Articles 10.3, 11.2 and 11.4 TFEU). Therefore, the public should be encouraged to take part in the making of health policy and to make a collective informed decision through risk communication on the acceptable level of health protection.

Similarly, at the international level, the concept of public awareness and participation is also respected in Article 23 of the *Cartagena Protocol on Biosafety*.[49] The Cartagena Protocol is an instrument renowned for its mechanism of regulation on importing genetically modified organisms (GMOs).[50] The PA has been laid down as a foundation of the mechanism. In addition, the Codex Alimentarius also stresses the element of 'risk communication'

74   *Current landscape*

in risk regulation, which indicates the exchange of information between relevant important stakeholders.[51] A more elaborate illustration of the mechanism will be addressed in Chapter 4.

In summary, the element of 'margin of safety' which is associated with the determination of the appropriate level of protection can be particularly influenced by public engagement. The acceptable level of risk differs in different communities, thus it requires social debates within specific communities to determine the appropriate level of health protection. The stimulation of public debate is an ongoing process, and thus no absolute rules or answers to particular issues exist (Pellerano and Montague 2006; Whiteside 2006). Constant refining and review are necessary to examine the appropriateness and effectiveness of the adopted approach. I will proceed to apply the non-scientific elements of the PA in compulsory licensing in Chapter 6 (section 6.3.4).

After the introduction of the Prescriptive PA and Information Disclosure PA, the last common classification of the PA is also noteworthy: weak versions versus strong versions are divided either in terms of the trigger threshold or the allocation of burden of proof.

3.3.3. Strong or weak

Commentators have expressed the polarities of this spectrum in terms of 'strong' and 'weak' versions in a great variety of formulations of the approach. Tinker expresses the view that:

> At its *strongest*, the precautionary principle may be interpreted to prohibit virtually all use of natural resources and all human activities of any kind in certain ecosystems. Such a moratorium could continue indefinitely, until such time as sufficient scientific knowledge develops about the effects of such activities or use. At its *weakest*, the precautionary principle may be mere hortatory language intended to guide states as they adopt national legislation and plans, allowing a permissive approach to use of resources and human activities and a balancing of interests which may favour development or quality of life choices over conservation of biodiversity or other preventive action.
>
> (Tinker 1996b: 56–7)

Some commentators avoid using potentially negative connotations associated with the terms 'weak' and 'strong'. For example, VanderZwaag refers to different strengths of formulations as 'ecocentric' or 'strict', and 'utilitarian' or 'permissive' and the like (VanderZwaag 1994).

This book follows a traditional classification and divides the 'weak' and 'strong' versions in terms of two criteria, the trigger threshold and burden of proof, and then concludes with an alternative version of the *'moderate'* PA.

(1) Trigger threshold

The standard to distinguish strong and weak versions of the PA is whether precautionary measures are required once a certain risk is identified or only permitted in the absence of scientific certainty (Kolitch 2006: 221–56). In the context, a prescriptive version of the approach is referred to as a strong one, and an argumentative version is accordingly a weak one. The strong PA requires mitigating action by those who created the damage or risk;[52] the weak PA merely prevents lacks of scientific certainty from postponing mitigating measures. For example, the embodiment of the weak precautionary principle articulated in the Preamble of the *United Nations Convention on Biology Diversity*: 'Noting also that where there is a threat of significant reduction or loss of biological diversity, lack of full scientific certainty should not be used as a reason for postponing measures to avoid or minimize such a threat.'

Further, a strong version implies that once a certain minimal threshold of risk is met, 'a fundamental rethinking of regulatory policy' is required (Sunstein 2005: 18). As Freestone and Hey note: 'once a risk is identified the lack of scientific proof of cause and effect shall not be used as a reason for not taking action to protect the environment' (Freestone and Hey 1995: 13). Another strong version of the PA is defined by Perez as:

> [S]etting certain thresholds of scientific uncertainty and hazardous potential, which once met, would allow regulators to take appropriate regulatory actions (e.g., impose a ban on the introduction of a new technology), irrespective of the costs – measured in terms of benefits forgone.
> (Perez 2007, citing Welsh and Ervin 2006: 153–72)

Likewise, the TFEU describes the strong version in the following way:

> Union policy on the environment shall aim at a high level of protection taking into account the diversity of situations in the various regions of the Union. It shall be based on the precautionary principle and on the principles that preventive action should be taken, that environmental damage should as a priority be rectified at source and that the polluter should pay.
> (Article 191.2 TFEU)

Sunstein notes that: 'The most cautious ... weak versions suggest, quite sensibly, that a lack of decisive evidence of harm should not be a ground for refusing to regulate' (Sunstein 2005: 18). Consequently, he refers to the Rio Declaration as a weak version of the PA. On the contrary, a strong version of the PA is more aggressive than the Rio Declaration because it is not limited the application to a high threshold such as threats of serious or irreversible damage. For instance, the Wingspread Declaration does not require the element of 'serious or irreversible damage' as the trigger threshold.

Under international customary law, a weak version or an argumentative version of the PA would not be able to impose a duty on states to be responsible

76 Current landscape

for the protection of human health and the environment in its territory, thus the adoption of a weak version would probably only be lip service and a declaratory tool of policy-making without any mechanism of enforcement. It is therefore suggested by this book that the employment of the PA would achieve relatively satisfactory efficiency with a *strong* or a *prescriptive* version of the approach.

(2) Burden of proof

A strong version of the PA sometimes refers to the reversal of burden of proof on the proponents of a new technology. As Sands notes, the PA would 'tend to shift the burden of proof and require the person who wishes to carry out an activity to prove that it will not cause harm to the environment' (Sands 2003: 273). However, its application is far more complicated in court than in theory and is under debate. Jones and Bronitt note that: 'precaution, it has been argued, has the potential to strike at the heart of this evidential problem by modifying the burden of proof that objectors must satisfy' (Jones and Bronitt 2006: 139). Thus the reversal of burden of proof is context-dependent and should be considered on a case-by-case basis.

The shift of onus is of particular significance in the WTO. In WTO law, if the PA is regarded as *exclusion* from other Members' obligations, the defendant party enjoys the reverse of burden of proof; if the PA is treated as an *exception* to Members' obligations, then the burden of proof still lies with the defendant party. In particular, in the *EC – Biotech* case,[53] the Panel recognized the adoption of a provisional SPS measure as 'a *right* and not an exception from a general obligation' under the SPS Agreement (*EC – Biotech*, paras. 7.2969 and 7.2973). It implies that the burden of proof is to be shifted to the complaining party. The allocation of burden of proof will be further examined in Chapter 4 when we explore the difference in legal status between exceptions and exclusions to WTO obligations in WTO law (Section 4.3).

(3) Moderate PA

It is noteworthy that in addition to the traditional classifications of weak and strong precaution which represent two extremes, the WHO has proposed *moderate precaution*, which consists of presumptions about interventions being under 'weak precaution' but which allow flexibility in order to shift the burden on a case-by-case basis (WHO, The World Health Report 2002: 151). Table 3.3.3 demonstrates that *moderate precaution* appears to strike a balance between the two extreme versions of precaution, while accommodating the strengths of weak and strong versions by balancing the burden of proof, and giving considerations to free trade and individual preference. In the context of *moderate precaution*, precautionary action can only be adopted as *a last resort* to prevent misuse or protectionism under globalization. It can be concluded that this version has resonance with the requirement of proportionality and will sit well in the trade world.

We will now identify the general features of the PA by comparative studies of the above-mentioned models.

The development of the precautionary approach   77

Table 3.3.3 Views of precaution within different views of regulation

Weak precaution	Moderate precaution	Strong precaution
Intervention only on positive scientific evidence and demonstrated cost-effectiveness	Presumption about interventions as under 'weak prevention', but with case-by-case flexibility to shift burden of proof	Risk creator has to demonstrate safety of activity. Little acceptance of cost-effectiveness arguments
Presumption of risk management. Banning very rare	Underlying presumption of risk management. Banning possible, but only as *last resort*	Presumption of risk avoidance. Banning very likely
Presumption of free trade based on objective scientific criteria. Individual preferences and societal concerns given no weight	Underlying presumption of *free trade* on the basis of scientific criteria. Recognition that individual preferences and societal concerns do matter	No automatic presumption of free trade. Individual preferences and societal concerns are dominant

Sources: Adapted from WHO *The World Health Report* 2002: 151

COMPARISONS OF THE PRECAUTION FORMULA

We can compare Sunstein's four factors of the Anti-Catastrophe Principle with Sandin's formulation of prescriptive versions of the PA and Trouwborst's Precautionary Tripod. They all identify the basic elements of harm, uncertainty and the introduced tool/measure. There is a slight difference in their construction of the PA where Sunstein puts more weight on the magnitude of potential harm; likewise, Trouwborst focuses on the distinction between 'significant' harm and 'serious or irreversible' harm, while Sandin asks which type of hazards should apply in the formula. Sunstein further proposes the concept of 'margins of safety'; Sandin stresses different types of measures applied under various conditions, and Trouwborst argues for the PA to be established from the perspective of *the rights and duties of states.*

This book focuses on the comparative study of these three models of the PA and seeks to further refine a workable model to fit into the expedient application in a public health emergency. A normative prescriptive version of the PA is emerging from the above analysis in the following outlines:

- The fundamental elements of the PA consist of the trigger threshold, scientific uncertainty, and the precautionary action.
- The adoption of the PA is required to be proportionate and efficient.

78 *Current landscape*

- The PA is more efficient as a prescriptive version than an argumentative one.
- The PA adopted in international law can be established from the perspective of a state's rights and duties.
- The adopting state bears the duty to carry out ongoing monitoring and review of the measure and the feared risk.
- Non-scientific factors such as cost-benefit analysis and public engagement can be included in the consideration of the PA.

Sunstein's proposal appears to fit in with modern democratic society, yet the distinction between 'high probability of a serious harm' and 'low probability of a less serious harm' fails to enclose a full range of risks. For example, risks of 'low probability of a serious harm' exist in a risk spectrum which is not yet categorized in his model, for example, the imposing of an import ban on beef due to the outbreak of 'mad cow disease' (BSE) in the country of origin falls within the domain of 'low probability of a serious harm'.[54]

Sunstein's incorporation of the extra factors such as cost-benefit analysis, deliberate democracy, and distributive justice provides practical policy guidance on the implementation of the approach in contemporary society. This category of the PA focuses on people's right to information and the allocation of burden of proof, which are of vital importance in a democratic society, yet they still need to be accommodated in a given scenario in accordance with the characteristics of a specific risk. In the circumstance of an acute public health emergency, there may not be sufficient time to carry out full proper public engagement; however, the duty of review and information disclosure could still be imposed on the adopting party after the invocation of the approach.

In summary, in order to have an effective PA, a *prescriptive* and *information disclosure* version will be opted for in this work. Further, a *moderate* PA is preferred with a view to avoiding extreme versions and also to take into account concerns of free trade.

3.4. Legal status and terminology – precautionary approach or precautionary principle?

Precaution appeared in national legislation before it was introduced at the international level (Sands 2003: 266–79), and most states adopt it at the national level more than at international level. It first emerged from environmental protection in Germany; there is also evidence that it had been applied by US courts in connection with health, safety and environmental protection even before the appearance of the concept in Europe (Perrez 2008: 253).

At the international level, the legal status of PA is not yet settled (Boutillon 2002: 429), but its widespread use has implied that it is recognized as 'a legitimate approach in the field of environmental protection' (Barton 1998: 517). The *European Council Resolution on the Precautionary Principle* notes that the PA is 'gradually asserting itself as a principle of international law in the field of environmental and health protection' (para. 3).[55]

Notably in the international economic regime, the WTO Appellate Body has suggested that PA has been incorporated in the WTO SPS Agreement; however, its application and legal status appears to be relatively restrictive in WTO law. The Appellate Body in *EC – Hormones* indicated that PA was not yet an accepted principle of 'general' or 'customary international law' by stating that:

> The status of the precautionary principle in international law continues to be the subject of debate among academics, law practitioners, regulators and judges. The precautionary principle is regarded by some as having crystallized into a general principle of customary international environmental law. Whether it has been widely accepted by Members as a principle of general or customary international law appears less than clear. We consider, however, that it is unnecessary, and probably imprudent, for the Appellate Body in this appeal to take a position on this important, but abstract, question. We noted that the Panel itself did not make any definitive finding with regard to the status of the precautionary principle in international law and that the precautionary principle, at least outside the field of international environmental law, still awaits authoritative formulation.
> (WTO Appellate Body Report, *EC –Hormones*, para. 123)

While the Appellate Body in *EC – Hormones* avoided declaring the legal status of PA, it did imply that 'the 'precautionary approach' or 'concept' is 'an *emerging* principle of law' which may in the future crystallize into one of the 'general principles of law recognized by civilized nations' within the meaning of Article 38(1)(c) of the *Statute of the International Court of Justice* (para. 122). It also mentioned that commentators have noted that there is sufficient state practice of PA, and it can be recognized as *an evolving principle* in international law (note 92).

The legal status of the PA has a direct impact on the preference for the term 'precautionary approach' rather than 'precautionary principle' in this work, which will be addressed in the following section.

PP OR PA?

The distinction between the terms 'precautionary principle' and the 'precautionary approach' has been a topic of academic debates. Birnie *et al.* note that '… European treaties and EC law generally refer to the precautionary principle, whereas global agreements more often refer to the precautionary approach or precautionary measures' (Birnie *et al.* 2009: 152–64). Some observe that the Americans prefer the word 'approach' in order to underline that they do not accept that it has yet gained the status of customary international law,

80   *Current landscape*

while the Europeans prefer 'principle' to emphasize that they accept it as a concept entailing certain legal implications (Perrez 2008: 258–9; Whiteside 2006). Few commentators insist on the significance of distinguishing the precautionary approach from the precautionary principle; both terms often appear to be interchangeable.

Mascher has concluded that 'there is nothing to suggest that the terms "precautionary principle" and "precautionary approach" cannot be used interchangeably' (Mascher 1997: 70–79). Yet Orrego Vicuña has observed that the term 'approach' reflects a hint of flexibility in the role of precaution in relation to fisheries management:

> Since scientific uncertainty is normally the rule in fisheries management a straightforward application of the precautionary principle would have resulted in the impossibility of proceeding with any activity relating to marine fisheries. It is on these grounds that the concept of the 'precautionary approach' surfaced with a view to provide a more flexible tool for the specific needs of fisheries management.
>
> (Orrego Vicuña 1999)

It is noteworthy that there is a preference for using the word 'approach' rather than 'principle' in cases of fisheries management (ITLOS Nos. 3 and 4; Howarth 2008, 213). For example, the 1995 *Convention on Straddling and Highly Migratory Fish Stocks* preferred the term 'precautionary approach' by noting that '"approach" offers greater flexibility and will be less potentially restrictive than the "principle"'.[56] Judge Laing had expressed in another Separate Opinion the view that 'adopting an approach, rather than a principle imports a certain degree of flexibility and tends, though not dispositively, to underscore reticence about making premature pronouncements about desirable normative structures'.[57] Judge Treves seems to associate the term 'principle' with legally binding, customary status, as opposed to the alleged more neutral 'approach'.[58] It is therefore observed that the word 'approach' receives more acknowledgement than the term 'principle' in empirical studies in international environmental protection.

Perrez has concluded that 'at the practical level, there is no conflict or contradiction between the terms "principle" and "approach"'. The debate over whether precaution should be considered a principle or an approach is therefore more to do with symbols and semantics than substance' (Perrez 2008: 259).

In addition, the UK Nuffield Council suggests that 'there is not just one, but several principles or considerations that need to be considered' by adopting the term 'precautionary approach' rather than 'precautionary principle' (Nuffield Council on Bioethics 2007: 35–6). As Laurie and Hunter point out, '[T]he Council prefers the term "precautionary approach" and, in so doing, reflects the Department of Health's framework in suggesting that no one principle or consideration should be applied. The value of these instruments

The development of the precautionary approach   81

lies in both their procedural and substantive contribution to the decision-making process' (Laurie and Hunter 2009: 101–37).

In empirical studies, the word 'approach' appears to be preferable in international legal instruments in order to avoid extreme versions of the precautionary principle that demand absolute environmental protection regardless of the cost. An extreme version of the precautionary principle shows little acceptance of the cost-effectiveness arguments, and gives no presumption of free trade. However, in this book, the precautionary approach is suggested as being triggered by empirical risk assessment or science-based judgement.[59] The invocation of a PA in compulsory licensing will depend on scientific judgement or certain forms of cost-effectiveness evaluation, tempered by precaution.[60]

Taking into account the factor of risk assessment and the reconciliation of free trade and international health, this book avoids extreme interpretations of the precautionary principle, and will settle at the *moderate* version proposed by the WHO. Hence, the term 'approach' would demonstrate the 'moderate' and 'pragmatic' nature of this book.

The term 'approach' suggests a broader and more adaptive method than the term 'principle', which indicates an absolute implication. For the time being, considering the evolving nature and the unsettled debates on the legal status of the precautionary principle as discussed above (WTO Appellate Body Report, *EC – Hormones*, para. 122), and given the political expediency in the international setting, it would be more agreeable to adopt the term 'approach' to avoid disagreements in international fora.

Terminology is the first stepping stone for communication among different stakeholders, which aims at facilitating future reconciliation in the application of the PA in a public health emergency. Considering the political sensitivities, which can be extreme in different worlds of trade, health, IP, and human rights, it would be more satisfactory to all stakeholders to adopt the term 'approach' rather than 'principle' within the domain of this book.

Based on the above consideration, a practical and workable reading of the existing legal text is sought by this work with a view to reconciling trade and health. Though some may argue that the two terms are interchangeable, the term 'approach' appears to be more apt than 'principle' in empirical studies in international law. It is also observed that the slight distinction between these two terms is that PP implies a more dogmatic assertion to adopt certain measures regardless of the cost in order to shy away from uncertain risks, while PA reflects a hint of a more flexible application of precaution. I will choose the term 'approach' in this book to underscore the adaptability and flexibility of risk management in a public health emergency.

3.5. Conclusion

I have introduced the origins and recent development of the PA, which has been proliferated in international environmental protection in the past few decades. Evidence shows that the implementation of the PA has also been

82 Current landscape

extended to the scope of human health and food safety in international law. States are allowed to determine their own appropriate level of health protection to adopt the PA in international customary law.

SCHOLARLY APPROACHES TAKEN

We have also reviewed scholars' proposals on the definition of the PA. Evidence shows that adopting the term 'approach' instead of 'principle' will be more practical in an international setting for it implies a rather flexible spirit, and would be more adaptive in the current political setting. In order to underscore the adaptability of the employed precaution, the term 'precautionary approach' is preferred in this book. Specifically, based upon the above-mentioned formulations of the PA, this book will be developed from the foundation of *'States' precautionary entitlements'*, which was based on Trouwborst's theory of *'precautionary rights and duties of states'* in international law. Trouwborst divides states' precautionary actions into 'rights' or 'duties' in accordance with the gravity of the anticipated harm, yet this book considers 'significant harm' (to human health) as a general reasonable trigger threshold of the PA. The question as to whether to follow Trouwborst's distinction of precautionary 'rights' or 'duties' according to the severity of the harm is not within the domain of this book.

In the discussion described above, a model of the *'prescriptive'* and *'information disclosure'* versions of the PA will be preferred. The element of 'public engagement' of risk management would need to be carefully mapped out in the duration of a preparedness plan of a pandemic due to the inherent limitations of an emergency. The burden of 'information disclosure' may still be imposed on the adopting party to avoid abuse of the PA. Further, the model of a *moderate* PA will also be considered, which aims to avoid extreme versions of the approach and serves to reconcile different stakeholders. It is noteworthy that the invocation of the PA depends greatly upon the adopted measure and the characteristics of each individual threat. Thus the elements of the approach are identified as a general template, and still need to be adapted in the context of each particular risk.

ELEMENTS OF THE MODERATE PRECAUTIONARY APPROACH

We have also reviewed different definitions of the PA proposed by philosophers, lawyers and scientists. Three categories of the PA have been reviewed; it can be concluded that the basic elements of the PA consist of: (1) threat of harm; (2) uncertainty; and (3) precautionary action. We have also identified other basic elements of the PA in this book, which are supposed to act well in the interplay of health, trade and IP. In summary, the adaptive version of the moderate PA consists of the elements described below:

- A precautionary action is established from the perspective of a *state's precautionary entitlements* in international law.

The development of the precautionary approach   83

- States enjoy a broad margin of appreciation in exercising their precautionary entitlements.
- The adoption of the PA should be *necessary* to protect human health or safety.
- The adoption of a *provisional measure* is a means to the approach.
- The said PA should be based on a *risk assessment*.
- The adoption of the PA should take *proportionality* into account, which needs to be employed as *a last resort*.
- The PA should be in compliance with Members' obligation of 'Non-discrimination' to the WTO. The approach should not consist of any disguised restriction and should be *least restrictive* to international trade.
- Uncertainty: the PA should be applied within the domain of *scientific uncertainty*.
- Threshold of harm: the PA *may* be triggered when the unknown harm crosses the threshold of *significant* level of harm.
- Action: the PA should include an *effective* precautionary action.
- Ongoing duty of monitoring and review: according to the Information Disclosure PA, the adopting state bears the duty to update relevant information on the said measure.
- Burden of proof: the PA allows a reversal of burden of proof on a case-by-case basis. Particularly in an Information Disclosure PA, the onus is often shifted to the one promoting a new product/technology, which implies that the party who introduces/increases risks to society bears the burden of proof.
- Other non-scientific factors such as public participation, *consumers' tastes and habits*, and *civilians' social and cultural preferences* could be taken into account on a case-by-case basis. However, in the situation of an acute health emergency, public participation may be restricted due to time constraints.

The PA from the perspective of a public health emergency will be further defined to reshape the IP policy through the lens of precaution in following chapters [61]. After reviewing the development of the PA, I will assess how the PA has been developed to date in the WHO and the WTO regimes in the following chapter.

Notes

1 UK Nuffield Council on Bioethics (2007) *Public Health: Ethical Issues.*
2 Ibid., p. 33.
3 National Institute of Clinical Excellence (NICE) (2009) *Methods for the Development of NICE Public Health Guidance* (2nd edition), p. 118, available at: http://www.nice.org.uk/media/2FB/53/PHMethodsManual110509.pdf
4 The Wingspread Statement on the Precautionary Principle was established during a conference of experts in Wingspread, Wisconsin, USA in January 1998.

84 *Current landscape*

The full text of the Wingspread Declaration is reproduced in Raffensperger, C. and Tickner, J. (eds) (1999) *Protecting Public Health and the Environment: Implementing the Precautionary Principle*, Washington DC, US: Island Press, pp. 353–4. According to Naomi Salmon, the version in the Wingspread Statement is generally adopted by non-governmental organizations aiming at a more stringent approach to environmental and health protection.

5 The Intergovernmental Agreement on the Environment (IGAE) signed in May 1992 by all heads of government in Australia (s 3.5.1).

6 See Section 3.3.1.

7 ECJ Case C–236/01, *Monsanto Agricoltura Italia SpA and Others* v. *Presidenza del Consiglio dei Ministri and Others* (*Monsanto*), ECR 2003 I–08105, adopted 9 September 2003, para. 133.

8 'Uncertainty' refers to a situation under which it is possible to define all possible outcomes, but where there is no basis for the confident assigning of probabilities. 'Ignorance' refers to a situation under which it is possible neither to assign probabilities nor even to define all possible outcomes.

9 Justice Stein of the New South Wales (NSW) Land and Environment Court in *Leatch* v. *Director-General. National Parks and Wildlife Service and Shoalhaven City Council*, 23 November 1993, 81 LGERA, 1993, p. 270, at 282.

10 For example: *United Nations Convention on the Law of the Sea* (1982); *Convention on Early Notification of a Nuclear Accident* (1986); *Convention on the Regulation of Antarctic Mineral Resource Activities* (1988); *Vienna Convention for the Protection of the Ozone Layer* (1985); *Protocol on Substances that Deplete the Ozone Layer* (The *Montreal Protocol*, 1987), and *Basel Convention on the Control of Transboundary Movements of Hazardous Wastes and their Disposal* (1989).

11 ICJ Report 7.

12 The ICJ found that a state of necessity was, on an exceptional basis, a ground recognized by customary international law for precluding the wrongfulness of an act not in conformity with an international obligation, and relied on the formulation of draft Article 33 of the ILC's draft Articles on State Responsibility.

13 1991 *Convention on Environmental Impact Assessment in a Transboundary Context*, Article 1 (vi).

14 ITLOS Nos. 3 and 4.

15 Press Release No. 71/02, Judgments of the Court of First Instance in Cases T-13/99 and T-70/99, Press and Information Division, the Court of Justice of the European Communities, 11 September 2002.

16 WHO (2003) 'Annual Report of the Monitoring/Surveillance Network for Resistance to Antibiotics 2003', at: http://www.paho.org/English/AD/DPC/CD/amr-lima-2004.htm

17 *Pfizer Animal Health* v. *Council of the EU* (2002) Case T-13/39 and C-329/99, Judgment of the Court of First Instance (Third Chamber), 11 September 2002, paras. 135–73 (*Pfizer* v. *Council*).

18 Press Release No. 71/02, Judgments of the Court of First Instance in Cases T-13/99 and T-70/99, Press and Information Division, the Court of Justice of the European Communities, 11 September 2002.

19 *Alpharma Inc.* v. *Council of the EU* (2002) Case T-70/99, Judgment of the Court of First Instance (Third Chamber), 11 September 2002 (*Alpharma* v. *Council*).

20 See Section 4.4.3.

The development of the precautionary approach 85

21 Para. 111(a) *Land-Based Activities Action Programme* (1995) applies the precautionary principle to radioactive waste storage by outlawing such storage near the coastal and marine environment unless the absence of any 'unacceptable risk' is demonstrated. In para. 104 (b) (i) of the same document, it suggests that priority ought to be given to phasing out chemicals that pose 'unreasonable and otherwise unmanageable risks'.

22 *Concise Oxford English Dictionary*, 11th edn, Oxford University Press, p. 1341.

23 The commentary to the 1994 International Law Commission *Draft Articles on the Law of the Non-Navigational Uses of international Watercourses*, the commentary to Article 3 paras. 13–15 and the Commentary to Article 4, para. 7.

24 International Law Commission (2001) Commentary to Article 2 (a) of the *Draft Articles on Harm Prevention*, para. 4.

25 See Section 6.3.1.

26 HM Government (1999) 'A Better Quality of Life: A Strategy for Sustainable Development for the United Kingdom', at: http://collections.europarchive. org/tna/20080530153425/http://www.sustainable-development.gov.uk/ publications/uk-strategy99/index.htm

27 White Paper: 'This Common Inheritance: Britain's Environmental Strategy', September 1990.

28 See Section 3.2.2.1.

29 *Application of the Republic of Hungary* v. *The Czech and Slovak Republic on the Diversion of the Danube River*, para. 31.

30 Statements of Claim of Australia and New Zealand, *Southern Bluefin Tuna* case, International Tribunal for the Law of the Sea (ITLOS), 15 July1999, paras. 63–6.

31 International Law Commission (2001) Commentary on Article 1 of the *Draft Articles on Harm Prevention*, para. 2.

32 In the *Gabcikovo–Nagymaros* case, the ICJ noted that Hungary did not prove a '"real", "grave", and "imminent" "peril" existed'.

33 See Section 3.2.3 (3).

34 Written Response of the United Kingdom, para. 147, 15 November 2001. International Tribunal for the Law of the Sea (ITLOS) No. 10, *MOX Plant Case* (Request for Provisional Measures) (*Ireland* v. *United Kingdom*).

35 International Tribunal for the Law of the Sea (ITLOS) No. 10, *MOX Plant Case* (Request for Provisional Measures) (*Ireland* v. *United Kingdom*).

36 See also: *Monsanto Agricoltura Italia and Others*, Case C-236/01, Judgment of 2003, para. 106; *Commission of the European Communities* v. *Kingdom of Denmark*, Case C-192/01, Judgment of 23 September 2003, para. 49; *Commission of the European Communities* v. *French Republic*, Case C-24/00, Judgment of 5 February 2004, para. 56.

37 Cf. the WTO accepts that Members can adopt a level of protection on a zero-risk basis. See WTO Appellate Body Report, *Australia – Measures Affecting the Importation of Salmon (Australia – Salmon)*, WT/DS18/AB/R, adopted 20 October 1998, para. 125.

38 See WTO Appellate Body Report, *Australia – Measures Affecting the Importation of Salmon (Australia – Salmon)*, WT/DS18/AB/R, adopted 20 October 1998.

39 WTO Appellate Body Report, *EC – Measures Concerning Meat and Meat Products (EC – Hormones)*, WT/DS26/AB/R, adopted 16 January 1998.

40 See Section 3.2.3 (3).

86 Current landscape

41 Order of 27 August 1999, para. 77.
42 International Chamber of Commerce Commission on Environment, A *Precautionary* Approach: An ICC Business Perspective, 1997.
43 For example, see para. 186 of Joined Cases T-74/00, T-76/00, T-83/00 to T-85/00, T-132/00, T-137/00, NS T-141/00, Judgment of the EU Court of First Instance of 26 November 2002.
44 For example, the moratorium on commercial whaling adopted by the International Whaling Commission (IWC) in 1982; the moratorium on pelagic driftnet fishing agreed by the UN General Assembly; the European Union's de facto precautionary moratorium on the marketing of genetically modified food products from 1998, and the precautionary restrictions imposed on emissions of chlorofluorocarbons under the *Montreal Protocol* in order to prevent further depletion of the ozone layer.
45 For example, the application of ample safety buffers in the setting of catch levels and fishing effort limitations where uncertainty is great; the NAFO Fisheries Commission acknowledges 'The more uncertain the stock assessment, the greater the buffer zone should be' in its *Precautionary Approach Framework*. The Framework distinguishes between five different states − the safe zone, the overfishing zone, the cautionary zone, the danger zone and the collapse zone − and sets out the appropriate precautionary management action for each.
46 For example, the performance of an Environmental Impact Assessment (EIA) and monitoring are required during the period when risk exists. The European Council called on EU Member States and the Commission to 'attach particular importance to the development of scientific expertise'. WTO Members must 'seek to obtain the additional information necessary for a more objective assessment of risk' after adopting a provisional SPS measure.
47 See Section 4.1.2 (1) for the definition of risk analysis.
48 UNECE Convention on Access to Information, Public Participation in Decision-Making and Access to Justice in Environmental Matters, Aarhus, Denmark, 25 June 1998 (Aarhus Convention). Other references regarding public participation in international/European environmental law including: UNECE Convention on Access to Information, Public Participation in Decision-Making and Access to Justice in Environmental Matters (1998), available at: http://www.unece.org/env/pp/documents/cep43e.pdf; UNECE Compliance Committee Report, Compliance with regard to the European Commission, UN doc.ECE/MP.PP/2008/5/Add.10, available at: http://www.unece.org/env/documents/2008/pp/mop3/ece_mp_pp_2008_5_add_10_e.pdf; Council Directive Proposal, Access to Justice in Environmental Matters, COM (2003) 624, available at: http://eur-lex.europa.eu/LexUriServ/site/en/com/2003/com2003_0624en01.pdf
49 See Section 4.2.
50 Living modified organisms (LMOs) resulting from modern biotechnology are broadly equivalent to genetically modified organisms. The difference between an LMO and a GMO is that an LMO is capable of growing, and typically refers to agricultural crops. GMOs include both LMOs and organisms which are not capable of growing.
51 The text of the Codex Alimentarius is available at: http://www.codexalimentarius.net; see also: *Codex Alimentarius Procedural Manual*, 21st edn, at: ftp://ftp.fao.org/codex/Publications/ProcManuals/Manual_21e.pdf
52 For example, a strong precautionary principle is provided in the *Treaty on the European Union*, as amended by the *Maastricht Treaty*, 7 February 1992, Article 130r.

The development of the precautionary approach   87

53 *European Communities – Measures Affecting the Approval and Marketing of Biotech Products (EC – Biotech)* WT/DS291/R, WT/DS292/R, WT/DS293/R, adopted 29 February 2006.

54 Bovine spongiform encephalopathy (BSE) is commonly known as 'mad cow disease', and was first identified in the UK in November 1986. Scientists suspect that BSE had been transmitted from sheep to cow through contaminated feed. BSE attacks the brain and central nervous system of the host before killing it. The most well-known BSE-related disease that affects people is Creutzfeldt-Jakob Disease (CJD). Researchers conclude that the most likely cause of CJD is eating meat infected with BSE. Like BSE in cattle, CJD is always fatal to humans. See: '"Mad Cow Disease" 1980s–2000: How Reassurances Undermined Precaution', in *Late Lessons from Early Warnings: The Precautionary Principle 1896–2000*, European Environment Agency, Copenhagen 2001; see also: UK Food Standards Agency Website at: http://www.eatwell.gov.uk/healthissues/factsbehindissues/bse/#cat237257; Holer, J. and Elworthy, S. 'The BSE Crisis: A Study of the Precautionary Principle and the Politics of Science in Law', in Reece, H. (ed.) (1998) *Law and Science: Current Legal Issues Volume 1*, New York: Oxford University Press.

55 *European Council Resolution on the Precautionary Principle*, SN 400/00 ADD 1 20 EN Annex III, adopted 9 December 2000 (Nice) (*EC PP Resolution*).

56 See FAO (1994) *The Precautionary Approach to Fisheries with Reference to Straddling Fish Stocks and Highly Migratory Stocks*, UN Doc A/CONF.164/INF/8.

57 Separate Opinion of Judge Laing, *Southern Bluefin Tuna Cases (New Zealand* v. *Japan; Australia* v. *Japan)*, International Tribunal for the Law of the Sea, 27 August 1999, para. 19.

58 Separate Opinion of Judge Treves, *Southern Bluefin Tuna Cases (New Zealand* v. *Japan; Australia* v. *Japan)*, International Tribunal for the Law of the Sea, 27 August 1999, para. 9.

59 See above, note 51. The work of the Codex Alimentarius Commission defines 'risk assessment' as a scientifically based process consisting of the following steps: (i) hazard identification, (ii) hazard characterization, (iii) exposure assessment, and (iv) risk characterization.

60 See Section 6.3.1.

61 See Sections 4.4.3 and 6.1.

4 The precautionary approach in international law

The current practice of international health protection has incorporated the essence of precaution by adopting particular health measures for an appropriate level of health protection. Typical examples of the PA implemented in international health can be found in legal instruments such as the WHO *International Health Regulations* (IHRs); the WHO/FAO *Codex Alimentarius*, and the *Cartagena Protocol on Biosafety* (CPB), which will also be assessed against the analysis and template developed in the previous chapter. Relevant employment of the PA by the WHO will first be discussed.

4.1. The PA in the WHO

The WHO stands as the primary international organization for addressing global health concerns. The WHO is established under the UN system as the highest directing and coordinating authority of the health-related issues for the world's population. The goal of the WHO is to ensure the right of everyone to the enjoyment of the *highest attainable standard* of physical and mental health (the right to health).[1] The protection and promotion of human health and safety is regarded as the first priority in the WHO regime, thus the concept of precaution has been widely promoted in the WHO system.

As discussed in the previous chapter (Section 3.3.3), the WHO has proposed the version of '*moderate precaution*' by taking into account the requirements of 'free trade' in order to reconcile trade and health. In the fourth Ministerial Conference on Environment and Health, it was noted that:

> We affirm the importance of the precautionary principle as a risk management tool, and we therefore recommend that it should be applied where the possibility of serious or irreversible damage to health or the environment has been identified and where scientific evaluation, based on available data, proves inconclusive for assessing the existence of risk and its level but is deemed to be sufficient to warrant passing from inactivity to policy alternatives.[2]
>
> (WHO *Fourth Ministerial Declaration on Environment and Health*, para. 17a)

The precautionary approach in international law 89

It stressed that the guidelines to the implementation of the PA need to consider the element of cost-benefit analysis, possible legal constraints, and impediment to free trade.[3] Further, the WHO organized an expert meeting on precautionary policies in environment and health in 2005. The consequent 'Dealing with Uncertainty' Report (WHO Uncertainty Report)[4] was published to identify major urgent questions about uncertainty and precaution in the WHO.

The WHO has acknowledged the PA as a risk management tool, and thus recommended that it should be adopted under scientific *uncertainty* where *serious* or *irreversible* damage to health has been identified. The Uncertainty Report discusses relevant tools about the implementation of the PA such as: risk assessment, cost-benefit analysis, uncertainty analysis, alternative assessment, and public participation tools. Its aim is to provide guidance as well as to facilitate the implementation of the PA as a tool to protect public health. It starts with adopting the definition proposed by the European Environment Agency (EEA) which is a more proactive definition than other versions of the PA (WHO Uncertainty Report, p. 3). Particularly, compared to the moderate PA developed in Chapter 3, the element of 'alternative assessment' is a unique feature which could term the version a 'constructive' instead of a 'restrictive' PA for it evaluates a whole range of alternatives at the time risks are identified. This approach would 'change the current focus from studying the risk to investigating the solutions' (WHO Uncertainty Report, p. 22).

The main instruments demonstrating the PA in the WHO regime are the International Health Regulations (IHRs) and the Codex Alimentarius (Codex). The IHRs are equipped with the mechanism of 'additional health measures' which serves as a tool for minimizing risks of virus transmission and the Codex Alimentarius consists of the structure of 'risk analysis' which incorporates the precautionary thinking in the regulation of food safety. We will first introduce its relevant application in the IHRs in the following section in order to examine the role of science in the containment of global virus transmission.

4.1.1. *The PA in virus surveillance – the International Health Regulations (IHRs)*

The WHO Constitution and the United Nations Charter vest power in WHO to adopt treaties and regulations to which State Parties subscribe. The *International Health Regulations* (IHRs) are one of the major United Nations agreements that have attempted to regulate the activities of State Parties as they relate to infectious diseases. They have been revised to meet the emergence of newly discovered infectious diseases such as SARS in 2002 and the highly virulent strain of bird flu in 2003. The IHRs were revised in 2005 to follow a precautionary thinking in their legal framework in order to ensure the effectiveness of the global virus surveillance network. The IHRs aim at preventing and responding to acute public health risks that have the potential

90   *Current landscape*

to spread rapidly across borders. The IHRs build an international network of virus surveillance, and oblige State Parties to notify the WHO of any occurrences of notifiable diseases. The purpose of the IHRs is to ensure maximum security against the international spread of diseases along with minimum interference with world traffic (Article 2).

In the era of globalization, fast-spreading diseases have been aided by international travel and trade in goods and services among countries and continents. Efficient disease containment greatly depends upon immediate global cooperation.[5] In order to build global health security, states are granted a margin of appreciation in determining the adoption of additional public health measures, which aims at achieving an appropriate or acceptable level of protection (ALOP).[6] States are entitled to be more cautious with regard to issues of containing virus transmission than international standards require.

(1) State Parties' rights and obligations under a public health emergency

The PA employed in the IHRs acts to provide a safeguard to human health by allowing prompt response to managing risks under a public health emergency of international concern (PHEIC). The definition of 'public health emergency of international concern' will first have been discussed before introducing states' duties and rights in the IHRs and the precautionary mechanism of additional health measures.

DEFINITION OF PHEIC

The IHRs are equipped with a reporting structure to oblige State Parties to notify the WHO of all events which may constitute a PHEIC within its territory (Articles 7–9; Annex 2). The IHRs define a public health emergency as 'an extraordinary event which is determined, as provided in these Regulations: (i) to constitute a public health threat risk to other States through the international spread of disease [;] and (ii) to potentially require a coordinated international response' (Article 1). A 'public risk' means 'a likelihood of an event that may affect adversely the health of human populations, with an emphasis on one which may spread internationally or may present a serious and direct danger' (Article 1).

SCOPE OF PHEIC

After the revision in 2005, the scope of IHRs has covered a broader range of notifiable diseases to reduce the rate of global virus transmission (Annex 2). The scope of notifiable diseases encompasses both imminent and potential risks; it also includes a large range of newly emerging diseases including natural and artificial threats. State Parties are required to notify the WHO of all events that may constitute a PHEIC.[7] In general, the IHRs categorize the notifiable diseases into three classes: (1) known diseases whose outbreaks are

The precautionary approach in international law 91

unexpected and serious, such as a new influenza strain or SARS; (2) known diseases with a demonstrated ability to become emergencies, including the plague or Ebola; and (3) unknown or potential threats or any other kind (Annex 2).

After receiving notification of a potential PHEIC, the WHO will begin an investigation and deploy response teams through systems such as the *Global Outbreak Alert and Response Network (GOARN)*,[8] which is a technological collaboration of existing institutions and networks aiming at rapid identification, confirmation and response to a PHEIC. The Director General of the WHO will determine whether an event constitutes a PHEIC in accordance with the criteria and procedures set out in these Regulations on the basis of the information received (Article 12).

An example of the declaration of a PHEIC is the one which was made after a swine influenza A (H1N1) outbreak reported in Mexico and the United States in 2009. After receiving notification of a PHEIC, the WHO Director General soon convened a meeting of the Emergency Committee to assess the condition on 25 April 2009. The Committee decided that the situation constituted a PHEIC after reviewing all available relevant information, and the Director General also determined that the event constituted a PHEIC.[9] Following the WHO's determination and announcement of the state of a PHEIC, public health officials in the United States soon declared a national public health emergency in preparation for following public health strategies.[10]

The emergency declaration in the United States was made in order to empower the government to stockpile sufficient antiviral drugs with public resource reallocation. Other countries have opted for travel bans, plans for quarantine, pig culling, and banning foreign pork imports, etc.[11] States have been vigilant and have made every possible effort against the health threat, yet not every response is deemed legitimate under their obligations to the WTO: some responses are criticized as overreactive. For example, Russia's ban on pork imports from Mexico and the United States is regarded as groundless as the H1N1 virus cannot be transmitted by pork. The ban on pork imports therefore may violate Article 17 (d) of the IHRs which indicates that any health measure needs to be *least-restrictive to international trade and traffic*. It will also be regarded as non-compliant with its obligations under the WTO if Russia is a Member of the WTO (Fidler 2009).

After a brief explanation of a PHEIC, we will now examine in the following section State Parties' rights and duties under a PHEIC.

THE DUTIES AND RIGHTS OF STATE PARTIES UNDER A PHEIC

The IHRs establish guidelines on the WHO's role and responsibilities in the event of a PHEIC, as well as outline the roles and obligations of WHO State Parties when addressing such crises. The purpose of the IHRs is to prevent, protect against, control and provide a public health response to the

92 Current landscape

international spread of disease in ways that are commensurate with and restricted to public health risks, and which avoid unnecessary interference with international traffic and trade (Article 2).

The IHRs formally grant the WHO authority to issue recommendations for State Parties to follow (Mack 2006: 365). The WHO may make standing recommendations of appropriate health measures for State Parties' routine or periodic application, and temporary recommendation for adopting additional health measures (Articles 16, 43). These are established in the context of the defined rights and duties of State Parties as follows:

Duties of surveillance and notification   The IHRs impose obligations on the State Parties of the WHO. Annex 1 of the IHRs spells out the 'core capacity requirements for surveillance and response', and details State Parties' obligations under the IHRs. It places duties on State Parties by building a streamlined event reporting system and by importing binding aspects of international law into the health regulations (Milano 2006: 26). The IHRs' goals include the avoidance of 'unnecessary interference with world trade and travel' (Article 2), and appear to give public health higher priority over commercial interests (Milano 2006: 26).

Further, the decision instrument in Annex II identifies a limited set of criteria that will assist State Parties in deciding whether an event is notifiable to the WHO. The criteria are as follows.

- Is the public health impact of the event *serious?*
- Is the event unusual or unexpected?
- Is there a *significant risk* of international spread?
- Is there a significant risk of international restriction(s) to travel and trade?

(Annex 2 IHRs)

In other words, once the health impact of an event is identified as *serious*, the risk of international spread and the risk of international restriction(s) to travel and trade are *significant*, State Parties are obliged to notify the WHO if the event is unusual or unexpected. This also suggests that the WHO adopts the PA of imposing State Parties' duty to notification when the health impact of an unusual or unexpected event crosses the *serious* threshold and the risk is identified as *significant*. This requirement, however, appears to deviate from the example of *Information Disclosure PA*,[12] which favours a shift of the burden of proof to the one who introduces a new product/technology. It could be understood that the invoking party may be in a better position to collect relevant information of the risk in an emergency.

Similar to the previous WHO *moderate precaution* model,[13] this IHRs decision instrument also takes into account the impact on free trade by asking if there is a significant risk of international restriction(s) to travel and trade. Through this instrument, we can again observe that the WHO aims to reconcile

The precautionary approach in international law 93

health protection and free trade by adopting a *moderate* approach of precaution. It could be suggested that the deployment of the PA in international public health law is tailored in order to conform to the requirements of global free trade and travel. An adopted precautionary measure to avoid health risks is expected to be 'no more restrictive of international traffic and trade' than available alternatives that would achieve the appropriate level of health protection (Article 17 (d) IHRs).

Rights to quarantine The IHRs also lay out the rights that State Parties have with respect to the WHO and clarify domestic rights relating to public health emergencies. As indicated in the IHRs, 'States ... have the sovereign rights to legislate and to implement legislation in pursuance of their health policies' (Article 3.4 IHRs). The IHRs vest in State Parties the 'right to quarantine', which allows them to take some action to restrict and protect their populations as they see fit, and the WHO is not in a position to uniformly constrain quarantine policy.

The 2003 SARS outbreak in Singapore provides an example of State Parties' right to quarantine (Sapsin *et al.* 2004: 158–60).[14] Possible patients were required to report to treatment centres, remain in quarantine with electronic tagging, and destroy contaminated property. All of these above-mentioned measures are adaptive to circumstances in individual states and are deemed acceptable under the IHRs. However, every procedure to enforce quarantine inevitably results in compromise of civilians' human rights to a certain extent. It is therefore required that the health measures need to be 'not more intrusive to persons than reasonably available alternatives that would achieve the appropriate level of health protection' (Article 17 (d)).

(2) Additional health measures

PRECAUTIONARY ENTITLEMENTS TO ACHIEVE
A HIGHER LEVEL OF HEALTH PROTECTION

A state's right to determine its appropriate level of health protection has been paid due respect in international law.[15] Under the IHRs, State Parties may also enjoy the right to choose their appropriate level of health protection; they are free to choose the same or greater level of health protection than WHO recommendations (Article 43.1 (a)). There are *two tracks* of determining an appropriate level of health protection: Member States may choose either to follow the WHO's recommendations to adopt a general public health measure or to adopt an additional health measure to achieve a greater level of health protection (see Table 4.1.1). The application of additional health measures can be deemed another face of the PA in international health, which will be introduced in the following section.

94 *Current landscape*

Table 4.1.1 Two tracks of implementing public health measures in the IHRs

	Two Tracks of implementing public health measures in the IHRs	
	General public health measures	*Additional health measures*
Principles §3	1. Respect for the dignity, human rights and fundamental freedom of persons 2. Guided by the UN Charter and the WHO Constitution 3. Universal application 4. States have the sovereign rights to legislate and to implement legislation in pursuance of their health policies	
Legal ground	1. Routine or periodic application (§23–34) or 2. From the WHO's standing recommendation towards a specific public health risk (§53)	1. From the WHO's temporary recommendation towards a PHEIC (§15.1) or 2. State Parties implement health measures in accordance with their relevant national law and obligations under international law, in response to specific public health risks or a PHEIC (§43.1–2)
Public health measures	Health measures on arrival and departure (§ 23) Special provisions for conveyances and conveyance operators (§24–29) Special provisions for travellers (§30–32) Special provisions for goods, containers and container loading areas (§33–34)	1. Based on scientific principles, scientific evidence, scientific information, and WHO guidance or advice (§43.1-2) 2. Shall not be more restrictive of international traffic and not more invasive or intrusive to persons than reasonably available alternatives that would achieve the appropriate level of health protection (§43.1) 3. Review: shall review the measure within three months taking into account advice from the WHO and the criteria of §43.2 (§43.6) 4. Consultation with impacted State Party (§43.7)

ADDITIONAL HEALTH MEASURES

As discussed above, the IHRs attempt to balance a State Party's rights and duties in international law while implementing the PA in the global disease surveillance network. A State Party may still choose to adopt additional health measures for an appropriate level of health protection under scientific uncertainty (Article 43.2). The imposition of additional public health measures represents the respect of State Parties' autonomy and sovereignty under a PHEIC as it further recognizes the precautionary thinking in the IHRs. Even in the situation of insufficient scientific evidence, when the public health risk cannot be scientifically assessed or quantified, additional health measures can still be imposed. The adoption of such *additional health measures* is considered the application of the PA. This version of PA could be considered a *prescriptive* and *moderate* version in light of our discussion in Chapter 3, which requires a precautionary action and minimum interference to international trade, albeit the onus appears to remain on the invoking party.

Further, additional health measures can be implemented under the WHO's temporary recommendations in response to specific health risks or a PHEIC (Article 43.1). The issue of a temporary recommendation needs to avoid unnecessary interference with international traffic (Article 15.2). A higher level of health protection may be accepted on condition that the health measures are not more restrictive of international traffic and not more invasive or intrusive to individuals than reasonable alternatives that would achieve appropriate level of protection (Article 43.1). In determining whether to adopt additional public health measures, State Parties need to consider scientific principles, available scientific evidence of a risk to human health, available information, and specific guidance or advice from the WHO (Article 43.2). In other words, State Parties can still adopt a temporary health measure based on available pertinent information even if scientific evidence is insufficient.

In addition, in order to avoid misuse of this mechanism, if an additional public health measure adopted significantly interferes with international traffic (Article 43.3),[16] the implementing state bears the duty to provide the WHO with the public health rationale and relevant scientific information within 48 hours (Article 43.5). The implementing state is also obliged to review the measure within three months to make sure the public health measure is consistent with the advice of the WHO. The criteria for determining whether to implement the additional health measure include scientific principles, available scientific evidence of a risk to human health, or available information from the WHO or other international organizations, and any available specific guidance or advice from the WHO (Article 43.2).

(3) Elements of the precautionary approach in the IHRs

The surveillance network and the mechanism of additional health measures both demonstrate the significance of precaution in the IHRs. On the one hand, State Parties enjoy their sovereignty upon the implementation of public health policies in adopting the PA; on the other hand, they are required to act according to the principle of the IHRs, which aims to minimize the interference of international traffic and trade as well as retaining full

96 *Current landscape*

respect for the dignity, human rights and fundamental freedom of individuals (Article 3.1).

In summary, in order to achieve a greater level of health protection than the WHO's recommendations, State Parties are entitled to adopt the PA under prescribed conditions. The elements of the PA in the IHRs include:

- Uncertainty: the PA is applied when there is insufficient scientific evidence in virus surveillance and notification, which is based on scientific principles; available scientific evidence of a risk to human health; or, where such evidence is insufficient, available information from the WHO and other organizations, and relevant WHO guidance (Article 43.2);
- Harm: *significant* risk of *serious* harm to human health (Annex 2);
- Action: the adoption of additional health measures (Article 43);
- Duty to review: the adopting Party should provide health rationale and review the said measure within three months (Article 43.6);
- Burden of proof: the adopting State Party should provide public health rationale and relevant scientific information (Article 43.5);
- No more restrictive of international trade and no more invasive or intrusive to persons than reasonably available alternatives that would achieve the appropriate level of health protection (Article 43.1).

After the introduction of the PA in the IHRs, it is also noteworthy to discuss the employment of the approach in the regulation of food safety within the WHO regime.

4.1.2. The PA in food safety – the WHO/FAO Codex Alimentarius

The Codex Alimentarius Commission was set up by the WHO and the Food and Agriculture Organization of the UN (FAO) to develop food standards, guidelines and related texts under the Joint FAO/WHO Food Standards Programme. It establishes the structure of '*risk analysis*' for application in the framework of the Codex Alimentarius. States are not forced to follow the Codex guidelines and standards as they appear to be voluntary in international law; however, under the requirements of the WTO Agreement on the Application of Sanitary and Phytosanitary Measures (SPS Agreement), the Codex guidelines are mandated to harmonize states' national law into Codex (Verkerk 2009: 24). Specifically, the SPS Agreement requires states to base their sanitary and phytosanitary measures on international standards (Article 3.1); the Agreement expressly identifies the Codex Alimentarius as the international standards for food safety (Article 3 in Annex A). This is to say that under the international economic settings and the pressure of the WTO Dispute Settlement System (DSS), countries are often left with no option but to be in full compliance with the standards of the Codex Alimentarius. The Codex Alimentarius has thus emerged as the official international standard in food safety since the WTO SPS agreement came into force in 1995.

The PA is not officially introduced in the Codex Alimentarius system; yet the term 'precaution' is identified as an 'inherent element' of risk analysis in the *Codex Alimentarius Commission Procedure Manual* (*Codex Manual*).[17] In situations where health risks exist but scientific data are insufficient, the Codex Alimentarius Commission will not provide a 'standard' but a related 'text', such as a code of practice, which is based on available scientific information (*Codex Manual*: 108). Further, the adoption of a 'safety factor' is deemed as a form of precautionary measure in international law. In other words, the PA appears in the guise of the 'safety factor' when scientific uncertainty abounds; specifically, the structure of 'risk analysis' implies that the precautionary thinking is at the stage of risk management (*Codex Manual*: 106). This will be addressed below.

(1) Risk analysis

The Codex Alimentarius defines the structure of risk analysis, which comprises risk assessment, risk management and risk communication (FAO/WHO Report 1995: 6; *Codex Manual*: 107).[18] Each is defined by the FAO in the following paragraphs (see Figure 4.1.2):

- Risk assessment consists of four steps: hazard identification; hazard characterization; exposure assessment; and risk characterization. Risk assessment includes quantitative assessment and qualitative expressions of risk (FAO/WHO Report 1995: 6; *Codex Manual*: 109).
- Risk management is the process of weighing policy alternatives to accept, minimize or reduce risks and to select and implement appropriate options (FAO/WHO Report 1995: 6; *Codex Manual*: 110–12).
- Risk communication is a process of exchanging information and opinion on risk among various stakeholders. This can also be understood as 'public engagement' in the context of deliberate democracy (FAO/WHO Report 1995: 6; *Codex Manual*: 112–13).

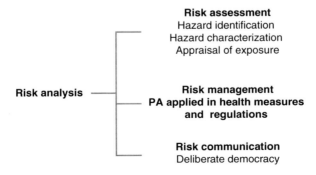

Figure 4.1.2 Risk analysis

98   *Current landscape*

Notably, the EU also recognizes that the PA should be considered in the structure of risk analysis, which comprises the three elements of risk assessment, risk management and risk communication in the EC's *Communication from the Commission on the Precautionary Principle*. This identifies four stages of risk assessment which should be performed before a precautionary action is taken: 'hazard identification, hazard characterization, appraisal of exposure, and risk characterization' (Annex III).[19] The PA is deemed particularly relevant to risk management for adopting public health measures after a scientific evaluation of a potential public health risk (see Figure 4.1.2). Specifically, the embodiment of the PA in the Codex Alimentarius is the adoption of a 'safety factor' in establishing a health standard at the stage of risk management, thus the PA in the Codex could also be deemed as a prescriptive PA which requires a precautionary action to be employed.

(2) A safety factor and 'additional safety factor'

The employment of safety margins is deemed a typical precautionary action in international environmental protection (Trouwborst 2006: 177–9). Based on the same rationale, in the process of risk management, the Joint Expert Committee on Food Additives (JECFA) of the Codex Alimentarius Committee uses the 'safety factor' as a margin of safety in establishing the standard of an Acceptable Daily Intake (ADI). The ADI is estimated by JECFA on 'the amount of a food additive, expressed on a body weight basis, which can be ingested daily over a lifetime without appreciable health risk'.[20]

In the determination of the standard of an ADI, the safety factor can be used in three ways: first, to choose a low 'no toxic effect' level as the 'no-observed-effect level';[21] second, an additional safety factor is often used by assuming humans are *ten times more sensitive* than experimental animals, which introduces a tenfold variation in sensitivity in the human population.[22] Third, it is also noted in a report of the Codex Alimentarius that a 'temporary ADI' which takes into account relevant public health risks and food technological aspects often uses an *additional safety factor*.[23] A 'temporary ADI' is defined by JECFA as one where the use of the substance is safe over a short period of time, but the safety data are insufficient to conclude that use of the substance is safe over a lifetime. In this case, a 'higher-than-normal safety factor' is used in establishing a temporary ADI.[24]

Hence, the spirit of precaution, particularly a prescriptive version of the PA, has been reflected in the Codex system through the adoption of a safety factor and an additional safety factor. We can therefore identify the relevant features of the PA in the Codex Alimentarius in the following section.

The precautionary approach in international law 99

(3) Elements of risk analysis in Codex Alimentarius

The Codex identifies the basic features of a risk analysis as follows:

- The adoption of a 'safety factor' of an ADI and an 'additional safety factor' of a temporary ADI is a form of a *prescriptive* PA in the Codex Alimentarius.[25]
- The standards or guidelines need to be evaluated and reviewed 'in the light of newly generated scientific data' (*Codex Manual*: 107). This requirement is consistent with the requirements of an 'Information Disclosure' PA, which demands that the precautionary measure is continually monitored.
- These guidelines and standards are based on principles of scientific analysis and evidence.[26]
- Health and safety aspects decisions should be based on risk assessment.[27]
- Legitimate factors relevant for the health protection of consumers and fair trade need to be considered (*Codex Manual*: 114).
- Legitimate concerns of governments when establishing domestic legislation need to be considered.[28]
- Health measures should not create unjustified barriers to trade (*Codex Manual*: 206).
- Health measures should be applied consistently, openly, transparently, and be documented (*Codex Manual*: 107).
- A 'functional separation of risk assessment and risk management' should be recognized (*Codex Manual*: 108).
- The function of 'food labelling' and constraints on the production or processing methods in developing countries should be considered.[29]

In summary, the Codex Alimentarius recognizes that the PA is applied in scientific uncertainty and is to be triggered by *risk assessment*. The Codex also favours a *prescriptive* PA which introduces a precautionary health measure; the duty of constant monitoring from an *Information Disclosure* PA and the duty of minimizing unjustified barriers to trade from a *moderate* PA are both recognized. However, in terms of allocation of the burden of proof, the Codex does not explicitly address whether a shift of the burden of proof is allowed. This may be referred back to the WTO SPS Agreement when disputes arise.

When scientific uncertainty persists, the Codex Alimentarius will not provide specific guidelines or standards but only relevant text based on available information (*Codex Manual*: 108). The structure of risk analysis indicates that the PA is particularly relevant to this stage of risk management. Though the PA is not officially written into the Codex Alimentarius, the requirements of its application appear to be more elaborate than the previous instrument in the IHRs. Common factors of the PA identified by the Codex Alimentarius and the IHRs include: the basis of scientific assessment or scientific information;[30] considering updated data by review and evaluation

100 *Current landscape*

(*Codex Manual*: 107; Article 43 IHRs); taking globalization into account by demanding the precautionary action does not create an unjustified barrier to trade (*Codex Manual*: 206; Article 43.1 IHRs). It also requires that the approach should be consistent, open and transparent (*Codex Manual*: 107; Article 42 IHRs).

In addition, it is also noteworthy that the Codex Alimentarius recognizes the function of 'food labelling', which may act to address the controversies of unknown risks to human health, such as food labelling on GMO products (*Codex Manual*: 205). When scientific evidence is insufficient or incomplete, food labelling may serve as a means to inform consumers so that they may distinguish potential health risks associated with a specific product (Cheyne 2009: 927).

After the discussion of the WHO's regulation on food safety, we will visit another important multilateral environmental agreement (MEA) regarding the regulation of the transboundary movement of biotechnology products. Attention will be turned to the Cartagena Protocol on Biosafety of which the PA is identified as playing a profound role in regulating health risks arising from biotechnology products.

4.2. The PA in the regulation of biotechnology – the Cartagena Protocol on Biosafety

In addition to the WHO system, many multilateral environmental agreements (MEAs) also incorporate the PA in their mechanisms to regulate risks to health and the environment (Bernasconi-Osterwalder *et al.* 2006: 266–7).[31] The Cartagena Protocol on Biosafety (CPB) was adopted at the Conference of the Parties to the Convention on Biodiversity on 29 January 2000, and entered into force on 11 September 2003. It is the first international instrument which provides a regulatory framework relevant to the PA to reconcile free trade and environmental protection. The use and release of genetically modified organisms (GMOs) in contemporary biotechnology has been aggressively expanding; however, the extent to which GMOs pose risks of adverse effects on human health still remains uncertain. Therefore trade conflicts have arisen over the regulation and labelling of GMO products. It is in this context that the Cartagena Protocol arises to provide a regulatory framework for the international trading of biotechnology products.

The CPB seeks to protect biological diversity from the potential risks posed by living modified organisms (LMOs) resulting from modern biotechnology. An LMO is defined in the Protocol as 'any living organism that possesses a novel combination of genetic material obtained through the use of modern technology' (Article 3 (g)). Modern technology means the application of *in vitro* nucleic acid techniques and cell fusion that overcome natural physiological reproductive or recombination barriers. Techniques used in traditional breeding and selection are excluded from the definition (Article 3 (i)).

4.2.1. The Advanced Informed Agreement (AIA) procedure

The Protocol devises the *Advanced Informed Agreement* (AIA) procedure as a new information-sharing mechanism under the Biosafety Clearing-House; this avails the Contracting Parties to conduct a risk assessment of imported LMOs (Articles 7–10, 12). The handling, use, or transboundary movements of LMOs that may have an adverse effect on the conservation and sustainable use of biological diversity can be regulated according to the PA (Article 1).

Under the AIA rules, the exporter is required to send written notification of the intended export to the importer (Article 8). The notification must contain specific information including a risk assessment about the potential adverse effects of the imported LMOs (Article 5, Annex I (K), and Annex II (j)). The importer is obliged to acknowledge receipt of the notification and to take a decision within 270 days on whether to allow import (Article 10.3). The importer can either: (1) approve the import and any subsequent imports; (2) prohibit the proposed import; (3) request additional information; or (4) extend the period for decision-making (Article 10.3). The importer has to set out the reasons for its decision unless the consent to import is unconditional (Article 10.4).

The mechanism of the AIA procedure still leaves a fair degree of flexibility for the importing state; for example, Parties may proceed according to the domestic regulatory framework (Article 9.2 (c)), adopt simplified procedures (Article 13.1 (b)), or enter into bilateral and regional agreements as long as these are consistent with the objective of the Protocol (Article 14.1).

4.2.2. Elements of the PA in the Cartagena Protocol on Biosafety

The AIA procedure requires that an import decision must be based on a risk assessment. A decision to ban or restrict the import of an LMO under the AIA procedure needs to be based on a 'risk assessment carried out in a scientifically sound manner' (Articles 10.1, 15, Annex III). Due to the lack of a clear consensus on the precise requirements for a risk assessment, the Protocol also sets out general principles and methodology, and points to a proper risk management (Annex III). It allows parties to take precautionary measures by stipulating that:

> Lack of scientific certainty due to insufficient relevant scientific information and knowledge regarding the extent of the potential adverse effects of a living modified organism … shall not prevent that Party from taking a decision, as appropriate, with regard to the import of the living modified organism … in order to avoid or minimize such potential adverse effects.
>
> (Articles 10.6, 11.8)

102 *Current landscape*

The Protocol is considered the most elaborate agreement on the PA in international law. It aims for the development of LMOs to be based on the PA to safeguard public health concerns from unknown risks of a novel technology (Winham 2003: 131). The notion of precaution has a pervasive influence on the CPB. Elements of the PA are reflected in several provisions of the Protocol, such as:

- the preamble, reaffirming 'the precautionary approach contained in Principle 15 of the Rio Declaration on Environment and Development;[32]
- Article 1, indicating that the objective of the Protocol is 'in accordance with the precautionary approach contained in Principle 15 of the Rio Declaration on Environment and Development;
- Article 10.6 and Article 11.8, which states: 'Lack of scientific certainty due to insufficient relevant scientific information and knowledge regarding the extent of the potential adverse effects of an LMO on biodiversity, taking into account risks to human health, shall not prevent a Party of import from taking a decision, as appropriate, with regard to the import of the LMO in question, in order to avoid or minimize such potential adverse effects'; and
- Annex III on risk assessment, which notes that: 'Lack of scientific knowledge or scientific consensus should not necessarily be interpreted as indicating a particular level of risk, an absence of risk, or an acceptable risk.'

Notably, the PA invoked in the CPB as an operational device to protect human health appears to have significant flexibility. The CPB follows the Rio Declaration on Environment and Development using the phrase 'precautionary approach' to describe the adoption of a precautionary concept on environmental and health protection. However, the Cartagena Protocol appears to be a stronger version than the Rio Declaration since it does not have the threshold requirement of 'threats of serious or irreversible damage' and 'cost-effective measures' (Mackenzie and Eggers 2000: 525–43).

The PA is adopted in the CPB as legitimate grounds to take a precautionary measure and is further limited by two conditions: the obligation of the importer to review the decision with the advent of new scientific information (Article 12), and the need for the measure to be only imposed to the extent necessary to prevent adverse effects within the territory of the importer (Article 16 (2)). It is noteworthy that 'social-economic considerations' also have a role to play in reaching an import decision regarding the value of conservation and sustainable use of biological diversity in the CPB. In addition, the Parties are also 'encouraged to cooperate on research on any social-economic impacts of LMOs, especially on indigenous and local communities' (Article 26).

The implementation of a precautionary measure is required to be in accordance with a risk assessment, but the importer's obligation to review does not

The precautionary approach in international law 103

have a specific time limit. In other words, the importer is not burdened with an ongoing obligation to keep the measure under review unless requested by the exporter to do so.

In summary, the features of the PA in the Cartagena Protocol comprise the following considerations:

- The trade decision is made under scientific uncertainty due to insufficient relevant scientific information and knowledge regarding the extent of the potential adverse effects of an LMO.
- The risks to human health of an LMO must be taken into account.
- The import decision is based on a risk assessment (Article 5).
- The risk assessment of the importing product can be expected to be carried out by the exporter (Annex I (k) and Annex II (j)). In other words, the burden of proof appears to be laid on the exporter.
- The importer has a duty to review the decision (Article 12).
- Trade measures need to be imposed only to the extent *necessary* (Article 16.2).
- Other 'social-economic considerations' must be taken into account, especially any impacts on indigenous and local communities (Article 26).

These features indicate that the PA in the CPB is also a *prescriptive* one by which the import decision is triggered by *risk assessment*. It appears to be a relatively *strong* version of the PA; however, it also states that a trade measure can only be imposed to the extent *necessary* to prevent potentially adverse effects on biological diversity. It may be fair to say that this version is more akin to the *Information Disclosure PA* with an emphasis on the duty to review as well as a shift of burden of proof.

4.3. The PA in the WTO

The precautionary approach (PA) has been emerging as a guiding norm in international environmental law, yet its application is relatively more reserved and restrictive in the international economic legal system. This is due to the intrinsic limitations of the WTO whose primary goals are the elimination of any possible restriction to trade and the promotion of a global market. In the following section, I will examine the PA in the WTO regime, specifically in the General Agreement on Tariffs and Trade (GATT 1947),[33] the Agreement on the Application of Sanitary and Phytosanitary Measures (SPS Agreement)[34] and the Agreement on Technical Barriers to Trade (TBT Agreement).[35] We shall see that, in contrast to the examples in the previous sections where the PA enjoys an assertive stance, the PA in the WTO regime is confined by ambiguous appearance – it is often unrecognizable as being under the heading of exceptions or exclusions to Members' obligations. However, the PA is found to have a more concrete presence in the SPS

104 *Current landscape*

Agreement, while WTO Members' determination to adopt a higher level of health protection has been recognized as a 'right' instead of a 'defence' in the trade world.

The WTO is the major institution that promotes global free trade. Its aim is to minimize trade barriers among countries in order to progress maximum economic interests. Trade liberalism, global market access and the elimination of tariffs as barriers to global trade and non-tariff barriers are primary concerns of the WTO. In order to preserve certain non-economic values including the protection of human health and environment under global world trade, the WTO system creates specific rules exempting Members from compliance with the general rules of its 'free trade' principle. Though the WTO has a very different mandate from the WHO, it has become one of the most important international organizations affecting international health issues due to its effective mechanism for dispute settlement (Kelly 2006: 79). The winning party of a dispute may be granted legitimate cause to issue trade sanction on the other party under the WTO Dispute Settlement System (DSS). Members of different organizations will resort to the WTO for resolving health-related trade disputes.

The PA provides a safety margin and appears in the WTO as exemption to free trade rules; however, this comes in different guises under different headings. Each iteration of the PA carries different weight in its legal instrument. Some appear in the exception provisions; others are reflected in the excluding provisions as the so-called 'conditional rights' (also known as excluding provisions), which enjoy a higher status in legal hierarchy than ordinary exception provisions (see Figures 4.3 and 4.3.1).

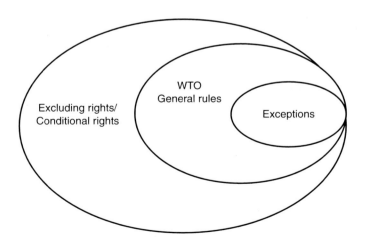

Figure 4.3 Exemption from WTO obligations

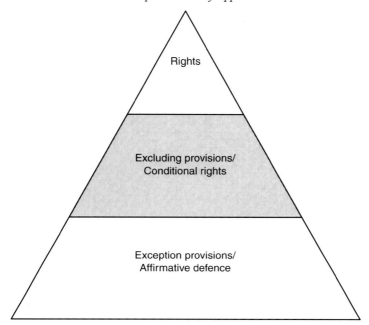

Figure 4.3.1 Legal hierarchy of exemptions from WTO obligations

THE LEGAL HIERARCHY OF EXEMPTIONS FROM WTO OBLIGATIONS

These exemptions from the WTO obligations have been placed into two categories: (1) provisions that establish an exception to a rule, which can be referred to as 'exception provision', and (2) provisions that exclude the application of other provisions, which can be regarded as 'excluding provision', which is also understood as 'conditional rights' that are only valid under certain circumstances (Grando 2006: 615; Charnovitz *et al.* 2004: 257; Figure 4.3).

The distinctions of these exemptions have special implications for their legal status. The Appellate Body of the WTO has distinguished the excluded rights as 'conditional rights', which enjoy a higher legal status than 'exception provision or affirmative defence' in WTO law (Charnovitz *et al.* 2004: 257). This is often demonstrated by the reversal of burden of proof when cases are associated with conditional rights (see Figure 4.3.1). As Grando notes, 'it implies the existence of a hierarchy between provisions where exceptions are placed at a lower level of the hierarchical pyramid' (Grando 2006: 615). Charnovitz *et al.* note that 'conditional rights' in WTO law 'are essentially provisions that read as exceptions but which are given a self-standing status in that the conditional rights carves out the general rules so that the general rule and the conditional right apply side by side, in a mutually exclusive manner' (Charnovitz *et al.* 2004: 257).

106   *Current landscape*

The distinction between 'exception rules' and 'excluding rules' is significant due to its implication for the legal status of the provision and designates the allocation of burden of proof. In the case regarding an exception rule, after the complainant's provision of prima facie evidence, the defendant has the burden of proving that it has complied with the requirements of the provision establishing an *exception* to that rule. The burden of proof is reversed for the complainant in an excluding provision. In this case, the complainant has the burden of proving that the defendant does not fall under the situation or has not complied with the requirements of a provision that *excludes* the application to the general rule (Grando 2006). For example, if compulsory licensing is deemed as an exception in TRIPS, the invoking party needs to prove that the public health emergency existed when the compulsory licence was issued in its territory; on the contrary, if compulsory licensing is deemed as an excluding provision, the onus is on the complaining party to prove that the public health emergency did *not* exist in the territory of the invoking party when the grant was issued.

INTERPRETATION OF EXCEPTION RULES

The understanding and interpretation of a treaty or an agreement shall be referred to its objectives and purposes in goodwill throughout the legal structure. According to 'general rules of interpretation' in the Vienna Convention on the Law of Treaties, 'A treaty shall be interpreted in good faith in accordance with the ordinary meaning to be given to the terms of the treaty in their context and in the light of its object and purpose' (Article, VCLT). In other words, the whole legal structure should be taken into account including its preamble, annexes, further instruments, subsequent agreements, subsequent practice and any relevant rules of international law. Moreover, when the textual approach referred to above still leaves the meaning ambiguous or obscure, then the preparatory work of the treaty may be used as a further means for interpretation (Crawford 2008: 383).

Interpretations of the PA in the WTO are accompanied by ongoing rulings of the Dispute Settlement Body when any new dispute arises. It is therefore necessary to analyse relevant cases and to sketch the outline of the approach applied by the WTO.

APPROPRIATE LEVEL OF HEALTH PROTECTION

The WTO has acknowledged WTO Members' rights to determine the level of health protection that they consider appropriate in a given situation.[36] The Appellate Body concluded that the SPS Agreement has incorporated precautionary elements, and noted that the PA is reflected in Article 5.7, in the sixth paragraph of the Preamble and in Article 3.3 (Appellate Body Report, *EC – Hormones*, para. 124). Specifically, the SPS Preamble recognizes Members' rights to maintain their appropriate level of protection (ALOP) of

The precautionary approach in international law 107

human, animal or plant life or health (paragraph 6). In addition, the Appellate Body in *EC – Asbestos* also stated: '... we note that it is undisputed that WTO Members have the right to determine the level of protection of health that they consider appropriate in a given situation' (Appellate Body Report, *EC – Asbestos*, para. 168). They are entitled to determine their level of health protection according to scientific and non-scientific factors.

Regarding the non-scientific factors in the determination of ALOP, scholars propose that risk regulation should include public perception of risk, which consists of citizens' preferences and domestic demand for regulation. These are supposed to be determined by democratic processes (Bohanes 2002: 323). According to Button's research, non-scientific factors represent social and cultural preferences which consist of a desired level of protection, economic feasibility, popular demands for regulations and the effect of regulation (Button 2004: 102–113). She further distinguishes various societal preferences into cultural traditions and public fear (Button 2004: 102–13). Public fear towards different risks varies in different cultures. Similarly, Sunstein also describes people and societies as 'selective in their fear' (Sunstein 2005: 13–15). It is self-evident that fear has an underlying subjective element reflected in different social contexts in accordance with the collective historic perception of a specific type of risk.

For example, the Europeans are aware of the residue of hormones in beef, while the Americans are afraid of BSE (Holer and Elworthy 1998).[37] Hence the willingness to accept a particular risk varies in different social contexts. The level of unacceptable health protection is anticipated to be determined by the community through an objective scientific assessment and a subjective process of public engagement. These examples illustrate that scientific findings are not the sole factor in risk regulations; civilians' social and cultural preferences in different contexts have arisen to play an important role in the policy-making of risk management. Ideally through public engagement, civilians' social and cultural preferences would serve as legitimate grounds to determine an appropriate level of health protection.

In addition to choosing its preferred level of health protection, a WTO Member is also allowed to act with prudence on the basis of *minority* opinion. The Appellate Body further expresses its view on minority opinion (Appellate Body Report, *EC – Asbestos*, para. 178). This demonstrates that the right of WTO Members to adopt the level of health protection they deem appropriate or acceptable is respected by the WTO. It also illustrates that Members are not obliged to base their decisions on majority scientific opinion. Further, in situations when neither majority opinion nor minority opinion is available or when it does not exist, the PA comes in to play a vital role in decision-making. In other words, the PA is to be activated within the scope of scientific ignorance or scientific uncertainty.

We will first introduce the PA in the GATT 1947 which appears in the context of the 'health exception' provision and the 'security exception' provision in the General Agreement, followed by the introduction to the PA in the

108 *Current landscape*

SPS Agreement, which is the main instrument for the regulation of health risks in WTO law.

4.3.1 *The PA in the General Agreement on Tariffs and Trade*

Precaution appears under the heading of 'exceptions' in the GATT. Though the wording of the GATT does not include explicit requirement of the role of science and precaution, it appears in the articles that WTO Members are left with sufficient space to employ precautionary measures to protect human life or health (Bernasconi-Osterwalder *et al.* 2006: 257). These include the health exception and the security exception (Article XX (b) and Article XXI GATT); both suggest the rationale of risk management on health and security grounds and lead to exemptions to free trade. Limited exceptions to general rules in the WTO regime are deemed legitimate while taking account of the interests of third parties.

The role of risk and precaution has been emerging as a topic of contentious debate in relation to the health exception provision of WTO law. Prominent cases involving the regulation of asbestos, hormones, pharmaceutical patents and biotechnology have arisen in recent years to test the clash of free trade and health protection (*EC – Asbestos*, *EC – Hormones*, *Canada – Pharmaceutical Patents*, *India – Pharmaceutical Patents*, *EC – Biotech, and EC – Continued Suspension (Hormones II)*). The WTO increasingly appears to be willing to leave leeway for health protection under scientific uncertainty in the trade world. However, the implementation of the PA on health and security grounds has still been highly restrictive for fear of such use resulting in protectionism.

According to the rationale of the PA, health and security measures are expected to be adopted promptly to cope with uncertain risks before the advent of the disaster. Its argument appears to legitimize exemption under the rules of free trade; however, if being adopted arbitrarily without transparency, the PA is susceptible to unilateral protectionism in international trade. Hence its application has been hesitant and fragmented in the WTO due to the lack of a clear definition and a harmonized mechanism for invocation. The following paragraphs will sketch the ambiguous face of the PA appearing under the health and the security exception headings in GATT.

(1) *Health exception in GATT*

Article XX (b) concerns measures which are *'necessary* to protect human, animal or plant life or health'. Members have the autonomy to adopt necessary precautionary measures to protect human, animal or plant life or health. The Appellate Body has also ruled that some important principles developed from the SPS Agreement are equally applicable under the health exception provision (Appellate Body Report, *EC – Asbestos*, paras. 167, 168 and 178; Bernasconi-Osterwalder *et al.* 2006: 257).

The precautionary approach in international law 109

PURPOSE OF THE HEALTH EXCEPTION PROVISION

The policy objective pursued by the precautionary measure at issue must be the protection of life or health of humans, animals or plants, and the said measure must be *necessary* to fulfil the policy objective (GATT XX (b)). The precautionary health measure inconsistent with the WTO obligations should be examined for its legitimate objectives within the interpretation of Article XX (b), and it should pass the necessity test and the proportionality test in order to prevent abuse of this article (Kapterian 2010: 89).

For the consideration of the necessity test and the proportionality test, it is noteworthy that the Appellate Body in *United States – Standards for Reformulated and Conventional Gasoline (US – Gasoline)*[38] introduced a two-tiered test: first, provisional justification by reason of characterization of the measure under XX (g); second, further appraisal of the same measure under the introductory clauses of Article XX (Appellate Body Report, *US – Gasoline*). Moreover, the Appellate Body further adopted a 'weighing and balancing' process as a *proportionality test* to relax the *necessity test* after *EC – Asbestos* (Appellate Body Report, *EC – Asbestos*, para. 172).

PRECAUTIONARY MEASURES UNDER THE HEALTH EXCEPTION PROVISION

Typical trade measures adopted to restrict free trade on health grounds include the banning of or restrictions on imported products which may constitute a risk to human health. Import bans or restrictions on products such as cigarettes, gasoline, asbestos and retreaded tyres arguably fall within the scope of 'the protection of life or health of humans'. However, such trade measures are hardly regarded as legitimate after the strict scrutiny of the necessity test and the proportionality test. Relevant cases will be examined respectively in the following sections in order to learn that only trade bans with scientific justification as well as without unnecessary intervention to trade will pass the scrutiny of the necessity test and the proportionality test. We will learn that the space for the PA appears to be rather vague and narrow and depends greatly upon the Panel's interpretation of the necessity test.

Thailand – Cigarettes   In *Thailand – Restrictions on Importation of Internal Taxes on Cigarettes (Thailand – Cigarettes)*,[39] the US argued that Thailand's quantitative restriction on the importation of cigarettes was inconsistent with the General Agreement. The Panel asked the WHO to comment on the health effects of cigarette consumption while considering the legitimacy of Thailand's restrictive measure (GATT Panel Report, *Thailand – Cigarettes*, paras. 50–57). The Panel accepted that smoking constituted a serious risk to human health and that consequently measures designed to reduce the consumption of cigarettes fell within the scope of Article XX (b) (GATT Panel Report, *Thailand – Cigarettes*, paras. 73 and 75). However, the Panel further concluded that there were other reasonable alternative measures consistent with the General

110   *Current landscape*

Agreement (GATT Panel Report, *Thailand – Cigarettes*, para. 81), hence the restrictive measure failed to meet the *necessity* test.

US – Gasoline   In *United States – Standards for Reformatted and Conventional Gasoline (US – Gasoline)*,[40] the Panel made an important clarification on the requirement of necessity: it is not the necessity of the policy objective that is to be examined, but the necessity of the disputed measure at issue to be examined. Consequently, the Panel examined whether there were reasonable alternative measures available which were 'consistent or less inconsistent' with the General Agreement (Panel Report, *US – Gasoline*, para. 6.25). The Panel agreed the necessity to decrease the consumption of gasoline to reduce pollution, but the US failed to prove the necessity of the applied measure. Therefore the US Gasoline Rule was found to be inconsistent with the necessity requirement in the WTO.

EC – Asbestos   The *EC – Measures Affecting Asbestos and Asbestos-Containing Products* Case (*EC – Asbestos*)[41] reaffirmed that a higher level of health protection of individual Members could be sustained by the PA in WTO law (Segger and Gehring 2003b: 289; Ruessmann 2002: 905). Asbestos has long been known for being a significant threat to human health. Exposure to chrysotile asbestos may increase the risk of asbestosis, lung cancer, mesothelioma or pneumocomiosis. These negative effects are also identified in a study by the WHO.[42]

In *EC – Asbestos*, France banned the importation and sale of asbestos from Canada for the reason of public health protection. France's ban of asbestos was proved to be without discrimination to both domestic and imported asbestos. However, Canada argued that the asbestos it exported was a 'like product' to substitute products used in construction and thus it should receive no less favourable treatment under the national treatment standard in GATT. Canada claimed that the measure was inconsistent with France's obligations under WTO law, but France's ban was proved legitimate after reasonable scientific evidence was provided to the DSB on chrysotile-cement products.

In addition, the Appellate Body adopted a *'weighing and balancing process'* as the *proportionality* test to supplement the necessity test.[43] In other words, the Appellate Body took more factors into consideration in determining the necessity of a measure. Besides 'the difficulty of implementation' of the alternative measure, the Appellate Body also referred to two factors in the weighing and balancing process: 'contribution of the measure to the realization of the value pursued' and 'importance of the value pursued' (Neumann and Turk 2003: 199–233).

Notably, the Appellate Body identified that several principles developed from the cases under the SPS Agreement were equally applicable under GATT XX. These include: Members have the right to establish their appropriate level of health protection; risks to human, animal or plant life or health

The precautionary approach in international law 111

must be assessed; risk assessment can be qualitative or quantitative; Members can rely on majority scientific opinions or minority opinions to adopt a trade measure (Appellate Body Report, *EC – Asbestos*, paras. 167, 168 and 178; Bernasconi-Osterwalder *et al.* 2006: 257).

Brazil – Retreaded Tyres Retreaded tyres are produced by reconditioning used tyres. In *Brazil – Measures Affecting Imports of Retreaded Tyres* (*Brazil – Retreaded Tyres*),[44] the EU challenged Brazil's restrictions on imported retreaded tyres from the EU. However, Brazil claimed that the ban was justified by Article XX (b) GATT, and argued that the import ban was aimed at reducing public health risks. Brazil contended that the import ban was designed to reduce waste tyre volume to reduce the incidence of dengue, cancer, environmental contamination, and other associated risks (Panel Report, *Brazil – Retreaded Tyres*, para. 4.11). Brazil argued that waste tyre accumulation threatens public health because it fuels mosquito-borne diseases and releases toxic chemicals into the environment (Panel Report, *Brazil – Retreaded Tyres*, para. 4.12). Brazil also submitted that it had suffered from epidemics of dengue, which the WHO has identified as 'a major international public health concern' (Panel Report, *Brazil – Retreaded Tyres*, para. 4.28).[45] Brazil explained that the ban was necessary and played an important part in the reduction of dengue. It was claimed that, following the Panel's statement in *EC – Asbestos*, the interests protected by the ban (the preservation of human life and health through the elimination, or *reduction* of health risks) were 'both vital and important in the highest degree' (Panel Report, *Brazil – Retreaded Tyres*, para. 4.16), and 'they weigh substantially in favour of the necessity of the measure' (Panel Report, *Brazil – Retreaded Tyres*, para. 4.44).

By contrast, the EU argued that the ban did not contribute to health and environmental protection. The EU claimed that there were no 'well-known and life-threatening health risks' posed by retreaded tyres (Panel Report, *Brazil – Retreaded Tyres*, para. 4.18), and the EU contested that the real aim of the import ban was not the protection of health but the protection of Brazil's domestic industry (Panel Report, *Brazil – Retreaded Tyres*, para. 4.19). Though Brazil imposed a ban on imported tyres, the court still granted a number of injunctions applied for by local retreaders, which were deemed by the Appellate Body as 'being applied in a manner that constitutes arbitrary or unjustifiable discrimination' (Appellate Body Report, *Brazil – Retreaded Tyres*, para. 258), and thus Brazil was not able to prevent the continued importation of used tyres (Epps 2008: 222–4).

In summary, the Panel and the Appellate Body found that the ban was necessary to protect human, animal, or plant life and health (Panel Report, *Brazil – Retreaded Tyres*, para. 7.215). However, the Panel also found that the quantity of imports of used tyres to the local retreading industry still seriously undermined the purpose of the ban (Panel Report, *Brazil – Retreaded Tyres*, para. 7.355), thus the ban was deemed to fail to meet the requirements

112 *Current landscape*

of the *Chapeau* of the GATT XX (b) and constituted *arbitrary or unjustifiable discrimination*, or a disguised restriction to trade (Panel Report, *Brazil – Retreaded Tyres*, para. 7.356).

RULES AND PRINCIPLES OF THE PRECAUTIONARY APPROACH
IN THE HEALTH EXCEPTION PROVISION

Following on from the above discussion, the structure of Article XX (b) includes the provision and the *Chapeau*. The examination of the disputed measure consists of three steps: first, to review whether the objective of the measure falls within the domain of the protection of 'human, animal or plant life or health'; second, the *Chapeau* requires that the applied measure should be *least inconsistent* with the obligations and be *least restrictive to trade*. The disputed measure should be applied in a non-discriminative way, and any disguised restriction on international trade is considered inconsistent with the *Chapeau*. Third, an analysis of weighing and balancing has been adopted by the Appellate Body to balance the values of the protected objectives and the cost of trade restriction. The Appellate Body started to take into account several other factors to relax the necessity test. Specifically, in *Brazil – Retreaded Tyres*, Brazil recalled the factors in determining the necessity of a measure as follows:

- the importance of the interests protected by the measure;
- the contribution of the measure to the end pursued;
- the trade impact of the measure; and
- the existence of reasonably available alternative measures (Panel Report, *Brazil – Retreaded Tyres*, para. 4.38).

In other words, the applied measure will be accepted as legitimate if it is considered *least restrictive to free trade*. If there exists an alternative measure that would achieve the same goal and is less restrictive to trade, then the alternative measure should be determined if it is reasonably available (Panel Report, *Brazil – Retreaded Tyres*, para. 4.38). Moreover, the Appellate Body has introduced a weighing and balancing process as a proportionality test into the necessity analysis. Any trade restriction aimed at protecting human health has to be in proportion to the benefits arising from the protection of human health.

In summary, Article XX (b) GATT appears to leave a fair space for Members' discretion in adopting the precautionary health measures; however, the space of the PA is in practice rather narrow after the interpretation of the Appellate Body. All of the above cases except for the *EC – Asbestos* case failed to pass the strict scrutiny of 'the necessity test'. Though the necessity test has been relaxed by the introduction of a weighing and balancing process for the proportionality test after *EC – Asbestos*, the necessity test in conjunction with the proportionality test still appears to be a relatively rigid and scientific-based

The precautionary approach in international law 113

approach to examine the legitimacy and validity of a trade measure in order to avoid disguised restriction on international trade.

In terms of the various types of the PA discussed earlier in Chapter 3, the PA in the health exception is also a *prescriptive* version as it allows a certain health-related trade measure to be implemented as long as the main objective falls within the scope of the Article, and passes the necessity test and the non-discrimination requirements in the *Chapeau*; due to the strict scrutiny of the necessity test of a precautionary measure, it could be deemed a *weak* PA. There is no shift of burden of proof should a dispute arise in relation to the legitimacy of the measure at issue: states that adopt the PA bear the onus of proving the necessity of the precautionary measure. Nevertheless, the interpretation of this Article has recourse to the rationale of the SPS Agreement – it can be suggested that the PA in the GATT is expected to be congruent to its application in the SPS Agreement.

Attention will now be turned to the discussion of the security exception provision in the GATT.

(2) Security exception

Contrary to the rigid application of the health exception provision, the invocation of the security exception provision appears to be rather subjective, broad and self-defining. The security exception provision lacks a clear mechanism, thus WTO Members enjoy a broad range of discretion in determining their 'security interests'. They are vested legitimate grounds to take actions which *they consider necessary* for the protection of their essential security interests. Consequently, the dispute settlement relies much on diplomatic pressure, which ultimately depends on the political power of the state.

Provisions involve 'national security' in the WTO laws including GATT XXI, General Agreement on Trade in Services (GATS) XIV *bis* (1),[46] TRIPS 73 (b) (iii), and Agreement on Government Procurement 23 (1). GATT XXI is a basic template for the interpretation of 'national security'. Trade measures adopted under such regulatory autonomy could be considered resonant with the rationale of risk management and the PA in WTO law. I will examine the mechanism of the security exception in GATT, and analyse the current state practice in the following paragraphs.

PURPOSE OF THE SECURITY EXCEPTION PROVISION

Definition and controversy   Article XXI (b) GATT allows Members to adopt or maintain measures relating to fissionable materials; measures relating to trade in arms or in other materials directly for military use, and measures taken in time of war or other emergencies in international relations which 'it considers necessary for the protection of its essential security interests'. Unlike Article XX, Article XXI does not have a chapeau to prevent misuse or abuse of the exceptions in Article XXI (Van den Bossche 2008: 664–9).

114   *Current landscape*

Members can apply Article XXI to protect their essential interests as *they consider necessary*.

The definitions of the terms and criteria of Article XXI deliberately remain vague in order to maintain a flexibility which Members can resort to in times of emergency. This also implies that states are allowed to have a greater margin of appreciation in exercising their *precautionary entitlements* in order to protect the essential interest of security under emergency situations. It may be fair to say that states' precautionary entitlements, or states' precautionary rights and duties to adopt a trade-restrictive measure, are deemed legitimate especially in a public health emergency. States' discretion in granting a precautionary compulsory licence based on their precautionary entitlements in international law will be discussed in later chapters.[47] The uncertainties of Article XXI may nevertheless result in unnecessary restrictions to trade which WTO Members may use for protectionism unilaterally.

The lack of clarity on the subjective phrasing of 'it considers necessary', 'essential security interests' and 'other emergency in international relations' makes the interpretation of this statute ambiguous. The concepts of 'security', 'diplomatic policy' and 'economic welfare' are thus often understood with confusion. On the flip side of the coin, as Article XXI functions as a safety valve in the GATT, Members will be more willing to participate in this trade agreement if it provides reserved flexibilities for exercising Members' autonomy in times of emergency.

Hence, it is fair to say that the security exception provision has been drafted without a clear mechanism on purpose. Relevant cases of the provision further indicate that the provision is adopted within a rather broad spectrum, and that the dispute resolution depends greatly on informal diplomatic negotiation in which the political power of a state inevitably plays a significant role. The PA in the security exception provision therefore appears to enjoy a broader application than that in the health exception provision.

PRECAUTIONARY MEASURES UNDER THE SECURITY EXCEPTION PROVISION

Sweden – Import Restrictions on Certain Footwear In Sweden – Import Restrictions on Certain Footwear,[48] the Swedish Government introduced the trade measure of a global quota system for leather shoes, plastic shoes and rubber boots from 5 November 1975.[49] The global quota system for shoes was introduced in order to allow time to 'remedy the serious difficulties' that had arisen in this sector of the shoe industry.[50] The Swedish Government claimed that the continued decrease in domestic shoe production had become a critical threat to the emergency planning of Sweden's economic defence, and it felt 'compelled to resort to temporary emergency measures to prevent a further deterioration of the domestic production capacity of shoes and rubber boots'.[51]

Although GATT XIX provides regulations regarding emergency action on imports of particular products, many Contracting Parties questioned the

The precautionary approach in international law 115

legitimacy of Sweden's act to invoke Article XXI. In recognition of international disapproval, Sweden promptly held negotiations and withdrew its measure of a quota system on shoes. This case demonstrates the importance of diplomatic pressure on the process of dispute settlement in Article XXI. An economic emergency within a specific industry therefore is not a legitimate cause to trigger the security exception provision.

Helms–Burton Act

The dispute settlement between the US and the EU about the Cuban Liberty and Democratic Solidarity (LIBERTAD) Act of 1996 (Helms–Burton Act) also demonstrates that the judgements of the WTO restrain Members from abusing the mechanism of the national security exception.

The US Helms–Burton Act is not considered consistent with Members' commitment to the WTO because it is motivated by foreign policy objectives, which are against the underlying principles of trade liberalization in the WTO trading system. On 20 February 1996, Cuba shot down two civil unarmed aeroplanes that violated Cuban airspace. The US soon adopted the Helms–Burton Act to impose economic sanctions on an extraterritorial basis on certain companies in other countries who trade with or invest in Cuba as a diplomatic revenge (Lindsay 2003: 1277). The Helms–Burton Act led to serious rejections from the US's primary trading partners including the EU, Canada and Mexico. The EU filed a complaint against the Helms–Burton Act to the WTO Dispute Settlement Body (DSB), and a Panel was held to settle this dispute.[52]

The US claimed that the legislation of the Helms–Burton Act was based on the ground of national security to invoke GATT XXI, and it asserted that it was not within the authority of the WTO to decide the domain of national security interests of the US.[53] There were also fierce debates about whether Cuba could constitute a real threat to national security (Lindsay 2003: 1277, note 149).[54] It seemed that the US held back on this Act because it would possibly challenge its legitimacy on the application of Article XXI by the DSB judgement, so the US negotiated with the EU and reached an agreement in April 1997. The EU promised to cease the procedure to the DSB Panel, and the US agreed to suspend the application of Titles III and IV of the Helms–Burton Act.[55] The case was closed due to the Panel being suspended for over twelve months.[56]

The resolution of the dispute on the Helms–Burton Act further demonstrates a peculiar approach to the dispute settlement of GATT XXI. Disputes in the WTO system can be resolved by other means of diplomatic negotiation as well as by the legal process in the DSB (Movsesian 1999: 775, 791–5). This may well be true if a dispute arises regarding the application of a PA in this provision. The trigger of a PA appears to be rather relaxed due to the subjective standard of '*it considers necessary*', and without a proper risk assessment and a clear allocation of burden of proof, the dispute settlement would

116   *Current landscape*

inevitably depend greatly upon political means. Resolutions using a diplomatic approach indeed provide flexibility in negotiations, and can be resolved more from a public point of view which would be more likely to reach mutual consensus. The strengths of the dispute settlement from diplomatic negotiations are not easily achieved by official judicial review, albeit diplomatic negotiation depends greatly upon the power of a state. Consequently, a weak state will often be forced to give in under the powerful economic influence of a strong state.

RULES AND PRINCIPLES OF THE APPLICATION OF THE
PRECAUTIONARY APPROACH UNDER THE SECURITY EXCEPTION

From the past experience of the *security exception* in Article XXI GATT, we can see that a 'one-size-fits-all' approach is not necessarily fit for purpose for Members' administration under a national emergency. States prefer to have more flexibility in their interpretation of the ambiguous implications of 'national security' and 'essential security interests'. GATT XXI is thus used as leeway for Members to exercise their authority when they think it necessary under circumstances of emergency. This could be linked to the discussion of *states' rights and duties* in Chapter 3.[57] When their 'national security' or 'essential security interests' are threatened by a particular health risk, states are granted more margin of appreciation in the interpretation of the PA.

In addition, a PA is only used as a policy tool in risk management while its application is to ensure that the concept of 'precaution' is employed under uncertainty (Motaal 2005: 483–501). Hence, similar to the function as a safety valve of GATT XXI in the WTO, the vagueness also demonstrates that a PA may be applied within a state's margin of discretion in risk management in accordance with a state's own particular policy objectives.

The current situation of a lack of a uniform definition as well as an ambiguous legal status of PAs in the security exception article does not deter its widespread application in risk management. A one-size-fits-all approach of the PA does not always satisfy the challenges of the multidimensional character of risks. Consequently, a tailored definition for a specific health risk will be proposed in order to facilitate further application and communication.[58]

GATT XXI is a highly controversial provision in the WTO regime due to its ambiguity of interpretation. Despite the fact that the phrasing appears to offer a broad interpretation, in reality its application needs to pass international political scrutiny. There are also follow-up discussions regarding the limitations of this Article. For example, Hahn argues that this Article was not designed to include the 'socio-economic consequence' resulting from the operation of GATT principles, nor was it designed to provide safeguards for 'vital industries' or to allow for the use of other protectionist measures (Hahn 1991: 558). He contends that Article XXI is not absolutely 'self-defining',

The precautionary approach in international law 117

and he suggests that Members should be required to provide the relevant facts and reasons with the proposed measure for protection of their essential security interests (Hahn 1991: 558).

In addition, in a later Decision adopted by Contracting Parties, the interests of third parties which may be affected was reckoned to be taken into consideration, and appropriate guidelines on the obligation to inform other affected Contracting Parties were established for its application. The Contracting Parties decided that 'contracting parties should be informed to the fullest extent possible of trade measures taken under Article XXI', and all Contracting Parties affected by such action should retain their full rights under the General Agreement.[59]

The General Agreement acknowledges that the Contracting Party has autonomy in the discretion of measures which involve its own essential interests. Nevertheless, the applied measure should be used as *a last resort* in order to prevent abuse of the provision.[60] Therefore it is imperative that a certain degree of judicial review remains to safeguard the provision from being abused or used arbitrarily. From case precedents and state practice of the security exception provision, if Members are to apply the PA under the national security provision, some clarifications about the ambiguity in the Article can be demonstrated in the following analysis:

- Members have *autonomy* to invoke GATT XXI and apply certain measures to protect their essential security interests.
- Members have the discretion to interpret their 'essential security interest' while taking into account the requirements in GATT XXI.
- Members are expected to avoid 'broad interpretation' to prevent the abuse of GATT XXI, and conform to the jurisprudence of 'limited interpretation of exceptions' in WTO laws (McRae 2000: 235–6).
- The adopted measure proposed under GATT XXI should be proportionate to the threat to Members' essential interests.
- Members are expected to inform other affected Members and the WTO.
- Affected Members retain their full rights in the WTO, such as the right to request a consultation and the process of Dispute Settlement in the WTO.
- The WTO has the authority to review the disputed measure proposed by GATT XXI, but the WTO is intrinsically not an appropriate mechanism to settle such highly political disputes (Horng 2005: 165).

Again, the PA in the security exception tends to be a *prescriptive* one in which a precautionary measure is taken on the grounds of national security; it can also be understood as relevant to the *Information Disclosure* PA for it expects the invoking state to inform other affected states and the WTO. In terms of a strong, weak or moderate version, the vague and subjective trigger 'it considers necessary' may initially indicate a relatively strong PA; however, evidence shows that the international political atmosphere indeed plays an

118   *Current landscape*

important role in the moderation of a strong PA. In order to avoid international conflicts of a precautionary measure, it may be fair to say that a *moderate* PA is more favourable than a strong PA under the national security exception heading.

Basically, Members prefer to reserve the ambiguity and flexibility of GATT XXI in order to exercise their autonomy and fulfil the needs of national essential interests in the circumstances of emergency. Members are left with a greater margin of appreciation in the exercise of the PA under this heading. Nevertheless, due to the intrinsic limitations of an unclear mechanism for operation and the subjectivity of interpretation, it inevitably depends more on the existing political dynamics in an international setting rather than the WTO DSB to resolve such disputes.

4.3.2. The PA in the Agreement on the Application of Sanitary and Phytosanitary Measures

The SPS Agreement was devised to introduce more elaborate rules for the application of the health exception rules in GATT XX (b) which relates to the use of sanitary or phytosanitary measures. The purpose of the SPS Agreement is to improve the human health, animal health and phytosanitary situation of WTO Members, and also to ensure that the SPS measures are not applied in a manner which would constitute a means of arbitrary or unjustifiable discrimination between Members (Para. 1 Preamble SPS Agreement). There is potential overlap between GATT XX (b) and the SPS Agreement. GATT XX (b) appears to cover general health measures that Members might adopt, while the SPS Agreement relates specifically to sanitary and phytosanitary measures. The SPS Agreement articulates that SPS measures which conform to the relevant provisions of the SPS Agreement need to be in accordance with Members' obligation under GATT XX (b) (Article 2.4). In other words, the SPS Agreement and the health exception in GATT stand in a mutually supportive way.

A Member's right to protect domestic public health was not officially recognized in the traditional GATT framework; health concerns in the GATT only serve as a general exception to the rule of free trade. It was not until the Uruguay Round of negotiations that the WTO introduced the SPS Agreement for a detailed framework of health protection in the WTO mechanism. On the one hand, the SPS Agreement grants Members the power to protect domestic human health issues and food safety by regulating risks arising from 'additives, contaminants, toxins, disease-causing organisms in food, beverages or feedstuffs' (Annex A, Article 1(b)); on the other hand, Members are obliged to follow relevant requirements in this agreement to avoid trade protectionism (Article 2). Following the framework developed in the Agreement, Members are free to adopt regulatory measures within their area of sovereignty with a view to protecting public health.

The precautionary approach in international law 119

(1) Appropriate level of health protection

The SPS Agreement affirms a Member's 'right' to take SPS measures 'necessary for the protection of human, animal or plant life or health', but the adopted SPS measure needs to meet several requirements:

- They must be applied 'only to the extent *necessary* to protect human, animal or plant life or health'.
- They must be 'based on *scientific principles* and ... not maintained without sufficient *scientific evidence*'.
- They must not 'arbitrarily or unjustifiably discriminate between Members where identical or similar conditions prevail'.
- They must be 'applied in a manner which would not constitute a disguised restriction on international trade' (Article 2).

The Preamble of the SPS Agreement recognizes Members' right to maintain the appropriate level of health protection. The international approved standard is generally recommended (Article 3.1; Article 3 of Annex A), but Members could adopt their ALOP accompanied by scientific justification based on the relevant international standards (Article 3.3). However, the SPS Agreement also provides leeway for a higher level of protection under scientific uncertainty by providing the mechanism of provisional SPS measures (Article 5.7). In other words, ALOP may be maintained with scientific justification, but provisional SPS measures may also be adopted if certain criteria are met under scientific uncertainty, which includes insufficiency in scientific evidence or causal relationship.

Under the SPS Agreement, a WTO Member is free to set its own health standard as long as the measure is applied by risk assessment based on scientific evidence (Articles 2.2, 2.5). Applications of international standards of health protection to the process of risk management are encouraged (Articles 3.1, 3.2, 3.3). However, a higher standard of protection than the international standard may also be accepted as a *conditional right* in conjunction with a valid risk assessment and scientific evidence (Articles 3.3, 5). Alternative measures can also be accepted as an equivalent if Members can prove they provide the same standard of health protection and are least restrictive to trade (Article 4).

Specifically, the Appellate Body suggested that the PA is reflected in the following three Articles in the SPS Agreement (*EC – Hormones*, para. 124):

- The sixth paragraph of the Preamble: Members can retain their appropriate level of health protection.
- Article 3.3: Members can introduce a higher level of health protection under scientific justification.
- Article 5.7: Members can adopt provisional SPS measures to manage health risks if scientific evidence is insufficient.

120 *Current landscape*

These Articles all recognize the *rights* of Members to determine the appropriate level of public health protection in WTO law. The Appellate Body has recognized the 'autonomous right' of a Member to establish a higher level of health protection (Appellate Body Report, *EC – Hormones*, para. 104). Under the framework of the SPS Agreement, Members can follow two tracks in order to adopt an SPS measure: track one is to follow available international standards; track two is at the discretion of Members. If Members wish to adopt a higher level of health protection for their population, scientific justification must be satisfied with risk assessment and scientific evidence. WTO Members are not prohibited from adopting a level of zero risk (Appellate Body Report, *Australia – Salmon*, para. 125).

In order to meet the requirements for adopting a higher level of health protection, Members need to take into account the objective of minimizing negative trade effects (Articles 5.3–5.6). Members are obliged to avoid arbitrary or unjust discrimination in the determination of the appropriate levels of health protection in different situations (Article 5.5). Relevant economic factors should also be assessed: the potential loss of production or sales in the event of the entry, the spread of a pest or disease, the costs of control for the importing Member and the cost-effectiveness of alternative approaches should be included (Article 5.3).

Furthermore, the PA has been embodied in provisional SPS measures in the SPS Agreement to manage unknown risks to human health. Provisional SPS measures can be adopted with a lack of scientific evidence in order to minimize the risk of a public health threat.

(2) Provisional SPS measures

The WTO Appellate Body concluded that '[t]hese explicitly recognize the right of Members to establish their own appropriate level of sanitary protection, which *level may be higher* (*i.e. more cautious*) than that implied in existing international standards, guidelines and recommendations' (italics added) (Appellate Body Report, *EC – Hormones*, para. 124). It also noted that in situations where there are risks of irreversible harm, for example, risks identified as life-terminating or damaging to human health, acts from *perspectives of prudence and precaution* may be adopted by responsible governments (Appellate Body Report, *EC – Hormones*, para. 124). In other words, in situations concerning risks of irreversible harm, the standard of application of the PA appears to be more relaxed. Scott hence contends that when the provisional measure is adopted to protect irreversible or life-threatening damage, Members' obligation to the WTO will be lessened (Scott 2009: ix).

The mechanism of provisional SPS measures was consequently drafted to be used in emergency situations where, for example, the spread of a disease has to be stopped urgently before it is feasible to complete a risk assessment (Marceau and Trachtman 2006). A Member may adopt provisional SPS

The precautionary approach in international law 121

measures on the basis of available pertinent information. In order to avoid misuse of this Article, after the adoption of a provisional SPS measure, Members are still obliged to obtain necessary additional information for a more objective risk assessment, and bear the duty to review the measure within a reasonable period of time (Article 5.7).

As the interpretations of the SPS Agreement depend greatly on the rulings of the Appellate Body, it is necessary to examine typical SPS cases in order to interpret the meanings of the legislation with respect to the PA. We will now familiarize ourselves with the procedural requirements of the precautionary mechanism in the SPS Agreement by examining the following cases.

(3) Case studies

JAPAN – MEASURES AFFECTING AGRICULTURAL PRODUCTS (JAPAN – VARIETALS)

In *Japan –Varietals*,[61] the United States filed a complaint against Japan relating to the quarantine requirement imposed by Japan for each variety of certain agricultural products (varietal testing requirements, 'VTR'). Japanese law provided that the prohibition on imported fruits can be lifted when the exporting country uses an alternative quarantine treatment that meets the same level of protection as the import ban. The United States complained that the testing for each variety of apples was lengthy, costly, and caused unjustifiable delay in marketing US products.[62] In particular, the United States challenged the requirement on the grounds that VTR was inconsistent with Japan's obligations under the SPS Agreement (Dunoff 2006: 155).

The Appellate Body in *Japan – Varietals* further found that the application of a precautionary SPS measure needs to meet four requirements.

> Pursuant to the first sentence of Article 5.7, a Member may provisionally adopt an SPS measure if this measure is:
>
> (1) imposed in respect of a situation where 'relevant scientific information is insufficient'; and
> (2) adopted 'on the basis of available pertinent information'.
>
> Pursuant to the second sentence of Article 5.7, such a provisional measure may not be maintained unless the Member which adopted the measure:
>
> (1) 'seek[s] to obtain the additional information necessary for a more objective assessment of risk'; and
> (2) 'review[s] the ... measure accordingly within a reasonable period of time'.

122 *Current landscape*

These four requirements are clearly cumulative in nature and are equally important for the purpose of determining consistency with this provision. Whenever *one* of these four requirements is not met, the measure at issue is inconsistent with Article 5.7.

(Appellate Body Report, *Japan – Varietals*, para. 89)

In addition to general requirements of an SPS measure such as *necessity*, *scientific justification*, and *non-discrimination* in international trade, this further set of requirements in the adoption of a provisional SPS measure is identified in the *Varietal* case. This set of requirements specifically demands that the provisional SPS measure be applied in situations of insufficiency of scientific information, based on available pertinent information; the adopting state is obliged to have an ongoing duty to gather updated information for monitoring and review. However, the Appellate Body did not explicitly indicate that there should be downstream obligations to change their policy or behaviour if fresh evidence is discovered.

In other words, in *emergency* situations where adequate risk assessment does not exist due to insufficiency of scientific information, Members can still implement provisional SPS measures based on available pertinent information. But in order to ensure the provisional measure does not constitute unnecessary restriction to international trade, it is noteworthy that after the adoption of a provisional measure, Members are obliged to obtain necessary information for a more objective assessment, and review the measure within a reasonable period of time. This has resonance with the duty to monitor the ongoing risks in the *Gabcikovo –Nagymaros* case.[63]

In *Japan – Varietals*, the Appellate Body noted that the VTR was not legitimate within the scope of Article 5.7. The Appellate Body found that Japan had not sought to obtain additional information, or to review the VTR within a reasonable period of time (*Japan – Varietals*, para. 92). The Appellate Body also explained that 'what constitutes a "reasonable period of time" has to be established on a case-by-case basis and depends on the specific circumstances of each case, including the difficulty of obtaining the additional information necessary for the review *and* the characteristics of the provisional SPS measure' (*Japan – Varietals*, para. 93).

The *Varietals* case indicates that the adopted PA should be accompanied with a set of requirements which aims to prevent abuse of this mechanism. It can also be inferred that the PA needs to remain adaptive to the characteristics of each particular risk, but that the adopting states are obliged not to cause any unnecessary interference to international trade. The set of requirements indeed serves as an objective safeguard to avoid misuse of the application of the PA in international trade, and it will further be applied in Chapter 6 when arguing for the PA to be extended to the realm of IP policy-making.

The precautionary approach in international law 123

EC – MEASURES CONCERNING MEAT AND MEAT PRODUCTS (EC – HORMONES)

In *EC – Hormones*,[64] the European Community invoked the precautionary approach to justify its ban on imports from the United States and Canada of beef treated with artificial hormones, where the impact on human health remains uncertain. The United States and Canada challenged the EC's ban on the sale and import of beef treated with growth hormones as a violation of the EC's obligation in the SPS Agreement.

Notably, the EC did not invoke the PA contained in Article 5.7. The Panel and the Appellate Body then had to explore if there could be elements of the PA in the SPS Agreement beyond what is contained in Article 5.7. They concluded that Article 3.3 allows Members to introduce a higher level of health protection than international standards. It is regarded as not only an exception, but as *a conditional right* or exclusion to WTO law. It serves as exclusion to Article 3.1 which expects Members to use international standards. This expresses that the act to adopt a higher level of health protection is a right instead of an exception in WTO law. To put it more accurately, the Appellate Body noted that:

> Article 3.1 of the SPS Agreement simply *excludes* from its scope of application the kinds of situations covered by Article 3.3 of that Agreement ... Article 3.3 recognizes the *autonomous right* of a Member to establish such higher level of protection, provided that that Member complies with certain requirements in promulgating SPS measures to achieve that level.
>
> (*EC – Hormones*, para. 104, emphasis added)

The Appellate Body suggests that the adoption of a higher level of health protection is an *autonomous right* of Members by excluding the application of Article 3.3 from Article 3.1. If Article 3.3 is treated as exclusion instead of exception to Article 3.1, the burden of proof would then rest upon the complaining party. In other words, Canada and the United States have to prove that the EC's ban is inconsistent with its obligations in the SPS Agreement.

The Appellate Body also noted that for '... a measure, to be consistent with the requirements of Article 3.3, [it] must comply with, *inter alia*, the requirements contained in Article 5 of the SPS Agreement' (*EC – Hormones*, para. 253). Article 5.1 requires Members to base their SPS measures on risk assessment, yet the Panel and Appellate Body both found that the EC ban was not based on a risk assessment, thus constituted a violation of the SPS Agreement. The Appellate Body consequently recommended that the EC bring its SPS measures into conformity with its obligations under the SPS Agreement (*EC – Hormones*, para. 255). This case demonstrates that Members need to base their decisions of a health policy on a risk assessment in order to avoid international conflicts.

124 *Current landscape*

UNITED STATES – CONTINUED SUSPENSION OF OBLIGATIONS
IN THE EC – HORMONES DISPUTES (HORMONES II)

Since the publication of the Appellate Body Report in *EC – Hormones*, the EC
has initiated 17 scientific studies to assess the risks to human health posed by
the hormones at issue (*Hormones II*, para. 10). However, the United States and
Canada have already requested that the DSB authorize suspension of the
concessions in relation to the EC.

The EC objected to the levels of suspension of concessions proposed by the
US and Canada, but the US and Canada had both obtained authorization from
the DSB to suspend concessions. The EC then notified the DSB of its adoption
of *Directive 2003/74/EC* and relevant reports which considered risk assessments that justified the permanent and provisional import prohibitions under
the SPS Agreement. The EC then claimed that it had implemented the DSB's
recommendations in the original *EC – Hormones* dispute, and considered the
suspensions of concessions by the US and Canada as not justified. However,
the US and Canada refused to lift the measure taken to suspend concessions or
other obligations, thus the EC filed a complaint (*Hormones II*, paras. 8–12).[65]

The Appellate Body noted that at the time of adoption of a provisional SPS
measure, the Member in question needs to identify the insufficiencies in the
relevant scientific evidence, and the steps it intends to take to obtain the
additional information to remedy these (*Hormones II*, para. 679). It also stated
that '[i]n emergency situations … a Member will take a provisional SPS
measure on the basis of limited information and the steps which it takes to
comply with this obligation to seek to obtain additional information and
review the measure will be assessed in the light of the exigencies of the emergency' (*Hormones II*, para. 680).

In summary, the *Hormones* case indicates the importance of basing a domestic SPS measure on decent risk assessment. The PA is deemed as a *right* not
an exception in the SPS Agreement; however, it will not be accepted
as legitimate without some sort of scientific evidence, and risk assessment
is regarded as a neutral measurement of the approach. In *Hormones II*,
the prerequisites to adopt a provisional SPS measure are further interpreted.
In addition to the above-mentioned requirements set out in *Varietals*,
the Appellate Body mentioned that the adopting state needs to identify the
insufficiency of scientific evidence and relevant following actions of monitoring
and review at the time of adoption. This shows that Members' rights to be
precautious link to their duties to continue gathering evidence over time.

EUROPEAN COMMUNITIES – MEASURES AFFECTING THE APPROVAL
AND MARKETING OF BIOTECH PRODUCTS (EC – BIOTECH)[66]

The controversies over the risks of genetically modified organisms (GMOs) to
human health and environment have been reflected in many anti-GMO
campaigns.[67] The EC as a whole and several independent Member States

The precautionary approach in international law 125

invoked the PA to adopt a general moratorium on approvals of biotech products imported from Argentina, Canada and the United States between October 1998 and August 2003. The moratorium was then challenged by Argentina, Canada and the United States.

The EC has two legal instruments to manage the risks of GMOs: the first is *EC Directive 2001/18* (the previous *EC Directive 90/220*), which governs 'the deliberate release into the environment of genetically modified organisms'; and the second is *EC Regulation 258/97*, which regulates 'novel foods and novel food ingredients'. These instruments set out procedures that need to be followed in order to obtain market approval for biotech products. They also allow Member States to provisionally restrict or prohibit the sale of a GMO product when they have 'justifiable reasons to consider that a product which has been properly notified and has received written consent ... constitute[s] a risk to human health or the environment' (Article 16 of Directive 80/220; Article 23 of Directive 2001/18).

However, the US, Canada and Argentina complained that the EC Member States did not adopt the provisional measures with scientific justification.[68] They argued that the EC's approval regime was influenced by public opinions instead of being based on scientific assessment. It was claimed that the EC Member States had violated Articles 5.1 and 2.2 of the SPS Agreement, and they applied arbitrary or unjustifiable restrictions on international trade.

It is noteworthy that the Appellate Body did *not* examine substantial controversies such as whether biotech products are safe or not; whether the biotech products are 'like products' with conventional products, or whether the EC has a right to require the 'pre-marketing approval of biotech products' (*EC – Biotech*, para. 8.3). The Appellate Body merely addressed procedural issues in relation to Directive 90/220 and 2001/18 being SPS measures within the meaning of the SPS Agreement (*EC – Biotech*, para. 8.4). The Appellate Body also found that the approval procedures resulted in *undue delay* to market (*EC – Biotech*, para. 8.6). The Appellate Body concluded that the EC had violated the SPS Agreement by applying a general de facto moratorium on the approval of biotech products. The DSU accordingly presumed the EC to have nullified or impaired benefits accruing to the complaining parties, and requested the EC to bring the relevant measures into conformity with its obligations under the SPS Agreement.

In the previous *EC – Asbestos* case, where the Appellate Body included a consumer's view in examining the 'likeness' of products, it was noted that 'consumers are, to a greater or lesser extent, not willing to use products containing chrysotile asbestos fibres because of the *health risks associated with them*' (*EC – Asbestos*, para. 145, emphasis added). It can be inferred that products carrying different health risks may not be classified as 'like products' (see Chapter 2). Regrettably, the Appellate Body of *EC – Biotech* did not address the like-product analysis of GMOs and overlooked the factor of 'consumers' taste and habits' in selecting GMO or non-GMO products.

126   *Current landscape*

In summary, the Appellate Body avoided commenting on the fundamental controversies of a biotech product, but only chose to examine the procedural legitimacy of the legislation within the scope of the SPS Agreement. It is a shame that the Appellate Body did not analyse whether or not the GMOs are 'like products' with non-GMOs, but only noted that the undue delay to market caused by the moratorium was regarded as inconsistent with the EC's obligations in the SPS Agreement. It may be fair to say that the Appellate Body avoided further analysis of the 'likeness' of GMOs and non-GMOs partly due to the insufficiency of existing scientific evidence. Nevertheless, the insufficiency of scientific evidence in such circumstances may be the exact legitimate grounds for the invocation of the PA.

(4) Rules and principles of the application of the PA in the SPS Agreement

As discussed above, the SPS Agreement sets the basic rights and obligations of Members (Article 2), and affirms that Members 'have the right' to take SPS measures 'necessary to protect human, animal or plant life or health' (Article 2.1). There are two tracks to adopting SPS measures: one is the general SPS measure, and the other is an expedient track for adopting provisional SPS measures. In order to meet the requirements, general SPS measures must:

- be applied 'only to the extent necessary to protect human, animal or plant life or health' (Article 2.1);
- be 'based on scientific principle and ... not maintained without sufficient scientific evidence' (Article 2.2);
- not 'arbitrarily or unjustifiably discriminate between Members where identical or similar conditions prevail' (Article 2.3); and
- not 'be applied in a manner which would constitute a disguised restriction on international trade' (Article 2.3).

Further, the SPS Agreement defines the necessity test in such a way that any alternative measure:

- must achieve the appropriate level of sanitary or phytosanitary protection;
- must be reasonably available taking into account technical and economic feasibility; and
- must be significantly less restrictive to trade (footnote 3).

Hence, the necessity test in the SPS Agreement is considered more flexible than that in GATT XX (b). It includes the consideration of technical and economic feasibility of Members, and the alternative measures need to be 'significantly' less restrictive to trade (footnote 3). However, Members are obliged to base their SPS measures on certain risk assessments that indicate the necessity of those measures in order to reach appropriate levels of health protection (Article 5.1).

The precautionary approach in international law 127

Again, the PA in the SPS Agreement is a *prescriptive* version,[69] by which states can adopt provisional SPS measures. It could also be understood as a *moderate* PA,[70] for the necessity test is relatively more relaxed than it is in the health exception. It is also akin to the *Information Disclosure* PA[71] for an emphasis is made on the duty of the adopting state to monitor and review the adopted measure. It is noteworthy that due to the legal status of a provisional SPS measure being within the domain of 'conditional rights' in the WTO, the burden of proof is therefore reversed onto the complaining state.

The SPS Agreement articulates that SPS measures which conform to the relevant provisions of the SPS Agreement shall be in accordance with Members' obligations under GATT XX (b) (Article 2.4). Yet the allocation of burden of proof in a dispute in relation to the SPS Agreement is different from that in relation to the GATT XX (b) due to their different legal status (Grando 2006: 615) (see Figures 4.3 and 4.3.1). The right to adopt SPS measures is deemed an 'autonomous right' by the WTO (Article 2.1), while GATT XX (b) is deemed an exception to any existing rule (Charnovitz *et al.* 2004: 257). Under the current rule, the burden of proof lies with the defendant who invokes an exception, but the burden of proof is on the complainant who challenges the measure which is adopted following an autonomous right. Therefore, the complaining party has to prove the adopted measure is not consistent with the SPS Agreement. An SPS measure is assumed consistent with the SPS Agreement if the complainant fails to prove otherwise.

4.3.3. The PA in the Agreement on Technical Barriers to Trade

The Agreement on Technical Barriers to Trade (TBT Agreement) was established alongside the SPS Agreement as an evolution of the GATT rules specifically on domestic regulatory autonomy (Marceau and Trachtman 2002: 881). The TBT Agreement concerns domestic technical regulations, standards and conformity assessment procedures which extend beyond sanitary and phytosanitary measures covered in the SPS Agreement (Articles 1.5, 1.6 TBT Agreement). WTO Members are encouraged to base their national measures on international standards with a view to harmonizing national norms and minimizing protectionism (Article 2.4 TBT Agreement; Marceau and Trachtman 2002: 814).

While international standards and conformity assessment systems are preferred, the TBT Agreement also recognizes that countries should be able to take necessary measures to ensure the quality of their exports or for the protection of health and the environment, to achieve an appropriate level of protection (ALOP) (paras. 4, 6 of the Preamble).

(1) Technical regulations

The TBT Agreement requires WTO Members to ensure that technical regulations shall not be more trade-restrictive than necessary to fulfil a legitimate objective, which may include national security requirements; the prevention

128   *Current landscape*

of deceptive practices; protection of human health or safety, animal or plant life or health, or the environment (Article 2.2). In considering the adoption of a measure, it is suggested that Members take account of the risks non-fulfilment would create. Available scientific and technical information, related processing technology or intended end-uses are all relevant elements in assessing such risks (Article 2.2).

A technical regulation covers a wide variety of product regulation, such as physical characteristics, labelling or production process (Lester *et al.* 2012: 601). In recent years, states have adopted labelling, marking or packaging schemes as a tool for managing uncertain risks arising from biotechnologies and climate change (Cheyne 2009: 927; Droge *et al.* 2004: 161). By providing information and choice to consumers from a labelling scheme, some costs of regulation may be transferred from regulators to industry and to consumers (Cheyne 2009: 931–2).

Technical standards fall into the following three categories: product standards, which determine characteristics of a product; product-related standards, which are related to the characteristics of a product by the production methods and are incorporated into the product; and non-product-related standards, which are relevant to the production methods but not to the product (Annex 1.1 and 1.2 TBT Agreement; Droge *et al.* 2004). It is held that products and processes and production methods (PPMs) are criteria for the differentiation of products, but non-product-related criteria cannot be used as the basis for 'unlike products' under the TBT Agreement and GATT (Droge *et al.* 2004: 164).

Labels can be further distinguished between voluntary and compulsory labels: voluntary labels offer an option for individual producers to decide whether to meet the criteria for a specific programme and to use that criteria for marketing purposes; compulsory labels are of command and control measures, which require producers to meet certain standards or market access will be denied. The adoption of mandatory labels needs to meet the requirement of non-discrimination in WTO law (Droge *et al.* 2004: 171). Article 2.1 sets out a basic non-discrimination requirement by stipulating that Members shall ensure that technical regulations imposed on imported products should offer no less favourable treatment than those on domestic products. Article 2.2 further raises the necessity test and addresses the issue that technical regulations are not used with the effect of creating unnecessary obstacles to international trade, and such regulations shall not be more trade-restrictive than necessary to fulfil a legitimate objective. The following cases will explore the Appellate Body's recent decision on whether the mandatory nature of labelling schemes constitutes technical regulations.

(2) Case study

EC – TRADE DESCRIPTION OF SARDINES (EC – SARDINES)[72]

In 1989, the EC decided that *sardinops sagax*, which is found primarily off the Western Pacific coasts of Peru and Chile, could only be sold under the

The precautionary approach in international law 129

technical term '*Sardinops sagax*', but not the general term 'sardines'. This measure would make it more difficult to sell the product. As an international standard, Article 6 of Codex Stan 94 sets out labelling conditions for sardines, and allows for the marketing of the *sardinops sagax* as sardines. The Appellate Body decided that the burden of proof rested with Peru to demonstrate that Codex Stan 94 is an effective and appropriate means to fulfil the EC's legitimate objectives. It was concluded that Peru adduced sufficient evidence to demonstrate that Codex Stan 94 would not be ineffective or inappropriate for the fulfilment of the legitimate objectives pursued by the EC Regulation, and that a Member must follow international standards unless that Member could justify the reason not to do so.

UNITED STATES – MEASURES AFFECTING THE PRODUCTION
AND SALE OF CLOVE CIGARETTES (US – CLOVES)[73]

The Appellate Body considered whether a US tobacco control measure which prohibits cigarettes with 'characterizing flavours' other than tobacco or menthol constitutes a violation of the TBT obligations. Section 907(a)(1)(A) of the Federal Food, Drug and Cosmetic Act (FFDCA) outlines special tobacco product standards, which results in a ban on flavoured cigarettes, including clove cigarettes primarily imported from Indonesia, but not to locally produced menthol cigarettes.

The Appellate Body examined whether clove cigarettes and menthol cigarettes are like products, and whether there was 'less favourable treatment' for imported clove cigarettes. The Appellate Body stated that:

> [A] panel must further analyze whether the detrimental impact on imports stems exclusively from a legitimate regulatory distinction rather than reflecting discrimination against the group of imported product. In making this determination, a panel must carefully scrutinize the particular circumstances of the case, that is, the design, architecture, revealing structure, operation, and application of the technical regulation at issue, and, in particular, whether that technical regulation is even-handed, in order to determine whether it discriminates against the group of imported products.
>
> (*US – Clove Cigarettes*, para. 182)

The Appellate Body then examined the design, architecture, revealing structure, operation, and application of Section 907(a)(1)(A), and concluded that the measure reflects discrimination against the group of like products imported from Indonesia and results in the detrimental impact on competitive opportunities for clove cigarettes (paras. 224–6).

130   *Current landscape*

UNITED STATES – MEASURES CONCERNING THE IMPORTATION,
MARKETING AND SALE OF TUNA AND TUNA PRODUCTS (US – TUNA II)[74]

The Appellate Body considered whether the mandatory 'dolphin-safe' label-ling scheme adopted by the US constituted technical regulations and whether it was compliant with the obligations under the TBT Agreement. The Appellate Body analysed this issue in two parts: first whether the labelling scheme modified the conditions of competition in the US market to the detri-ment of Mexican tuna products; second whether any detrimental impact reflected discrimination against the Mexican tuna products (para. 231). The Appellate Body questioned whether the difference between tuna caught outside or inside the Eastern Tropical Pacific Ocean (ETP) in the conditions necessary for acquiring a 'dolphin-safe' label was a legitimate regulatory distinction (para. 284). By taking into account both the discriminatory effect of the labelling conditions of this measure and its intent, the Appellate Body then concluded that the labelling measure caused detrimental impact on Mexican tuna products.

It is clear that the TBT Agreement encourages Members to adopt available international standards. The TBT Agreement states that a standardizing body shall use existing international standards as a basis for the standards it develops, except where such international standards are ineffective or inap-propriate (Paragraph F of Annex 3). WTO Members will be expected to justify and publish the rationale of their TBT measures if international stand-ards are not chosen. A TBT measure would thus be deemed a prescriptive and an *Information Disclosure Precautionary Approach* (IDPA) in this regard.[75] The burden of proof appears to stay with the adopting state as they bear the responsibility to disclose the rationale of the said measure, albeit in some cases the shift of onus is observed. Any precautionary measure under the TBT obligations will need to satisfy the necessity test of the non-discrimination requirement; technical regulations aiming to protect health and safety are to be no more trade-restrictive than necessary.

4.3.4. *Interim conclusion: the legal hierarchy of exemptions from WTO obligations*

Though the WTO has gradually recognized the importance of the precau-tionary approach in environmental and health protection in recent years, its implementation appears to be rather ambiguous and rigid, which is narrower than what we see under the UN regime due to the inherent constraint of promoting free trade and eliminating trade barriers.

The PA under the exception headings in the WTO system includes the health exception provision and the security provision. Both are *prescriptive* versions of the PA. The interpretation of the Appellate Body shows that the PA in the health exception appears to be a *weak* version, while it appears to be a relatively *strong* one in the security exception, albeit that moderation

The precautionary approach in international law 131

from the international political settings exists to constrain its use. Both have the prerequisite of 'necessary': the definition of 'necessary' in the health exception rule is considered objective and requires scientific justification. By contrast, the definition of 'it considers necessary' in the security exception appears to be self-defining and leaves more flexibilities for Members' discretion. This is to say that the PA may enjoy broader employment in the security exception; however, the lack of a transparent mechanism in the security exception provision inevitably results in controversies which may only be resolved through political negotiation.

It has been stated previously that exception rules in WTO law are expected to be applied restrictively. Though Members enjoy a certain degree of autonomy to interpret the PA within the domain of the security exception, they are still under pressure from the international political setting. The application is also required to be 'limited interpreted' and adopted as *a last resort*. The invoking Member bears the burden of proof and is expected to inform other affected Members to the fullest extent possible.

In addition to the limited application of precaution in exception provisions of GATT, the SPS Agreement, which is considered the most elaborate agreement on health issues in WTO law, is thought to embody the PA in the guise of provisional SPS measures. The Appellate Body has also indicated that the principles developed from the SPS Agreement are equally applicable under GATT XX.

As different PAs exist in both exception provisions and excluding provisions in WTO law, they can be further distinguished in terms of legal status. The PA in exception provisions acts only as an affirmative defence in which the onus remains on the defendant; on the contrary, the PA in excluding provisions can also be understood as a 'conditional right' in WTO which enjoys a shift of the burden of proof. In other words, when the PA is identified

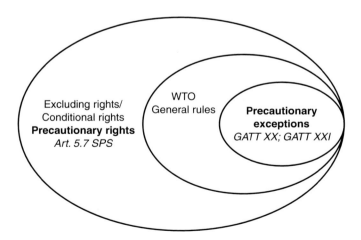

Figure 4.3.4 Precautionary actions in the WTO

132 *Current landscape*

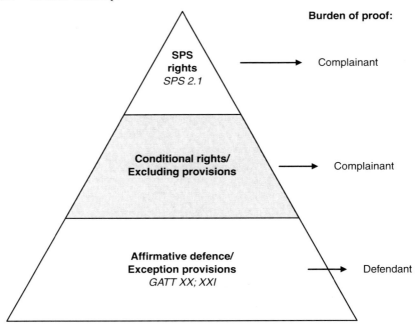

Figure 4.3.4.1 Legal hierarchy of the precautionary approach in the WTO

as a 'conditional right', the burden of proof is reversed onto the complaining party. For example, a precautionary measure in the health or security exception could only serve as a defence if the defendant is able to prove the necessity of the health measure; however, if a precautionary SPS measure (or a provisional SPS measure; Article 5.7) is deemed a conditional right by the WTO, it enjoys a higher level of legal status, and the complaining party bears the onus to prove that the adopted measure is inconsistent with Members' obligations to the WTO.

The SPS Agreement aims to help WTO Members set up a standard system of risk management for imported food and produce. It also requires Members to conform to their obligations in WTO law to ensure that the principle of non-discrimination is protected (para. 1 of the Preamble). In addition to dealing with the situation of scientific uncertainty, the PA is embodied in the SPS Agreement through the imposition of a provisional SPS measure to manage uncertain health risks under a public health emergency (Article 5.7). The WTO Appellate Body has identified the function of provisional SPS measures as 'a temporary "safety valve" in situations where some evidence of a risk exists but not enough to complete a full risk assessment under a health emergency' (*EC – Hormones II*, para. 678). It further stated that: 'In emergency situations, for example, a WTO Member will take a provisional SPS measure on the basis of limited information' (*EC – Hormones II*, para. 680). Therefore, it can be

The precautionary approach in international law 133

argued that this version of the PA is closest to the version that exists in compulsory licensing on the grounds of a public health emergency. If the legal status of compulsory licensing is considered a 'conditional right' instead of being an 'affirmative defence', the PA model in the SPS Agreement can then be mapped in the compulsory licensing scenario.

From the above SPS cases, it can be observed that the implementation of the PA is comparatively restricted by a set of procedural requirements of the SPS Agreement. Fundamental requirements of the PA are identified in *Japan – Varietals*; the *EC – Hormones* case suggests the importance of basing Members' ALOP on a risk assessment; and the *EC – Biotech* case indicates that a Member's domestic provisional SPS measure should not result in the said product's undue delay to market.

Similarly, the TBT Agreement sets out the rights of Members to ensure the quality of their exports or for the protection of health at the levels they consider appropriate by adopting domestic labelling schemes. Interestingly, it recognizes that Members' entitlements to adopt TBT measures are relevant to the protection of their essential security interests (para. 7 of the Preamble, Article 2.2), of which the application has recourse to the inter-pretation of the security exception of GATT where states have a broader margin of appreciation in determining the adoption of a precautionary measure. Such adoption, unsurprisingly, should also be in compliance with the fundamental requirements of the WTO, including taking into account international standards and available scientific and technical information (Articles 1.1, 2.2, 2.4); it should not be applied with the effect of creating unnecessary obstacles to international trade (Article 2.2); not be more trade-restrictive than necessary (Article 2.2); and should comply with the duty of notification (Articles 2.9, 2.10, 5.6) and the duty to review (Article 15).

In summary, three versions of PAs have been examined in the WTO context, which can be further distinguished by their legal status (see Table 4.3.4). These are all *prescriptive* versions, while PAs in the exception provisions are only affirmative defences, but in the SPS Agreement it is a *conditional right*. WTO Members' *right to protect* public health has been recognized and developed in the SPS Agreement and TBT Agreement, and the PA in the SPS Agreement is more concrete and sophisticated than others. It appears that the PAs in WTO exceptions are at two extremes, and that the PA in the SPS and TBT Agreements appears to be a *moderate* mechanism.

It is also noteworthy that in order to avoid misuse and create unnecessary substantial barriers to trade, the invocation of a provisional SPS measure is subject to a set of procedural requirements which aims to avoid disguised protectionism in international economic law. This default set of procedural requirements of the PA arising from case precedents could be accommodated into the IP regime through the application in compulsory licensing discussed in Chapter 6.

134 Current landscape

Table 4.3.4 Precautionary approaches in the WTO

Version of PA		Prescriptive	Information Disclosure	Reverse burden of proof	Strong/ Weak/ Moderate
Exception provision	Health exception	V			Weak
	Security exception	V	V		Strong
Excluding provision (Conditional right)	Provisional SPS measures	V	V	V	Moderate
	TBT measures	V	V	V	Moderate

In summary, the PA in the WTO regime appears to be restrained by the tension between health and global free trade. The Appellate Body adopts a cautious approach to the interpretation of the PA. Some features of the PA in the WTO regime can be identified as follows:

- The measure needs to be *necessary* to protect human life or health.
- The measure needs to be consistent with the requirements of *non-discrimination* in international trade, and should not cause any undue delay to market.
- A *provisional measure* needs to be adopted in the situation of insufficiency of scientific evidence.
- A provisional measure needs to be based on available pertinent information.
- The adopting state is required to have an ongoing duty of monitoring and review, and anticipated steps of review should be identified at the time of adoption. However, the Appellate Body does not explicitly impose a duty to change approach with the discovery of new evidence.

4.4. Conclusion

States' health measures have evolved and been recognized as a *right* or *a conditional right* in the world trade system. Moreover, based on the rationale of *'State responsibility'* and *'State stewardship'* in protecting public health, states may be obliged to seek a high level of health protection as well as to protect the population from pending health threats. They are free to exercise their *precautionary entitlements* to safeguard their civilians when confronted by unknown risks, of which the damages are identified as crossing the *significant* threshold. Yet trade supremacy under globalization at times overshadows the

The precautionary approach in international law 135

protection of public health, specifically with regard to the regulation of uncertain risk.

4.4.1. *Trade supremacy in the regulation of uncertain risk*

The PA appears to be common sense to the lay public; however, it is often criticized as ill-defined and a hindrance to scientific progress and international trade (Peterson 2006: 595–601). In addition to the lack of a clear consensus on its definition, the unsettled debate over the legal status of PAs in international law is further restricted by trade supremacy in international law.

The legal framework for regulating technologies should not be one-size-fits-all, but should be able to reflect the ethical differentiation of technologies in response to their individual implications for society (see Chapter 2). Legitimate factors of differentiation would include public interests, public policy, national emergency, risk management, and deliberative democracy. These factors are supposed to be weighed against legitimate trade objectives on a case-by-case basis. Yet the concern of risks to human health is often constrained by the primacy of international trade, and the value of free trade often overrides health factors in the WTO regime unless there is solid scientific justification. The regulation of uncertain risks is often subordinated to the principles of non-discrimination, which inevitably leads to a presumption: products are presumed safe until proven otherwise.

On the one hand, states' discretion in the regulation of health issues is restricted by the universal employment of 'international standards', such as the Codex referred to by the SPS, which greatly relies upon scientific evidence in risk management. On the other hand, the established international standards are intended to be globally applicable; thus this framework of risk management needs to avoid rigidity. It should allow an 'ample' or 'adequate' margin of safety to be taken by states at different levels of social-economic development (De Sadeleer 2008: 131). An ample margin of safety to cover the full range of diverse risks to human health, as well as taking into account the flexibilities of individual development and various social-economic backgrounds, should be well considered in risk regulation. Therefore, the prevention or reduction of *uncertain risks* to human health ought to be taken into consideration in the protection of public health. Uncertain risks which have the potential to result in *significant* damage to human health should be regarded as valid until proven otherwise.

For example, following on from the *Biotech* case, it can be observed that the WTO does not directly tackle the substantial health concerns raised by a given product; it only serves as a trade mechanism to regulate the free movement of health-related commodities. Under the current framework, products that give rise to potential concerns of uncertain impact to human life or health will not be banned in the first place without scientific evidence. In other words, *food is assumed not harmful to human health unless proven otherwise*

136 *Current landscape*

(Baetens 2007: 276). However, from past experience, many harmful effects without scientific evidence are subsequently proved. For example, the European Environment Agency has identified 12 'late lessons' from early warnings including the regulations regarding X-rays, asbestos, sulphur dioxide, chemical contamination, Tributyltin, hormones as growth promoters, mad cow disease, and so on.[76] Scientific justification for regulations or banning at times comes after the product has entered the market. Unfortunately, the damage is usually irreversible. This is exactly where the PA should come into play a vital role in covering the gap of scientific uncertainty or scientific ignorance before the scientific justification of regulation is completed.

The WTO Appellate Body's apparent lack of awareness of uncertain risks to human health in failing to address the like-product debate of GMO and non-GMO products in the *Biotech* case implies that the regulation of uncertain risk has not been distinguished in the trade world. The focus on the significance of the potential damage also helps to ensure a proportionate response with respect to any IP rights which might be in play. It is therefore argued in this book that technologies or products associated with risks to human health *do* pose unique implications for society, thus they should receive differential treatment in order to adopt an ample margin of safety. This is to say that products associated with *significant* risks to human life or health should *not* be categorized as 'like products' with other products in international trade. In such cases, if the public health risk is derived from harmful products, the IP system may be reflective on the risk by the restriction of the product/technology. By the same token, if the risk is from natural disasters/epidemics, the IP system needs to be reflective on the risk by the promotion of access to the product/technology (see Figure 1.1.2, Research parameter: Precaution lens).

Likewise, the IP regime also shows an imbalance between health and trade protection. TRIPS shows a tendency to stress the intact protection on private property rights, while the status of exclusions to IP on grounds of public interests, regulation of risks to public health or public policy remains relatively vague in state practice, yet such legitimate factors which reflect the spirit of public interest need to be able to step in to balance rights and obligations of right holders and promote the social and economic welfare of IP (Articles 7 and 8 TRIPS). This is where the function of the PA comes into play for harmonizing private and public interests in a sustainable trade/health regime (Li 2013).

4.4.2. Regimes conflict and the precautionary approaches

The implementation of the PA has been inconsistent in different regimes. It is observed that the discrepancies of PAs exist not only between national and international planes; regimes conflict also appears in individual legal instruments in international law (Helfer 2004: 1). Research shows that *domestic*

The precautionary approach in international law 137

health or environmental regulations often allow a comprehensive employment of a PA to safeguard human health (De Sadeleer 2008: 196; Sunstein 2010: 227); however, at the *international* level, when global trade interests are considered of paramount importance, and the risks often undervalued, the application of a PA in the protection of public health thus appears sporadically. The following paragraphs consider the examples of regimes conflict of the PA.

(1) IHRs versus SPS Agreement

The features of PAs in the IHRs are similar to those in the WTO SPS Agreement. These are both *prescriptive* and *moderate* versions of the PA; the need of *information disclosure* is also recognized in both instruments. Some common elements of scientific uncertainty have been identified: risks to human health; based on available information; the adoption of a specific health measure for a higher level of health protection; the adopting party is obliged to review the measure within three months; and the measure should not be more restrictive to international trade than reasonably available alternatives. However, there are three major differences between these two instruments:

- The burden of proof appears to remain on the invoking state in the IHRs.
- Regarding the enforcement mechanism, the IHRs are only equipped with consultation between states (Article 43.4), while the WTO Members can resort to its Dispute Settlement System (DSS), which is regarded as binding and effective in international dispute settlements. State Parties of both organizations may ultimately choose the WTO DSS for an efficient resolution. The WTO enforcement mechanism thus plays an important role in ensuring that states take measures in compliance with the IHRs (von Tigerstrom 2005: 35).

(2) Cartagena Protocol versus SPS Agreement

The most prominent regimes conflict appears in the Cartagena Protocol and the WTO SPS Agreement. The Cartagena Protocol has potential inconsistency with the SPS Agreement in the regulation allowing banning of the import of GMOs. State Parties of both legal instruments may find conflicts in prescribing relevant national laws (Covelli 2003: 773). The PA invoked in the Cartagena Protocol is an operational device with more flexibility to safeguard human health. Specifically, the procedural requirements of GMO importation are more stringent in the AIA procedure in the Cartagena Protocol than those in the SPS Agreement. The burden of proof under the Cartagena Protocol appears to be allocated to the exporting party since the Protocol allows the importing party to require a risk assessment from

138 *Current landscape*

the exporting party (Article 15.2). The importing party may also require the cost of risk assessment to be borne by the exporting party (Article 15.3).

Further, the implementation of a precautionary measure is not necessarily based on scientific justification; the obligation of the importer to review does not have a specific time frame in the Cartagena Protocol; while in the SPS Agreement, any provisional measure is obliged to be reviewed within a *reasonable period of time* (Article 5.7). According to the Cartagena Protocol, the importer does not have a constant obligation to keep the measure under review unless requested to do so by the exporter (Article 12). For example, the EC was challenged by the US, Canada and Argentina in the recent WTO *EC – Biotech* case on its regulations of GMOs imports. The EC claimed that its import suspension of GMOs was consistent with its obligations in the Cartagena Protocol, while the US, Canada and Argentina cited its 'undue delay' as a violation of the requirements in Article 8 and Annex C (1) (a) of the SPS Agreement.

In order to avoid inconsistency with other international agreements, the Preamble of the Cartagena Protocol suggests that trade and environmental agreements should be mutually supported, and the interpretation of the Protocol should not lead to a change in the rights and obligations under existing international agreements. A complementary relationship between trade-related provisions of environmental treaties and WTO law has been implied, and conflicts should be avoided through conciliatory interpretation (Mackenzie and Eggers 2000: 525). However, in terms of dispute resolution, similar to the clash of the IHRs and the SPS Agreement, states of these two legal regimes will also resort to the WTO for enforcement. It is therefore suggested to harmonize the requirements of the PA in the two organizations to avoid conflicts and contradiction in international public health law.

4.4.3. Elements of the precautionary approach in the international health regime

Evidence shows that the PA has been widely implemented in the regulation of health risks arising from virus transmission and biotechnology in international public health law. Although being employed without a uniform name, *prescriptive* PAs have appeared in different guises of risk management in contemporary society. The IHRs incorporate the mechanism of 'additional health measures' which aims to prompt detection of disease transmission; the Codex Alimentarius consists of the structure of 'risk analysis' which focuses on managing the risk from food and the adoption of 'safety factor' or 'additional safety factor' for the establishment of a temporary ADI; and the Cartagena Protocol includes an 'Advance Informed Agreement' (AIA) system (Articles 7–12) which attempts to monitor the transboundary movement of GMO products. All the above devices are deemed as the employment of a *prescriptive* PA and risk management in the international public health regime.

The precautionary approach in international law 139

In summary, it can be concluded that a single approach which comprises a *prescriptive, information disclosure and moderate* version of the PA is preferred in the international public health and intellectual property law regime. A precautionary measure triggered by risk assessment is essential in this model, a need to restrain the use to avoid unnecessary interference to international trade and traffic is identified, and the requirement of information disclosure is recognized, albeit that the shift of burden of proof is to be determined on a case-by-case basis. To conclude, the PA employed in this book comprises the following common features:

- There is scientific uncertainty or potential adverse impact on human health.
- Additional health measures or additional safety factors can be adopted.
- Risk assessment is suggested to be the trigger of a health measure; if scientific evidence is insufficient to carry out a full risk assessment, the health measure should be based on scientific principle, available pertinent information or suggestions from international organizations.
- There is a duty to review the health measure within a reasonable period of time.
- The health measure should be *necessary*, which means it should be no more restrictive of international trade and traffic than reasonably available alternatives.
- Other legitimate concerns including the protection of consumers, fair trade, government domestic regulation, social-economic impact may also be taken into account.

It is noteworthy that the health measure should pay due respect to free trade and avoid creating unnecessary barriers to international trade. This has resonance with the WHO '*Moderate Precaution*' model which aims to reconcile health protection and global free trade.[77] It can therefore be assumed that a *prescriptive, moderate* model, as well as an *information disclosure* model which has a special emphasis on the duty to review, could sit well in the trade word.[78]

4.4.4 Redefinition of the precautionary approach

The PA is not opposed to science and evidence; rather it supplements the blind spot or ignorance of science. It is used as a policy tool in risk management while its application is to ensure the concept of a 'safety factor' employed in circumstances of scientific uncertainty or insufficiency in scientific evidence. In other words, the PA is supposed to stand side by side with science and evidence; both act in a mutually supportive way to provide a safeguard to human health in case of scientific uncertainty.

To avoid possible controversies over the applications of the PA, which may amount to discrimination in free trade, a structural mechanism is proposed for a systematic application which starts with a scientific evaluation of risk.[79]

140   *Current landscape*

> (1) a health threat, which is (2) under scientific uncertainty, then (3) some public health measure for achieving an appropriate level of protection (4) should not be postponed.

Figure 4.4.4 PA formula

Moreover, from the previous analysis, the definition of the PA in the international public health law regime tends to be a *prescriptive* one, which requires specific public health measures to be instituted to regulate the unknown risks to human life or health. An *information disclosure* version could also shed some light on our model with regard to its mandate for the introducing party of a new product or technology to monitor and disclose any risk to the public. A *moderate* version is favoured as a strong version of the PA tends to opt for intervention regardless of potential costs and a weak one does not require any action for intervention. A moderate version would therefore reconcile both extremes, and it is in favour of adopting the least restrictive measure (LRM) to free trade, given that globalization has arisen to play an important role in international health. Consequently, a revised formulation based on Sandin's prescriptive version can be further illustrated by Figure 4.4.4 (Sandin 1999: 889).

Further, the requirement of minimizing restriction to international traffic and trade can also be accommodated into the formula. In order to accommodate a workable PA in the context of this book, the outline of the PA will be sketched in this section with a view to reconciling the needs of the trade and the health worlds. Thus this refined version of the PA from an international health law perspective can be elaborated as shown in Figure 4.4.4.1.

The PA should be triggered once the unknown risk is identified as passing the *significant* threshold. States have the precautionary entitlement to adopt health measures to achieve their appropriate level of public health protection. However, considering the possible adverse effects of unnecessary interference to international trade, I also suggest that the health measure be a LRM to trade. It is anticipated that applications of the PA in international public health can be recast using this formula. Some additional conditions including the duty to review, a cost-benefit analysis, public engagement and the burden of proof may be imposed respectively according to the various characteristics of individual health risk. Specifically, the implementation of the PA in the intellectual property regime will be examined in the following chapter.

> When confronted with *significant* threats of harm to human health, scientific uncertainty should not postpone the adoption of a precautionary public health measure for an *appropriate* level of public health protection while avoiding *unnecessary* interference to international trade.

Figure 4.4.4.1 Redefinition of the PA in international health law

Notes

1 The State Parties of WHO adopted important principles with regard to public health that are enshrined in the preamble to its Constitution. Hence, the Constitution establishes as a fundamental international principle that enjoyment of the highest attainable standard of health is not only a state or condition of the individual, but '... one of the fundamental rights of every human being without distinction of race, religion, political belief, economic or social condition ...'.

2 WHO (2004) *Fourth Ministerial Declaration on Environment and Health*, EUR/04/5046267/6, Budapest, Hungary 23–25 June, para. 17a.

3 Ibid., para. 17c.

4 WHO (2005) *Dealing with Uncertainty: Setting the Agenda for the 5th Ministerial Conference on Environment and Health, 2009*, EUR/06/5067987, Copenhagen, Denmark, 15–16 December (WHO Uncertainty Report).

5 WHO (2007) 'Issues Paper – Invest in Health, Build a Safer Future', p. 16.

6 'Appropriate level of protection' is also understood as 'acceptable level of protection'. See Section 2.1.2 (1).

7 WHO (2005) 'What Has Changed in the International Health Regulations', available at: http://www.who.int/csr/IHRS/revisionchange/en/print.html. The decision instrument identifies a limited set of criteria that will assist State Parties in deciding whether an event is notifiable to the WHO.

8 http://www.who.int/csr/outbreaknetwork/en/

9 Statement by WHO Director General, 25 April 2009, available on WHO website, Swine Influenza, http://www.who.int/mediacentre/news/statements/2009/h1n1_20090425/en/index.html

10 'U.S. Declares Public Health Emergency over Swine Flu', *New York Times*, 26 April 2009, available at: http://www.nytimes.com/2009/04/27/world/27flu.html

11 'The World Response to Flu Crisis', *BBC News*, 9 May 2009, available at: http://news.bbc.co.uk/1/hi/world/americas/8022516.stm

12 See Section 3.3.2.

13 See Section 3.3.3 (3).

14 In April 2003, Singapore amended its Infectious Disease Act to 'require persons with [possible SARS] to report to designated treatment centres, ... enforce home quarantine with electronic tagging and forced detention, and allow the quarantine and destruction of SARS-contaminated property'.

15 See Sections 2.1.2 (1) and 3.2.3 (1). The WTO recognized Members' right to pursue a higher level of health protection in *EC – Hormones*, Appellate Body Report, para. 124. Article 95.3 of the *EC Treaty* also provides that: 'The Commission, in its proposals envisaged in paragraph 1 concerning health, safety, environmental protection and consumer protection, will take as a base a high level of protection, taking into account in particular any new development based on scientific facts.'

16 Significant interference generally means refusal of entry or departure of international travellers, baggage, cargo, containers, conveyances, goods and the like, or their delay, for more than 24 hours.

17 *Codex Alimentarius Commission Procedural Manual*, 21st edn, Joint FAO/WHO Food Standards Programme, FAO, Rome, 2013 (Codex Manual).

142   *Current landscape*

18 Report of the Joint FAO/WHO Expert Consultation (1995) *Application of Risk Analysis to Food Standards Issues*, Geneva, Switzerland, 13–17 March, WHO/FNU/FOS/95.3 (Food Standard).

19 *Communication from the Commission on the Precautionary Principle* (2000) Commission of the European Communities (CEC), Brussels, 2 February. See Section 3.2.3 (2).

20 WHO Environmental Health Criteria Document No. 70 (1987) *Principles for the Safety Assessment of Food Additives and Containments in Food*, Geneva.

21 If a toxic effect is found at the 2 per cent level and a 'no toxic effect' at 1 per cent level, the 1 per cent level will be the 'no-observed-effect level'. In this case, the no-observed-effect level lies between the 1 per cent and 2 per cent levels. If no toxicological evaluations are done at intermediary levels, the choice of the 1 per cent level as the no-observed-effect level introduces a safety factor. See Codex Alimentarius Document (1989) *Guidelines for Simple Evaluation of Food Additive Intake*, CAC/GL 03-1989, p. 3 (Codex Guidelines).

22 Ibid., Codex Guidelines, p. 3.

23 Codex Alimentarius Document, *Glossary of Terms and Definitions* (Residues of Veterinary Drugs in Foods), CAC/MISC 2-2012 (Codex Glossary).

24 Ibid.

25 Ibid.

26 *Statement of Principle Concerning the Role of Science in the Codex Decision-Making Process and the Extent to which other Factors are Taken into Account*, Decision of the 21st Session of the Commission, 1995.

27 *Statement of Principle Relating to the Role of Food Safety Risk Assessment*, Decision of the 22nd Session of the Commission, 1997.

28 See above, note 26.

29 See above, note 26.

30 See above, note 27; Article 43.2 IHRs.

31 For example: 1992 Convention on Biodiversity (CBD); the 1992 Framework Convention on Climate Change; the 1989 Basel Convention on the Control of Transboundary Movements of Hazardous Wastes and Hazardous Substances; the 1996 Protocol to the Convention on the Prevention of Marine Pollution by Dumping of Wastes and other Matter.

32 The Rio Declaration on Environment and Development, UN Doc.A/CONF.151/26, Vol. I, Annex I, 1992 (Rio Declaration).

33 The General Agreement on Tariffs and Trade (GATT 1947 or GATT).

34 WTO Agreement on the Application of Sanitary and Phytosanitary Measures (SPS Agreement); Marrakesh Agreement Establishing the World Trade Organization, Annex 1A: Multilateral Agreements on Trade in Goods.

35 WTO Agreement on Technical Barriers to Trade (TBT Agreement); Marrakesh Agreement Establishing the World Trade Organization, Annex 1A: Multilateral Agreements on Trade in Goods.

36 See Sections 2.1.2 (1) and 3.2.3 (1).

37 See Chapter 3, note 54.

38 *United States – Standards for Reformulated and Conventional Gasoline (US – Gasoline)*, WT/DS2/R, Report of the Panel, 29 January 1996; WT/DS2/AB/R, Reports of the Appellate Body, 29 April 1996.

39 GATT Panel Report, *Thailand – Restrictions on Importation of and Internal Taxes on Cigarettes*, 7 November 1990, BISD 37S/200.

40 See note 38.

The precautionary approach in international law 143

41 *European Communities – Measures Affecting Asbestos or Products Containing Asbestos (EC – Asbestos)*, WT/DS135/R; WT/DS135/AB/R, adopted 12 March 2001.

42 WHO International Programme on Chemical Safety (IPCS) (1998) *Environmental Health Criteria 203 – Chrysotile Asbestos*, para. 144.

43 The Appellate Body Report of *Korea – Beef* was the first WTO ruling to introduce some relaxing elements into the necessity test. *Korea – Measures Affecting Imports of Fresh, Chilled and Frozen Beef (Korea – Beef)*, WT/DS169/AB/R, adopted 10 January 2001, para. 161.

44 *Brazil – Measures Affecting Imports of Retreaded Tyres (Brazil – Retreaded Tyres)*, WT/DS332/R; WT/DS332/AB/R, adopted 3 December 2007.

45 WHO (1999) 'Guidelines for Treatment of Dengue Haemorrhagic Fever in Small Hospitals' (ix).

46 General Agreement on Trade in Services (GATS). Services from architecture to voicemail telecommunications and to space transport are also included into the production of most goods after Uruguay round of negotiation.

47 See Sections 5.3.2 (2) and 6.3.

48 L/4250, 17 November 1975.

49 Although Sweden never formally invoked Article XXI, its position was supported by the exception.

50 Notification by the Swedish Delegation, Introduction of a Global Import Quota System for Leather Shoes, Plastic Shoes and Rubber Shoes, L/4250, p. 2.

51 Notification by the Swedish Delegation, Introduction of a Global Import Quota System for Leather Shoes, Plastic Shoes and Rubber Shoes, L/4250, p. 3.

52 WTO Panel Named in Helms–Burton Dispute; Dispute Settlement Body, Minutes of Meeting, WTO/DSB/M/78.

53 Guy de Jonquie'res (1997) 'US Dodges Brussels Onslaught: Washington Buys Time as Anti-Cuba Law Dispute Goes to World Trade Body', *Financial Times* (London), 21 February, 6.

54 Whether Cuba really represents a national security threat to the United States is an issue that is still being debated. At least one person suggests that perceptions of Cuba's threat linger from the Cold War and are maintained for political reasons (e.g. the common belief that Florida is an important swing state).

55 Under the Helms–Burton Act, the president has the authority to suspend application of Title III for up to six months if he gives notice to the appropriate congressional committees and '[the] suspension is necessary to the national interests of the United States and will expedite a transition to democracy in Cuba', 22 USCA Section 6085(c) (West Supp.2002). The president may make additional suspensions as necessary.

56 WTO (1997) Communication from the Chairman of the Panel, *United States – The Cuban Liberty and Democratic Solidarity Act*, WT/DS38/5.

57 See Chapter 3, Section 3.2.1.

58 See Section 4.4.4.

59 Decision Concerning Article XXI of the General Agreement, Decision of 30 November 1982 (1982), General Agreement on Tariffs and Trade, L/5426, 2 December. Available at: http://www.wto.org/gatt_docs/English/SULPDF/91000212.pdf

60 In the discussion on the complaint by Czechoslovakia against export restrictions imposed by the US, it is noted that: '... every country must be the judge in the last resort on questions relating to its own security. On the other

144   *Current landscape*

hand, every contracting party should be cautious not to take any step which might have the effect of undermining the General Agreement.' Corrigendum to the Summary Record of the Twenty-second Meeting, Contracting Parties Third Session, General Agreement on Tariffs and Trade, GATT/CP.3/SR.22, Corr.1, 20 June 1949, available at: http://www.wto.org/gatt_docs/English/SULPDF/90060101.pdf

61 Appellate Body Report, *Japan – Measures Affecting Agricultural Products (Japan – Varietals)*, WT/DS76/AB/R, 22 February 1999.

62 Under the legal regime, after extensive testing, Red Delicious apples from the United States were approved for import in August 1994; however, separate and different testing for different *varieties* of apples including Gala, Granny Smith, Jonagold, Fuji and Braeburn apples was still ongoing in 1998 when the dispute was being heard in a WTO dispute settlement.

63 See Section 3.2.2 (1).

64 *EC – Measures Concerning Meat and Meat Products (EC – Hormones)*, WT/DS26/AB/R, WT/DS48/AB/R, adopted 13 February 1998.

65 Appellate Body Report, *United States – Continued Suspension of Obligations in the EC – Hormones Dispute (Hormones II)*, WT/DS320/AB/R, adopted 16 October 2008.

66 *European Communities – Measures Affecting the Approval and Marketing of Biotech Products (EC – Biotech)* WT/DS291/R, WT/DS292/R, WT/DS293/R, adopted 29 February 2006. See also: Covelli, N. and Hohots, V. (2003) 'The Health Regulation of Biotech Foods under the WTO Agreements' 6(4) *Journal of International Economic Law* 773–95.

67 For example, Greenpeace and Friends of the Earth have clearly expressed their concerns about GMO products. See Greenpeace International, 'Say No to Genetic Engineering', at: http://www.greenpeace.org/international/campaigns/genetic-engineering; see also Friends of the Earth Europe European GMO Campaign, at: http://www.foeeurope.org/GMOs/Index.htm

68 Nine safeguard measures were at issue in this case: Australia – T25 maize; Austria – Bt-176 maize; Austria – MON810 maize; France – MS1/RF1 oilseed rape (EC-161); France – Topas oilseed rape; Germany – Bt176 maize; Greece – Topas oilseed rape; Italy – Bt-11 maize (EC-163), MON 810 maize, MON809 maize, T25 maize; and Luxembourg – Bt-176 maize.

69 See Section 3.3.1.

70 See Section 3.3.3 (3).

71 See Section 3.3.2.

72 Appellate Body Report, *European Communities – Trade Description of Sardines (EC – Sardines)*, WT/DS231/AB/R, 26 September 2006.

73 Appellate Body Report, *United States – Measures Affecting the Production and Sale of Clove Cigarettes (US – Cloves)*, WT/DS406/AB/R, 4 April 2012.

74 Appellate Body Report, *United States – Measures Concerning the Importation, Marketing and Sale of Tuna and Tuna Products (US – Tuna II)*, WT/DS381/AB/R, 16 May 2012.

75 See Section 3.3.2.

76 European Environment Agency, *Late Lessons from Early Warnings: the Precautionary Principle 1896–2000*, Environmental Issue Report, No. 22, Copenhagen 2001.

77 See Section 3.3.3 (3).

78 See Sections 3.3.1, 3.3.2 and 3.3.3 (3).

The precautionary approach in international law 145

79 As the EC Communication has suggested, this mechanism should also include the sub-principles of proportionality, non-discrimination, consistency, review and transparency. *Communication from the Commission on the Precautionary Principle*, Commission of the European Communities, Brussels, COM/2000/1, 2 February 2002 (Annex 2 IHRs).

5 The different faces of the precautionary approach in intellectual property

5.1. Precautionary entitlements in TRIPS

The role of science has been widely discussed in the context of the granting of exclusive patent rights to novel technologies; for example, the morality or patentability of stem cell, human genome and biotechnology has been subject to great debate (Laurie 2004: 59; Laurie 1996; Porter *et al*. 2006: 653). However, the study from the view of a precautionary approach (PA) or risk management after the granting of intellectual property (IP) has seldom been carried out. This chapter therefore aims to explore the role of the PA in TRIPS with an extended discussion on compulsory licensing. It is argued that a risk factor arising from the PA has a role to play in the IP regime, and that in contemporary society it is essential and legitimate to employ the PA in compulsory licensing of pharmaceutical patents under a public health emergency.

Under the TRIPS umbrella, WTO Members (Members) are required to provide minimal standard of IP protection on commodities including pharmaceutical products. Though the TRIPS Agreement creates inbuilt flexibilities in order to protect human health, the comprehensive protection of IP has given rise to many ethical debates. Notably, the issue of pharmaceutical patents has drawn commentators' attention to the interpretation of the flexibilities in the TRIPS mechanism. These flexibilities include objectives and principles of TRIPS; transitional periods for implementation; exhaustion of rights; exceptions to patent rights; and compulsory licensing (Matthews 2011: 17). Yet the current international political atmosphere and the WTO retaliation mechanism have deterred Members from taking full advantage of the flexibilities recognized in the TRIPS Agreement.[1]

In the following section, we will explore another guise of precaution first by visiting the flexibilities in TRIPS on health and security grounds. Similarly to the approach taken in Chapter 4 in examining the legal status of the PA in the General Agreement on Tariffs and Trade (GATT 1947), the Agreement on Technical Barriers to Trade (TBT Agreement) and the Agreement on the Application of Sanitary and Phytosanitary Measures (SPS Agreement),[2] we will see that PAs in the TRIPS are also distinguished between exceptions and

The different faces of the precautionary approach in intellectual property   147

exclusions to IP (Figure 5.3.2). Exclusions enjoy a higher legal status than exceptions (Figure 5.3.2.1). Particularly, the granting of a compulsory licence is argued to be exclusion to IP and a precautionary entitlement of states through the explicit interpretation of the Doha Declaration on the TRIPS Agreement and Public Health (Doha Declaration).[3] This chapter also observes a trend towards adopting the PA in recent state practice of compulsory licensing. The PA under the health and security exception provisions in TRIPS will first be discussed.

5.2. Health exceptions in TRIPS

The understanding of the exception rules in the TRIPS Agreement is essential to comprehend the limitations of Members' obligations in WTO law. If a Member's specific determination of the level of IP protection falls within the scope of exceptions, it would not be deemed non-compliant with its obligations to TRIPS.

5.2.1. Exceptions to rights conferred

TRIPS exceptions are applied with significant limitations. Examples of legitimate exceptions to patent rights include experimental-use exceptions, research or teaching exceptions and the Bolar exception, which is also known as an 'early working' exception which allows generic drug producers to initiate the process of marketing approval of generic drugs before the expiry date of the patent.[4] It helps consumers to obtain generic drugs at lower prices immediately thereafter. Bolar exception has been established in many countries to promote access to medicines and to support the development of a generic pharmaceutical industry. While an experimental-use exception aims for technology innovation, a research and teaching exception is for diffusion of knowledge; the Bolar exception in particular is created to promote competition and access to medicines. The detailed interpretation of the scope of Article 30 TRIPS is in the WTO Panel Report on *Canada – Patent Protection of Pharmaceutical Products (Canada – Pharmaceutical Patents)*,[5] where The WTO Panel specifically interpreted the wording of 'limited exception' in Article 30 of the TRIPS Agreement.

CANADA – PHARMACEUTICAL PATENTS

On 11 November 1998, the EC and their Member States filed a complaint to the Dispute Settlement Body (DSB) of the WTO against Canada's Patent Act regarding the protection of inventions in the area of pharmaceuticals. Canada's Patent Act Section 55.2 creates some exceptions to patent protections under certain circumstances. The first paragraph of Section 55.2 is known as the 'Regulatory Exception', which concerns the exception of users

148 *Current landscape*

related to the development and submission of information required under domestic law, and the second paragraph is the 'Stockpiling Exception', which provides legitimate grounds for competitors in the market to manufacture and stockpile the patented product before its patent expires.

The Panel elaborated that the examination of exception to IP is subject to the 'three-step test'. First, the exception needs to be limited; second, the exception must 'not unreasonably conflict with a normal exploitation'; third, the exception does 'not unreasonably prejudice the legitimate interests of the right holder, taking account of the legitimate interests of third parties' (para. 7.20, Articles 13, 26(2) and 30 TRIPS).

The EC alleged that the exception violated Canada's obligation under Article 28.1 with Article 33 of the TRIPS Agreement. Canada asserted that the word 'exception' in TRIPS Article 30 should be interpreted according to the conventional dictionary definition, such as 'confined with definite limits', or 'restrictive in scope, extent, amount'. However, the EC interpreted the word 'limited' to connote a narrow exception, which could be described such as 'narrow, small, minor, insignificant or restrictive' (para. 7.28). The Panel agreed with the EC and adopted the narrow interpretation of the word 'limited'. The Panel concluded that the interpretation 'should be justified in reading the text literally, and focusing on the extent to which legal rights have been curtailed, rather than the size or extent of the economic impact' (para. 7.31). Rodrigues, however, contends that the interpretation of Article 30 TRIPS would need to balance commercial, social and environmental considerations of WTO values, and criticizes the ruling by noting that 'the Panel interpreted the terms of the document as if the TRIPS Agreement focused exclusively on commercial goals' (Rodrigues 2012: 96).

The *Canada – Pharmaceutical Patents* case indicates that the exception in TRIPS 30 should be interpreted in a limited manner, and the exception should not curtail substantial rights of the patent holder. This case shows that the PA in Article 30 TRIPS is a *prescriptive* but *weak* version. The exception rule in the TRIPS, like its application in the GATT 1947, is again required to be applied restrictively.

5.2.2. Security exception

Further to the above discussion in Chapter 4 with respect to the security exception in the GATT,[6] it is observed that the concept of 'national security' has shifted from a purely military to a much broader concept, which Gross and Aolain argue encompasses almost all areas of human endeavour (Gross and Aolain 2006). One of the most important causes for the transition of the concept of national security is the reality of increasing global interdependence. National security consideration constitutes one of the general exceptions to international trade agreement in GATT XXI, and the language used has been described as 'broad, self-defining, and ambiguous' (Jackson 1997: 230).

The different faces of the precautionary approach in intellectual property 149

In the IP regime, Article 73 of the TRIPS Agreement is another provision which allows Members to take action deemed necessary for the protection of 'essential security interests' in particular situations. The provision states that the Agreement cannot be construed as preventing Members from taking action in pursuance of a Member's obligation under the United Nations (UN) Charter for the maintenance of international peace and security (Correa 2007: 520). The wording of this Article echoes GATT XXI and thus the jurisprudence developed thereof may be of relevance for the interpretation of Article 73 of the TRIPS Agreement.

According to the above discussion of security exception in GATT XXI, Members are left with a considerable margin of appreciation in the interpretation of 'national security interests'; however, their determination may not be exempt from the scrutiny of the international political settings and the Dispute Settlement Body (DSB) of the WTO. Further, as Correa maintains that 'a health crisis or a natural disaster may justify the invocation of such an exception' (Correa 2007: 520), a public health emergency of international concern (PHEIC)[7] thus may constitute legitimate grounds for security exception in WTO laws. In the context of major human rights conventions, national security is also viewed as a legitimate ground for restricting certain rights and freedom. Cases before the European Court of Human Rights have demonstrated states' wide discretion in the sphere of national security as grounds for limiting human rights (Gross and Aolain 2006: 218–19). It may also be argued that states are left with a broader margin of appreciation in trimming IP in association with security concerns. Following Sunstein's theories of 'Anti-Catastrophe Principle' and the 'Trimming exercise' as discussed in previous sections (Sunstein 2009: 1049),[8] a health framework for IP protection would need to steer between the polar positions to minimize possible damages. A safety margin is thus recommended to be adopted in the IP regime for risk management in times of emergency.

However, the PA adopted under an exception provision is merely deemed an 'affirmative defence' to the obligations to TRIPS. The burden of proof lies with the defendant to prove the existence of a public health emergency. Thus the trimming measure of IP in the security exception is assumed inconsistent with the obligations to TRIPS unless the defendant can prove otherwise.

PAs which are exercised within the domain of excluding provisions, namely the *conditional rights* in the IP regime, are discussed below.

5.3. Health exclusions in TRIPS

Excluding provisions of IP enjoy a higher legal status in WTO law than that of exception provisions; Members could adopt health-related regulatory measures at their discretion to trim IP within their sovereignty.

150 *Current landscape*

5.3.1. **Pre-grant measure**

According to Article 27.2 of the TRIPS, WTO Members may choose to adopt precautionary exclusions to patentable subject matter based on morality, public order (or public policy), public health, and serious environmental harm (Carvalho 2005: 209–10; Kolitch 2006: 221–56; Diebold 2008: 43). Morality might simply be a principled objection to an invention; however, precaution implies a desire to eliminate or prevent a risk. In other words, precautionary actions based on risk assessment or evaluation of available pertinent information would appear to be a means for risk management, which is deemed more grounded in scientific justification than morality claims or objections to a technology.

'Human health' is considered as a sub-species of *ordre public* (Correa 2007: 289). The European Patent Office (EPO) has distinguished '*ordre public*' relating to public interests from morality, which is referred to as the physical integrity of individuals (Correa 2007: 288). For example, the issues of the patentability of human genetics (Brownsword 2004; Rowlandson 2010: 67) and software patent protection (Leith 2007, 2004; Guadamuz 2006: 196; Taylor 2009) have recently drawn the debates on the legitimate exclusion to IP on morality grounds.

It is observed by Correa that WTO Members enjoy a wide range of discretion in determining the situation of '*ordre public*' according to their particular values and social background that needs special protection. Specifically, he argues that 'a country devastated by an epidemic may consider that adopting measures to combat it may be a matter of "*ordre public*"' (Correa 2007: 288). This indicates that states may have the autonomous right to employ health measures to contain virus transmission on '*order public*' grounds in times of public health emergencies. This echoes the argument of the legitimacy of a state's trimming exercise of IP under a pending threat to national security interests.

In addition, many nations have incorporated the PA into their patent laws to varying degrees in order to protect human health (Kolitch 2006: 245). For example, the Indian Patents Act makes exclusions to patent granting for inventions of which the primary or intended use would be contrary to law or morality or injurious to public health (Article 3(d) Patents Act 1970).[9]

(1) Patentability

The debate over the incorporation of a stricter criterion for patentability is highlighted in the India *Novartis* case. In India *Novartis* (*Novartis AG, NATCO Pharma Ltd and M/S Cancer Patients Aid Association* v. *Union of India and Others*),[10] the Supreme Court elaborated the consideration of invention and the patentability tests in Section 3(d) of the Patents Act. The Supreme Court reaffirmed the Patent Office's rejection of an application for grant of patent for imatinib mesylate in beta crystalline form as a secondary patent.

The different faces of the precautionary approach in intellectual property 151

In a review of the reform of the Patents Act, the Court stressed that 'the same patent law would operate differently in two countries at two different levels of technological and economic development, and hence the need to regulate the patent law in accordance with the need of the country' (para. 37). It was further noted that the design of a patent law would need special reference to the economic condition of the country, its scientific and technological advancement, and factors for minimizing the abuse of patent monopoly (para. 38). It was suggested that inventions should be precisely defined in order to identify whether the grant of patents would retard research or industrial progress, or be detrimental to health, or make those inventions non-patentable (para. 39). The Court noted that prior to the WTO TRIPS Agreement, monopoly was rarely granted to important articles of daily use such as medicines or food, which are vital to health. It was considered that the refusal of patents would enlarge competition and thus result in the production of these products in sufficient quantity and at accessible cost to the public (para. 42).

Section 3(d) of the Patents Act explicitly excludes patentability of 'the mere discovery of a new form of a known substance which does not result in the enhancement of the known efficacy of that substance'. The Supreme Court interpreted that the test of efficacy in the case of a medicine would refer to 'therapeutic efficacy' and that the 'therapeutic efficacy' of a medicine must be judged strictly and narrowly (para. 180). It is worth noting that 'bioavailability' refers to 'the degree to which a drug or other substances become available to the target tissue after administration' (para. 184). The Court further differentiated 'bioavailability' from 'therapeutic efficacy' by stating that whether an increase in bioavailability leads to an enhancement of therapeutic efficacy must be specifically established by research data (para. 189). The Court thus concluded that the beta crystalline form of imatinib mesylate failed in the tests of invention and patentability.

Considering the *Novartis* decision, Stiglitz and Jayadev commented that 'there is a growing consensus among economists that the current IP regime actually stifles innovation', and stated that the Indian Supreme Court's decision is an 'effort at rebalancing a global intellectual property regime that is tilted heavily toward pharmaceutical interests at the expense of social welfare' (Stiglitz and Jayadev 2013).

PRE-GRANT OPPOSITION

It is also noteworthy that the Indian Patents Act retained pre-grant opposition, which allows third parties to oppose patent applications prior to grant (Section 25). Any person can express to the Controller opposition to the grant of a patent on the ground that the applicant wrongfully obtained the invention; that the invention has been published or does not involve any inventive step; that the subject of the claim is not an invention; or that the applicant has failed to disclose the required information.

152 Current landscape

(2) Brazil National Health Vigilance Agency (ANVISA)

Due to the high prevalence of HIV/AIDS in its population, Brazil has been at the forefront in advancing the 'right to health' in international society. It has adopted a series of reforms in patent law to promote access to medicines.[11] It is also noteworthy that the Brazilian patent law provides a number of statutory exclusions from patentability, essentially limiting the definition of patentable subject matter to exclude various categories of inventions for policy reasons.[12] Particularly, a self-developed scheme of National Health Vigilance Agency (ANVISA)[13] has been introduced to incorporate a role for the health agency into the process of pharmaceutical patent granting. ANVISA is a unique scheme to deliberately trim IP protection prior to patent granting on public health grounds, which can be deemed a means for adopting a margin of safety in the IP regime.

ANVISA has the power of veto over patent granting when it considers the said patent is harmful to human health. This scheme is regarded as an action to take full advantage of the flexibilities in TRIPS on health and security considerations.

PRIOR CONSENT MECHANISM OF ANVISA AS A PRECAUTIONARY
ACTION FOR THE PRE-GRANT EXEMPTIONS

The Brazilian exclusions to patentable subject matter are typical of precautionary exclusions in the patent laws for WTO Members. The ANVISA includes public health concerns to limit patent applications on public health grounds. The aim of this trimming exercise of IP granting is to provide an *additional safety factor* in the IP regime, thus it can be deemed a precautionary measure. According to the legislation, the concession of patents for pharmaceutical products and processes will depend on the prior approval of ANVISA (Article 229-C of Law 9.279/96). The prior consent mechanism of 'anuencia previa' (prior approval) from ANVISA has been adopted since 2003 to examine substantive patentability criteria.

In other words, the creation of 'anuencia previa' requires two government agencies, the National Institute for Industrial Property (INPI) and ANVISA to work together in the examination and granting of pharmaceutical patents. The significance of the prior consent requirement is that it partly vests 'the competence of regulating pharmaceutical patent applications within ANVISA' (Rodrigues and Murphy 2006: 423). ANVISA has the power of veto over the granting of any pharmaceutical patent while considering the impact on societal interests relating to public health of a pharmaceutical patent (Rodrigues and Murphy 2006: 423). The requirement of 'anuencia previa' has been a novel programme to differentiate pharmaceutical patent application from other patents, and it can be seen as a precautionary measure to manage risk to human health. 'The prior approval' of ANVISA was devised to suggest the unique and important implication of pharmaceutical patents for society, and to ensure that

The different faces of the precautionary approach in intellectual property 153

the granting of pharmaceutical patents receives special examination. However, this consequently gives rise to a question: Is it acceptable in the WTO that pharmaceutical patents are not regarded as 'like products' with other patents and receive differential market treatment (Article 27.1 TRIPS)?[14]

PURPOSE AND DEFECT OF ANVISA

The novel device of ANVISA aims to pursue the harmonization of IP granting and public health by limiting pharmaceutical patentability when taking into account societal interests relating to public health of a pharmaceutical patent from the notion of risk management and precaution. ANVISA has the power of veto if the granting of a particular pharmaceutical patent is considered contrary to public health. It appears to have wide discretion in the use of the term 'contrary to public health' while it adopts a strict standard in consenting to the patentability of health-related inventions.

However, there still exist some problems in the mechanism which also attract discussion and criticism. In addition to the legitimacy issue on the distinction of the 'likeness' of pharmaceutical patents and other patents, the main conflict is the different mandates and responsibilities of INPI and ANVISA which create tension in the process of granting patents. INPI's primary goal is to apply the norms of Brazil's Industrial Property Law, which is industry-oriented and adopts guidelines more similar to those of developed countries. Yet, ANVISA's purpose is 'to protect the health of the public' and 'to control products and services that involve risk to the public health' (Articles 6 and 8 Law No. 9782/99). Consequently, the review of ANVISA is based on a public health oriented guideline which adopts a stricter standard in consenting to the patentability of inventions that meets higher standards of non-obviousness and novelty (Rodrigues and Murphy 2006: 423). If the two institutions have disagreements with a patent application, the process is blocked and results in a delay of the grant. TRIPS requires that procedures concerning the enforcement of IP rights shall not entail unwarranted delays (Article 41.2 TRIPS), yet the conflicts of INPI and ANVISA could have significant results in delaying the granting of some applications. It may consequently cause 'undue delay' to the market for a significant period. This results in a possible violation of the TRIPS.

In summary, though the effectiveness and possible violations of the TRIPS of ANVISA remain to be explored, the reform of pharmaceutical patenting in Brazil demonstrates that developing countries have striven to take full advantage of the flexibilities in TRIPS. The prior consent requirement suggests that ANVISA is a *prescriptive* PA. The ANVISA scheme can be categorized as a *strong* PA due to the wide discretion in consenting to the patentability of inventions. In addition, ANVISA also requires a manufacturer to present relevant documents in the registration process at ANVISA.[15] It could then be understood that ANVISA reflects an *Information Disclosure* PA.[16]

154 *Current landscape*

5.3.2. *Post-grant measure*

Following on from the consideration of patentability of an innovation, there exist symmetrical trimming exercises in IP protection after patent granting. These comprise post-grant opposition to patent granting and compulsory licensing.

(1) *Post-grant opposition*

Similarly to the function of the pre-grant opposition adopted in India,[17] the European Patent Convention (EPC) incorporates a post-grant opposition mechanism for a third party to give notice to the European Patent Office of opposition to a patent (Article 99(1)). In the United States, the Hatch–Waxman Act of 1984 provides incentives for generic companies to challenge pharmaceutical patents that they believe were improperly issued (Sampat *et al.* 2012: 414). The US Patent Law also adopts the post-grant review system by introducing the Leahy–Smith America Invents Act (35 USC § 321).

(2) *Compulsory licensing*

TRIPS provides flexibilities for governments to fine-tune the granted exclusive protection in order to meet other social agendas. It allows governments to evoke suspension on the exclusiveness of patent holders' rights during certain periods in national emergencies provided certain conditions are fulfilled. The relationship between TRIPS and public health has been widely discussed with regard to developing countries (Sell 2004: 363, 2002: 193; Helfer 2004), but has hardly been explored in a developed country setting. Yet, in recent years, the use of compulsory licensing for redressing health concerns is increasing in developed countries due to emergent PHEICs[18] under globalization. For example, France has implemented an *ex officio* licence for national public health reasons in its patent act (Article L. 613-16 of Law No. 92-597, the Intellectual Property Code), and Belgium has proposed a special compulsory licence regime for national health reasons (Articles 31–4 Patent Law; Overwalle 2007: 251).

In the case of 'other use without authorization of the right holder' in Article 31 TRIPS, also known as 'compulsory licensing', the exclusiveness of patent rights may be temporarily suspended to meet the needs of public interest under a public health emergency. Compulsory licensing can be regarded as a tool for limiting IP protection in an attempt to achieve a better balance of rights and obligations of IP (Article 7 TRIPS; Li 2013). From the lens of risk management, the *provisional* suspension of the exclusiveness of patent protection in a public health emergency can be regarded as a precautionary measure in IP. It has been adopted as a means for redressing the dilemma of 'access to essential medicines' in a public health emergency, albeit in practice its operation has been highly controversial.[19]

The different faces of the precautionary approach in intellectual property 155

Taubman notes that the Doha Declaration has provided a political solution to these debates arising from compulsory licensing (Taubman 2010: 48–9);[20] however, it is observed that, even with the interpretation of the Doha Declaration, Members still tend to bypass this measure on the grounds of public health emergency or other circumstances of extreme urgency. The following section will review the Doha Declaration and the more recent development of compulsory licensing in empirical studies. This suggests that a PA reading of the text would practically meet the need for stronger political and moral arguments for this measure, which is not only in line with the Doha Declaration, but also workable within the existing legal framework.

COMPULSORY LICENSING AS A PRECAUTIONARY ACTION
FOR POST-GRANT EXEMPTIONS

It can be argued that, under certain circumstances, compulsory licensing of pharmaceutical patents under a public health emergency can be regarded as a precautionary health measure as it is a provisional measure to suspend the exclusiveness of IP protection due to the greater need of public health. Similarly to the above-mentioned precautionary measures, specifically that of the SPS Agreement,[21] the granting of a precautionary compulsory licence must be accompanied by a series of procedural requirements to restrain excessive abuse. Under current international law, states are free to determine their appropriate level of health protection (ALOP) and thus have autonomy to exercise the discretion to strike a balance between public health and IP protection.[22]

The function of compulsory licensing could also be understood from the above-mentioned 'Trimming' concept proposed by Sunstein, who argues for the incorporation of a safety net in emergency situations (Sunstein 2009: 1049). In extreme situations, states may be left with no other choice but to 'trim' IP protection by compulsory licensing in order to safeguard public interests of health and security. Compulsory licensing thus provides a margin of safety under a public health emergency where the exclusiveness of IP may be temporarily suspended to protect public health.

It can be further argued that even in situations where there is a lack of information, 'being humble and uncertain about the right result' (Sunstein 2009: 1061), it may still lead states to choose to trim IP protection to minimize possible damage to public health. It can be suggested that in the uncertainty of extreme situations, it is appropriate to steer between the polar situations of IP protection. Questions arise that ask what kinds of measures might be deployed in the trimming exercise. What limits or flexibilities might be used to avoid polarization? Such concerns and the policy-making of IP protection in a public health emergency will be further addressed in the following chapter.

The conditions and procedures prior to the granting of a compulsory licence are set out in Article 31 TRIPS. For instance, the proposed user needs

156 *Current landscape*

to obtain authorization from the right holder on reasonable commercial terms and conditions unless a national emergency or other circumstances of extreme urgency exist. In situations of national emergency or other circumstances of extreme urgency, the right holder shall be notified as soon as is reasonably practicable. The scope and duration of such use needs to be limited to the purpose for which it was authorized; such use needs to be non-exclusive; it requires to be authorized primarily for the supply of the domestic market,[23] and adequate remuneration needs to be paid to the patent right holder (Taubman 2008b). Moreover, the granting of a compulsory licence is subject to judicial review or other independent review by a higher authority.

As a general rule, it requires the competent authorities of the WTO Members to decide each compulsory licensing case and establish conditions that are intended to prevent the granting of sweeping compulsory licences across a broad range of inventions. For example, in subparagraph (b) of Article 31, before an application may be considered, the proposed user must first obtain a voluntary licence on reasonable terms and conditions within a reasonable period of time. The requirement of the obligation of the proposed user to first make an effort to obtain authorization from the right holder can be waived in cases of national emergency or other circumstances of extreme urgency, yet similarly to the security exception in GATT,[24] the condition of 'national emergency or other circumstances of extreme urgency' is not clearly defined in TRIPS.

In the later round of negotiations in Doha in 2001, WTO ministers stressed that it is important to implement and interpret the TRIPS Agreement in a way that supports public health (Doha Declaration on the TRIPS Agreement and Public Health, Doha Declaration).[25] The Declaration has emphasized that the TRIPS Agreement should not prevent member governments from acting to protect public health. It also affirms governments' right to use the Agreement's flexibilities, such as compulsory licensing.

DOHA DECLARATION ON THE TRIPS AGREEMENT AND PUBLIC HEALTH

In agreeing to launch a new round of WTO trade negotiations, trade ministers adopted the Doha Declaration on 14 November 2001 (Abbott 2002: 469; Sun 2004: 123; Baker 2004: 613; Ansari 2002: 57; Attaran 2002: 859; Chang 2007: 553). The Declaration sought to alleviate developing countries' dissatisfaction with the TRIPS regime. It committed WTO Members to the interpreting and implementing of the Agreement to support public health and to promote access to medicines (para. 4). It also affirmed the *right* of Members to use the flexibilities in the TRIPS Agreement to promote these goals (para. 4).

For example, the paragraph in the Doha Declaration that stresses WTO Members' right to take advantage of the flexibilities of TRIPS has resonance with the flexibilities used to protect public health in Article 27.2 TRIPS:

The different faces of the precautionary approach in intellectual property 157

We agree that the TRIPS Agreement does not and should not prevent Members from taking measures to protect public health. Accordingly, while reiterating our commitment to the TRIPS Agreement, we affirm that the Agreement can and should be interpreted and implemented in a manner supportive of WTO Members' right to protect public health and, in particular, to promote access to medicines for all. In this connection, we reaffirmed the rights of WTO Members to use, to the full, the provisions in the TRIPS Agreement, which provide flexibility for this purpose.

(Para. 4, Doha Declaration)

The interpretation of the Doha Declaration implies that Members' right in deciding an ALOP is an *'autonomous right'* and deciding the exclusion to patent rights is conferred. On the one hand, from the view of state *sovereignty* and national autonomy in international law (Brownlie 2003: 287; Raustiala 2003: 842; Oesch 2003: 635; Cottier 1998: 83; Condon 2006: 233), the Doha Declaration has reaffirmed that the granting of a compulsory licence under a public health emergency falls within the scope of domestic sovereignty. State sovereignty has been adopted as a reason to limit Members' obligations to the WTO (Condon 2006: 233). On the other hand, this also has resonance with the argument of state responsibility and the protection of civilians when an unknown risk to human health is suspected.

The Doha Declaration has stated that each WTO Member has the right to grant compulsory licences and the freedom to determine the grounds upon which such licences are granted (para. 5(b)); each Member has the right to determine what constitutes a national emergency or other circumstances of extreme urgency. It articulates that public health crises, including those relating to HIV/AIDS, tuberculosis, malaria, and other epidemics, can represent a national emergency or other circumstances of extreme urgency (para. 5(c)). In view of this, Carvalho noted that 'WTO Members are entitled to rely on their own legal system and practices' to issue compulsory licences (Carvalho 2005: 151).

In addition, WTO Members' right to determine an ALOP has been reaffirmed in the Dispute Settlement System (DSS) rulings.[26] Members are allowed to take a more cautious approach to health risk than international standards require. Specifically through the interpretation of the Doha Declaration, arguably, it can therefore be inferred that the notion of precaution has been incorporated, or at least accepted, in TRIPS.

The Declaration also reminds Members to apply the customary rules of interpretation of public international law: each provision of the TRIPS Agreement needs to be read in the light of the objectives and principles of the Agreement as stated in Articles 7 and 8 of the general provisions in the Agreement (para. 5(a)). The objectives of the TRIPS Agreement clearly state that the protection and enforcement of IP should contribute to the mutual advantage of producers and users and in a manner conducive to 'social economic welfare', and a balance of rights and obligations. In Article 8 regarding its principles, it stipulates that Members may adopt measures 'necessary to protect public health', and to promote the 'public interest' in sectors of vital importance to their socio-economic and technological development (Li 2013).

Further, the principles of the TRIPS Agreement state that Members may adopt measures 'necessary to protect public health', yet, according to the interpretation of the Doha Declaration, the necessity test in Article 8.1 TRIPS has distinguished itself from that of GATT XX(b).[27] The interpretation of paragraph 5(c) of the Doha Declaration implies that the granting of a compulsory licence is a *conditional right*, or an 'exclusion provision' in TRIPS (see Figure 5.3.2) which enjoys a higher legal status in the WTO legal hierarchy than 'exception provisions', the so-called 'affirmative defence' in the general exception provision (see Figure 5.3.2.1).

In addition, Correa also argues that paragraph 5(c) of the Doha Declaration shows an important and different implication from the GATT/WTO jurisprudence of 'the necessity test' outside of the TRIPS context (Correa 2002b: 16–17). Likewise, Carvalho also notes that 'the word "necessary" seems to be redundant in Article 8.1 and … [has] no practical meaning' (Carvalho 2005). From the above analysis, it can therefore be concluded that the burden of proof of such cases is reversed to the complaining Member (of compulsory licensing) to prove that such emergency conditions do not exist with the accused party (Correa 2002b: 16–17).

The Doha Declaration has reaffirmed that a WTO Member has the right to determine the grounds to grant a compulsory licence. The right to determine an ALOP is regarded as an 'autonomous right' in WTO law which therefore requires the complainant to bear the burden of proof that the defendant does not fall within the category of emergency situation.

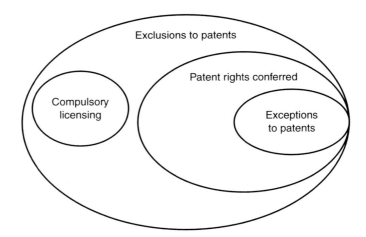

Figure 5.3.2 Exemptions to WTO patent rights

The different faces of the precautionary approach in intellectual property 159

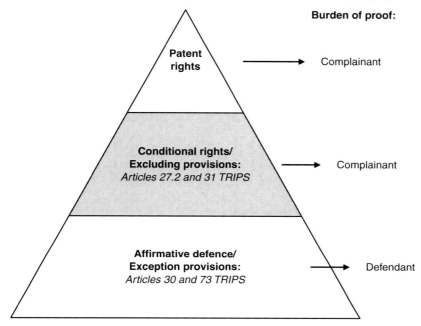

Figure 5.3.2.1 Legal hierarchy of the precautionary approach in TRIPS

From this perspective, the WTO appears to open a door for public health concerns to legitimize the flexibilities which Members can apply to their discretion (Sherman 2004: 353). This also manifests in Members' autonomy being paid due respect in the public health dimension of international economic law (ie. Appellate Body Report, *EC – Hormones*, para. 104). In particular, Bloche argues that the WTO system has come to treat protection of health as a de facto interpretative principle when disputes arise over Members' treaty obligations. He notes that especially since the global AIDS pandemic, world politics has pushed the WTO to identify an emerging pattern of deference to *national autonomy* when Members' domestic health policies conflict with other values protected by trade agreements (Bloche 2002: 825–48). It is also noteworthy that the ongoing amendment of Article 31(f) which introduces a notification system for triggering compulsory licensing in order to export/import patented drugs is also an attempt to embody the flexibilities in TRIPS.[28] It is in this context that I observe in this book a trend towards adopting the PA to promote access to medicines in compulsory licensing in state practice.

In summary, in terms of legal status, the PA in compulsory licensing is akin to the PA in the SPS Agreement:[29] both are exclusions to Members' obligations to the WTO. It can further be concluded that precautionary compulsory licensing is a *prescriptive* PA; it can also be categorized as an *Information*

160 *Current landscape*

Disclosure PA for the adopting state needs to notify the right holder and also bears the responsibility to review the grant in due course (paras. (b), (g), (i) Article 31 TRIPS). Further, in order to achieve a *moderate* PA, it is suggested that the precautionary template in the SPS Agreement be adapted in the application for a precautionary compulsory licence. This will be explored in the following chapter.[30] Attention will be paid to relevant cases where the PA has been observed to be accommodated into compulsory licensing.

TREND OF COMPULSORY LICENSING

The recent implementation of compulsory licensing seems to broaden its scope in states' practice. In recent years, it had been employed to cope with potential disease outbreaks under the threat of anthrax in the US and Canada, as well as avian flu in Taiwan. Moreover, the issuance of compulsory licences has extended to chronic disease drugs. Thailand granted compulsory licensing of a heart disease drug by claiming that heart disease has resulted in a national financial emergency. This was followed by India's first compulsory licence of a cancer drug in 2012. Yet, despite the interpretation of the Doha Declaration, there is no clear or objective mechanism for the invocation of a compulsory licence; thus such application still gives rise to debates on the legitimacy of the grant. Relevant cases are discussed in the following sections.

UNITED STATES AND CANADA

In 2001, the US and Canada were threatened with a terrorist attack of a particular strain of anthrax that would be resistant to penicillin and other common antibiotics, but possibly treatable by ciprofloxacin, an antibiotic which is patented under a German company, Bayer Inc. The recommended stockpiles for ciprofloxacin (Cipro) did not exist and the patent owner could not meet the demand for nearly two years. In the fear of an imminent outbreak, the US public health authorities considered calling off the protection of the Cipro patent under Bayer, but decided to wait rather than to buy readily available generics from outside the US.[31]

At the same time, under the threat of a possible outbreak, the Canadian government also considered issuing a compulsory licence for the generic manufacture of the antibiotic Cipro.[32] The conflict ceased when both the US and Canada reached an agreement with Bayer who promised a price reduction on the drug.[33] This anthrax case may imply that the threat of a possible pandemic outbreak is a legitimate ground for compulsory licensing of patented drugs.

TAIWAN

The WHO, on its website, has consistently warned that there has been a high possibility of an avian flu outbreak since Spring 2005, and should a serious

The different faces of the precautionary approach in intellectual property 161

outbreak happen, the high mortality rate of avian flu H5N1 could result in millions of deaths worldwide.[34] The WHO considered the H5N1 outbreak in 2005 to be a Phase 3 'pandemic alert phase'.[35] The WHO thus recommended that countries should stockpile the appropriate antiviral at least sufficient for 10 per cent of the population, to contain the spread of the virus.[36]

Tamiflu (Oseltamivir), the patented drug under Roche, is regarded as the most effective antiviral treatment for H5N1, and was in short supply in 2005 when the WHO made its stockpiling recommendation.[37] Roche, as the single manufacturer, was increasing its production capacity, but still would not be able to meet the global demand for several years. In order to secure sufficient stockpiles of Tamiflu, after negotiations with Roche broke down, Taiwan's Department of Health (DOH) considered it necessary to obtain compulsory licensing of the antiviral to eliminate possible shortages due to an outbreak or Roche's failure to supply the antiviral in good time. Consequently, the DOH filed the compulsory licensing application with the Taiwan Intellectual Property Office (TIPO). TIPO granted compulsory licensing of Tamiflu on 25 November 2005, the first case of compulsory licensing in the light of a threat of an avian flu pandemic (TIPO Rule No. 09418601140). The grant took effect immediately and was to operate until December 2007 unless a licensing agreement was reached between Roche and the DOH.

According to the WHO, the potential H5N1 outbreak in 2005 was a Phase 3 pandemic alert phase, which means that a virus new to humans is causing infections, but does not spread easily from one person to another.[38] The evolution or mutation of the virus to the next human-to-human phase is not predictable with current technology. Under such global risks, every government would face the dilemma of balancing the industrial development of the pharmaceutical sector with public health needs.

The issue is how to properly apply the concept of 'national emergency' under international economic law, and how to validate the granting of compulsory licensing. The Taiwanese government claimed that the grant was based upon special consideration of scientific and non-scientific factors. It was claimed that its special geographical location and diplomatic isolation were the main factors in rendering the grant.

Since 2003, Taiwan has not suffered a bird flu outbreak, unlike neighbouring South East Asian countries,[39] but has claimed that it is a high-risk country that merits surveillance of the pandemic due to its special geographical location and not being a Member State of the WHO. In the previous SARS outbreak, Taiwan was excluded from the global disease surveillance system, and could not receive support from the WHO in the first place because it was not a member of the WHO.[40] In light of its past experience of isolation from the international surveillance network, Taiwan claimed that its dilemma of diplomatic and political isolation necessitated extra protection in order to prepare for the disease outbreak, thus the Taiwanese government considered that the threat of the possible outbreak constituted the condition of 'national emergency', and that it was necessary to apply *extra* caution in preparation for the upcoming outbreak of avian influenza. In order to stockpile enough doses of Tamiflu to prepare for a pending pandemic, the DOH insisted that the compulsory licensing of Tamiflu was legitimate and necessary.

The validity and legitimacy of granting a compulsory licence for a potential public health threat requires further scrutiny, although the previous US and Canadian cases on Cipro seem to indicate that the absence of a bird flu outbreak is not an excuse to prevent Taiwan from considering that this risk of a potential outbreak constitutes a national emergency under TRIPS Article 31(b). The above Cipro cases in the consideration of the granting of a compulsory licence under the anthrax threat seem to suggest that the so-called 'national emergency' does not necessarily be an ongoing catastrophe.

THAILAND

Thailand is the first country to test the boundaries of compulsory licensing of medications for chronic diseases. On 25 January 2007, Thailand granted compulsory licences of patents for the heart disease drug Plavix (clopidogrel bisulphate). Thailand argued that the production of the generic Plavix by the government-owned Government Pharmaceutical Organization (GPO) constituted a 'public non-commercial use' rather than that of 'national emergency or other circumstances of extreme urgency' in TRIPS Article 31(b). Thailand also alleged that under TRIPS 31(b), the requirement of prior negotiation was waived in cases of public non-commercial use, and that this provision only obliged the government to inform the patentee promptly.

On the one hand, civil society and the NGO have expressed support for Thailand's move on compulsory licensing for chronic diseases treatment (Love 2007b).[41] On the other hand, critics have condemned Thailand's act of compulsory licensing of Plavix as overstepping the appropriate application of compulsory licensing.

However, there seemed to be a consequence after the grant: the patent owner of Plavix, Abbott Laboratories, announced that it would no longer market new pharmaceutical products in Thailand, and even withdrew seven registration applications for four new pharmaceutical products.[42] In April 2007, the US placed Thailand on its Special 301 Priority Watch List, which was deemed to be a trade sanction.

INDIA

Following on from Thailand's attempt at issuing compulsory licences for chronic disease drugs, the Indian government granted the first compulsory licence for kidney cancer and liver cancer drug Nexavar in 2012 (Compulsory License Application No. 1 of 2011). The Court stated that: '[f]rom its very nature, a right cannot be absolute. Whenever conferred upon a patentee, the right also carries accompanying obligations towards the public at large. These

The different faces of the precautionary approach in intellectual property   163

rights and obligations, if religiously enjoyed and discharged, will balance out each other' (para. 1). The Court decided the case by processing the following three substantial issues in this application: whether the reasonable requirements of the public have not been satisfied; whether the patented invention is not available to the public at a reasonable affordable price; and whether the patented invention is not worked in the territory of India (para. 9).

In considering these questions, the Court held that the number of patients requiring treatment by this drug is higher than the patentee expected and that that patentee's conduct of not making the drug available to the public during four years since the grant of the patent is not justifiable. The Court questioned why the patentee did not provide *differential pricing* for different classes of the public. The Patents Act requires that 'patents are granted to encourage inventions and to secure that the inventions are worked in India on a *commercial* scale and to the fullest extent that is reasonably practicable without undue delay' (Section 83(a)) and that the Controller has the power to issue a compulsory licence on the grounds that the patented invention has not been worked in India (Section 86(1)). The Court held that the patentee's conduct of not importing the drug till 2008 and only importing in small qualities in 2009 and 2010 was unjustifiable. It was thus held that the invention was not worked on a commercial scale and to an adequate extent.

Thailand made the first attempt at testing the threshold of the provision by granting compulsory licences for chronic disease drugs, but it experienced the backfire of trade retaliation. Trade sanctions and retaliations by drug companies may create chilling effects following governments' acts of compulsory licensing for pharmaceutical patents.[43] It is noteworthy that India's first compulsory licence has led to fierce protest by pharmaceutical companies, but the WTO Director, Pascal Lamy, appeared to support India's decision by saying that 'decisions made by an independent judiciary have to be respected as such' and that 'TRIPS provides flexibilities that allow countries to issue compulsory licences for patented medicines to address health urgencies' (Sen 2013).

However, the above cases have shown a trend in adopting a PA into compulsory licensing. The recent occurrences of public health emergency also demonstrate that the employment of compulsory licensing for pharmaceuticals is no longer limited to developing countries; developed countries could also face the dilemma of patent right protection and the access to drugs debates under a public health emergency. Both the United States and Canada threatened to issue compulsory licences of Cipro at the time of the anthrax threat, and Taiwan granted a compulsory licence of Tamiflu in preparation for a possible avian flu outbreak. These cases also imply that the incorporation of precaution in compulsory licensing has been an inevitable option to tackle a public health emergency. Moreover, from the perspective of *states' duties and rights*,[44] states may be obliged to take certain precautionary health measures to protect their civilians under a public health threat, even if there is no full scientific certainty (Ruessmann 2002: 905). In order to minimize Members'

164   *Current landscape*

reluctance for compulsory licensing, this book focuses on the enhanced use of existing tools and stronger political and ethical arguments for this measure rather than on the exploration of a new legal doctrine. For example, Chapter 2 deals with the justification of the need for differential treatment for medical technology in compulsory licensing by establishing how the 'like-product' analysis enables a new reading of the discrimination/differential treatment distinction made in TRIPS Article 27.1.[45]

COMMENTS ON THE PRECAUTIONARY APPROACH IN TRIPS

Patent protection is a two-edged sword for encouraging or stifling innovation. Pharmaceutical patents are vital to the innovation of new technology in drug production, but how to strike the right balance between the right to health and patent protection requires an *organic* IP system which is equipped with constant adapting and fine-tuning. International pharmaceutical industries strive to reduce the practice of compulsory licensing by urging that the scope of compulsory licensing should be limited to certain diseases (Outterson 2008: 279).[46] They claim that the necessary investment in the research and development of new drugs is the main reason for the high cost of antivirus drugs (Love and Hubbard 2007: 1519). However, in most developing and underdeveloped countries, the enormous health burden appears to be too overwhelming to consider the protection of IP (Nanda and Lodha 2002: 581; Mercurio 2006: 1; Love 2007a: 679; Opderbeck 2005: 501).

The controversy over the inclusion of pharmaceutical products in the IP regime has raised ethical debates. From a historical perspective, many countries with the most innovative pharmaceutical industries, such as France, Germany, Italy, Sweden and Switzerland, did not provide pharmaceutical patents until the industries were established (Alsegard 2004). TRIPS is the first international agreement that provides patent protection for pharmaceutical products, and it has been challenged by the developing world for offering excessive patent protection for life-saving drugs, which leads to the postponing of efficient therapy for resource-poor patients.

It is in this context that the scheme of compulsory licensing has been developed to address the dilemma between human rights to health and IP. However, empirical studies show that it has been scarcely used, especially on the grounds of 'national emergency or other circumstances of extreme urgency' due to the ambiguity of its definition. Instead of serving as an objective and transparent mechanism to redress the imbalance of IP, compulsory licensing has been constantly used as a diplomatic threatening tool for drug price reduction in many countries such as South Africa, Brazil, Thailand, the US and Canada (Abbott and Reichman 2007: 921).[47] Thus the consequences of its application inevitably rely much on power play in international settings.

From the above analysis, based on the distinction between 'excluding provisions' and 'exception provisions' in WTO law, the mechanism of

The different faces of the precautionary approach in intellectual property 165

compulsory licensing can be considered exclusion to IP, which is deemed Members' 'conditional right' in the WTO regime. The question of how best to achieve Members' ALOP by compulsory licensing then arises. Members are entitled to exercise this right to establish their ALOP by means of compulsory licensing if certain conditions are satisfied.

The Doha Declaration clarified and interpreted the terms of compulsory licensing. It reaffirmed Members' autonomy in determining an ALOP under a public health emergency, such as AIDS/HIV, tuberculosis, malaria, and other epidemics. Paragraph 5(c) of the Declaration indicates that the device of compulsory licensing has an important and different implication from the WTO jurisprudence of 'the necessity test'. It also implies that Article 31 is an 'excluding provision', which excludes other provisions in the TRIPS Agreement. It suggests that the right to grant compulsory licences is an 'autonomous right' in the WTO. Charnovitz *et al.* describe an excluding provision (also called conditional right) standing in a mutually exclusive manner with the general rule (Charnovitz *et al.* 2004: 257).[48] In view of the principles of exception rules applied in the WTO system, a Member is required to prove that the adopted health measure is *necessary* in order to eliminate public health risk through scientific justification. However, compulsory licensing can be deemed an 'excluding provision', thus the burden of proof is laid on the complainant who needs to provide evidence that a public health emergency does not exist. In this analogy, compulsory licensing is deemed compliant with the obligation to TRIPS unless the complainant proves otherwise.

However, the application of compulsory licensing of pharmaceuticals has always been controversial in international fora due to its lack of a clear threshold for invocation. Resource-poor states are hesitant and reluctant to invoke the provision for fear of trade retaliation from developed states. In order to promote a balanced trimming exercise of IP and to restrain a sweeping use of the PA in compulsory licensing, an objective and transparent mechanism is required to prevent its abuse. Relevant conditions to restrict the application of the PA will be further addressed in the following chapter.

5.4. Conclusion

In the previous chapter, it has been observed that there are two forms of operation of the PA according to its legal status in the WTO regime: one is in the guise of exception provisions, and the other excluding provisions. The PA appearing as an excluding provision which enjoys a higher legal status than that of an exception provision.

Following the same analogy, the PA in TRIPS can also be categorized into exception provisions and excluding provisions. Particularly, this chapter scrutinizes the mechanism of compulsory licensing and argues that the concept of precaution has been incorporated into compulsory licensing since

166 *Current landscape*

the specific interpretation of the Doha Declaration. The Doha Declaration has indicated the flexibilities of compulsory licensing, which may have implications for the PA in health risk management in TRIPS. It is argued that WTO Members have the precautionary entitlement to grant a compulsory licence under a public health emergency. In addition, recent state practice has also demonstrated a trend towards the employment of the PA which broadens the scope of compulsory licensing in promoting access to medicines. It is therefore important to apply the scheme of compulsory licensing in a way that differs from the traditional approach of 'the necessity test' in other WTO exception rules.

In summary, the mechanism of compulsory licensing of pharmaceutical patents under a public health emergency can be considered related more to the scheme of the provisional SPS measures due to their legal status and common characteristics of the rationale of risk management in a public health emergency in WTO law. They are both *provisional* health measures adopted under a public health emergency within the domain of scientific uncertainty. These two instruments can be regarded as the excluding provisions in WTO law; both enjoy a higher legal status than that of exception provisions. States' domestic sovereignty and flexibilities at discretion should be paid due respect when confronting a public health emergency.

Accordingly, WTO Members may argue for a precautionary entitlement to trim IP through compulsory licensing in a public health emergency. The mechanism of adopting a provisional SPS measure is suggested to be adapted into the precautionary granting of a compulsory licence. In view of this, further recommendations to embody the PA in compulsory licensing will be made in the following chapter.

Notes

1 See Section 1.2.3 (1).

2 See Sections 4.3.1 and 4.3.2.

3 *Doha Declaration on the TRIPS Agreement and Public Health* (Doha Declaration), adopted by the fourth Ministerial Conference of the World Trade Organization in Doha, Qatar, on 14 November 2001. WT/MIN(01)/DEC/2 of 20 November 2001. See Section 5.3.2.(2).

4 WHO, WIPO, and WTO (2013) 'Promoting Access to Medical Technologies and Innovation: Intersections between Public Health, Intellectual Property and Trade', p. 174. http://www.wto.org/english/res_e/publications_e/who_wipo_wto_2013_e.htm

5 *Canada – Patent Protection of Pharmaceutical Products (Canada – Pharmaceutical Patents)*, WT/DS114/5, WT/DS114/R, 12 March 2000.

6 Section 4.3.1 (2).

7 See Section 4.1.1 (1).

8 Section 3.3.2.

9 Other nations whose patent laws are known to include a statutory public health exclusion are Costa Rica, Ghana, Iran, Japan, Kenya, South Korea, Mongolia,

The different faces of the precautionary approach in intellectual property 167

Mozambique, Nepal, Nicaragua, Panama, Peru, Portugal, Saudi Arabia, Somalia, Taiwan, Thailand, Trinidad and Tobago, Uruguay, and Vietnam. See Teegarden (2004).

10 *Novartis AG, NATCO Pharma Ltd and M/S Cancer Patients Aid Association* v. *Union of India and Others*, Civil Appeal Nos. 2706–2716, 2728, 2717–2727 of 2013.

11 For example, Law 10196/2001 has introduced restrictions and amendments to Patent Law 9279/96.

12 In Brazilian law, the following are not patentable: anything contrary to morals, standards of respectability and public security, order and health; substances, materials, mixtures, elements or products of any kind, as well as the modification of their physical-chemical properties and the respective processes for obtainment or modification, when resulting from the transformation of the atomic nucleus; and all or part of living beings, except transgenic microorganisms that satisfy the three requirements of patentability – novelty, inventive step and industrial application – provided for in Article 8 and which are not mere discoveries.

13 Available at: http://portal.anvisa.gov.br/wps/portal/anvisa-ingles

14 See Section 2.1.2.

15 Resolution – RDC no. 25, 9 December 1999.

16 See Chapter 3, Sections 3.3.1, 3.3.2 and 3.3.3.

17 See Section 5.3.1 (1).

18 See Chapter 4, Section 4.1.1 (1).

19 See Chapter 1, Section 1.2.3.

20 See above, note 3.

21 See Section 4.3.4.

22 See Sections 2.1.2 (1), 3.2.3 (1), 4.3.2 (1).

23 This condition is now under amendment; see Chapter 1, Section 1.2.3 (3).

24 See Chapter 4, Section 4.3.1 (2).

25 See note 3, above.

26 See Chapter 4, Section 4.3.2 (1).

27 See Chapter 4, Section 4.3.1 (1).

28 See Section 1.2.3 WTO website: http://www.wto.org/english/tratop_e/trips_e/public_health_e.htm

29 See Section 4.3.4.

30 See Section 6.3.

31 'America's Anthrax Patent Dilemma', BBC News, 23 October 2001, available at: http://news.bbc.co.uk/1/hi/business/1613410.stm

32 CPTech, 'Ciprofloxacin: the Dispute over Compulsory Licenses', available at: http://www.cptech.org/ip/health/cl/cipro/

33 Bayer press release on Cipro deal, 25 October 2001, available at: http://lists.essential.org/pipermail/ip-health/2001-October/002261.html

34 See WHO website: http://www.who.int/mediacentre/factsheets/avian_influenza/en/index.html

35 WHO 'Pandemic Phase', see: http://www.who.int/csr/disease/swineflu/phase/en/

36 WHO (2005) 'WHO Global Influenza Preparedness Plan: The Role of WHO and Recommendations for National Measures before and during Pandemics', Department of Communicable Disease, Surveillance and Response, Global Influenza Programme, WHO/CDS/CSR/GIP/2005.5.

37 WHO (2006) 'WHO Rapid Advice Guidelines on Pharmacological Management of Humans Infected with Avian Influenza A (H5N1) Virus', WHO/PSM/PAR/2006.6, p. 43.

168   *Current landscape*

38 See above, note 36, p. 6.

39 Bird flu broke out in South East Asia; the more deadly bird flu H5N1 had killed more than 109 people in Indonesia, Vietnam, Cambodia, Thailand and China. See: The Writing Committee of the World Health Organization (WHO) Consultation on Human Influenza A/H5 (2005) 'Avian Influenza A (H5N1) Infection in Humans, 353 *New England Journal of Medicine* 1374–85.

40 Taiwan has been rejected as a member of the WHO due to China's opposition.

41 For example, Knowledge Ecology International (KEI) applauds the decision by Thailand's Ministry of Health, and they 'expect that Thailand will issue other compulsory licence[s] on medicines in the future'. The Joint Statement by 15 NGOs claims that the Minister for Public Health has acted according to the flexibilities laid out in Article 31(b) of the TRIPS Agreement, and even the US has applied the flexibilities in the past. They called the attempt to attack the legitimacy of the decision 'insulting and mischievous', Knowledge Ecology International Statement on Thailand Compulsory Licenses, 21 January 2007; 'Joint Statement by 15 NGOs, Thai Civil Society Supports the Health Ministers of Thailand and Brazil and Calls on Pharmaceutical Companies and Lobbyists to Stop Abusing their Power', available at: http://lists.essential.org/pipermail/ip-health/2007-May/011155.html, 10 May 2007.

42 Abbott Pharmaceuticals in Thailand: Fact Sheet, 13 April 2007.

43 Intellectual Property Watch (2008) 'Thailand Avoids Compulsory Licence on Cancer Drug; 3 More Drugs Undecided', available at: http://www.ip-watch.org/weblog/2008/01/31/thailand-avoids-compulsory-licence-on-cancer-drug-3-more-drugs-undecided/

44 See Chapter 3, Section 3.2.1.

45 See Sections 2.1.2 and 6.2.

46 In order to limit the scope of granting compulsory licences, the EU and the US have attempted to negotiate a list of diseases for which compulsory licences would be given. See 'Communication from the European Communities and Their Members to the TRIPS Council Relating to Paragraph 6 of the Doha Declaration on the TRIPS Agreement and Public Health' (2002) Brussels, 20 June 2002.

47 See Chapter 1, Section 1.2.3 (1).

48 See Section 4.3.

Part III

Recommendations

6 The precautionary approach in compulsory licensing

This chapter is divided into three parts. First, following on from the tailored model of the PA proposed in Chapter 4, which reflects the current limitations of the PA and the requirements of globalization, this redefinition will be further recast into the IP regime by means of adopting a margin of safety in compulsory licensing of pharmaceutical patents. Second, it is argued that pharmaceutical technologies should receive differential treatment by adopting the PA into compulsory licensing on the rationale of precaution and risk management. Finally, an expedient track of compulsory licensing of pharmaceutical patents based on the PA is also developed with a detailed set of sub-conditions in order to prevent abuse of this Article.

6.1. Redefinition of compulsory licensing through the precautionary approach

A precautionary approach (PA) reading of compulsory licensing is anticipated to make ample allowance for safety in the intellectual property (IP) regime in times of emergency. The precautionary action of adopting 'additional conservatism' is regarded as the embodiment of the PA in the structure of risk analysis (Goldstein and Carruth 2004: 492). In order to examine the legitimacy of adopting the PA and the structure of *risk analysis* in compulsory licensing, the legal status of this provision will first be analysed. We will then be able to explore to what extent WTO Members (Members) can exercise their *precautionary entitlements* in the determination of compulsory licensing in a public health emergency.

COMPULSORY LICENSING AS A STATE'S CONDITIONAL RIGHT IN TRIPS

As discussed in Chapter 5, through the clarification of the Doha Declaration on the TRIPS Agreement and Public Health (Doha Declaration),[1] compulsory licensing falls within the *rights* of WTO Members; put more specifically, it is identified as a *conditional right* in WTO jurisprudence. It indicates that states have *sovereignty* in the determination of compulsory licensing once

172   *Recommendations*

certain conditions are satisfied. These sub-conditions will be further addressed in the later sections of this chapter.

In addition, it is also argued in Chapter 5 that compulsory licensing can at times be deemed to be a form of precautionary measure which serves to constrain private IP in times of public health emergency. It is articulated in TRIPS that in the case of 'a national emergency or other circumstances of extreme urgency', individual patent protection may be *provisionally* limited for the greater needs of the public (Articles 31 (b) and (c) TRIPS). This is to say that compulsory licensing can serve as a means for achieving the nation's appropriate or acceptable level of protection (ALOP). By adopting the PA and the structure of risk analysis in compulsory licensing, this book would embody the flexibilities in TRIPS and boost states' confidence in compulsory licensing in a public health emergency. Based on the argument of '*precautionary entitlements of states*' and the '*State stewardship model*',[2] states may choose to grant a compulsory licence when the risk of harm to public health is identified as passing the '*significant/serious*' threshold.

Considering 'State responsibility' in international law, as well as their obligations in the WHO International Health Regulations (IHRs), every government has responsibilities to safeguard the global virus surveillance network by sharing viruses or specimens and protecting their civilians from virus attack by securing an essential drug supply under the threat of a potential public health emergency.[3] Specifically, the WHO has advised that states start the stockpiling of essential medicines and vaccines during the preparation period of a disease outbreak.[4] Research shows that global demand for vaccine would far outstrip production capacity at the time of a pandemic, and it could take years from the point of the identification of the virus strain to produce sufficient medication for global needs.[5] For effective pandemic containment, medications need to be delivered within three to four weeks of the start of sustained human-to-human transmission.[6] In the absence of voluntary licensing, compulsory licensing would thus inevitably be the essential avenue to ensure sufficient drug supplies within such a limited time period prior to an actual pandemic outbreak. Adopting a safety margin on the grounds of the PA in compulsory licensing is of vital importance in the preparedness for a public health emergency.

The Doha Declaration has reaffirmed Members' *conditional rights* to determine the ALOP in the IP regime,[7] which accordingly appears to accommodate the concept of precaution into the TRIPS Agreement. WTO Members have the conditional rights to show *more* caution when adopting a higher level of health protection than international standards suggest. Particularly, after the interpretation of the Doha Declaration, it can be argued that the scheme of compulsory licensing can be understood and rephrased from the perspective of precaution as shown in Figure 6.1

In other words, the PA could enable states to adopt a safety margin in compulsory licensing when the harm has crossed the *significant* threshold, but the scientific evidence is not yet fully established. The PA model adapted in

The precautionary approach in compulsory licensing 173

> When confronted with a public health emergency, if, on the basis of the best information available, there are reasonable grounds for concern that *significant* harm to human life and health may occur, scientific uncertainty should not prevent states' precautionary entitlements from adopting a temporary limitation on the exclusiveness of pharmaceutical patents to prevent/abate this harm for achieving an appropriate level of public health protection while avoiding unnecessary interference to international trade.

Figure 6.1 Redefinition of compulsory licensing through the lens of states' precautionary entitlements

compulsory licensing introduces a more objective mechanism to trigger the grant and boosts states' confidence in granting a compulsory licence during the preparatory stage of a public health emergency.

6.2. Differential treatment of adopting the PA in compulsory licensing of pharmaceutical patents

We will also need to examine whether the adoption of the PA and the structure of *risk analysis* in this provision will constitute 'discrimination' in the WTO regime. Following on from the discussion in Chapter 2, if the adoption can demonstrate legitimate differential treatment, it will then not be deemed as 'discrimination' by the WTO.[8]

The differential treatment in international trade can be demonstrated by the adoption of the PA in risk regulation. The adoption of a *differential track* of compulsory licensing (CL) of pharmaceutical patents in a public health emergency can be justified by the analysis shown in Figure 6.2.

Figure 6.2 demonstrates that the PA can be incorporated into compulsory licensing by establishing a differential track dealing with technologies

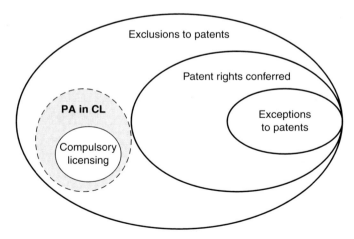

Figure 6.2 The precautionary approach in compulsory licensing and exemptions to patent rights

174   *Recommendations*

strongly associated with the elimination of significant risks to human life and health. In short, I argue that the protection of public health and security can serve as a legitimate factor for differential treatment in compulsory licensing.

6.3. Precautionary compulsory licensing in a public health emergency

Based on the proposed model of the PA, I will proceed to build a framework of the PA in compulsory licensing in the following paragraphs. First of all, the trigger threshold, or the domain to invoke the PA in compulsory licensing, needs to be considered. The following sections also address the fact that a sound framework for the PA in compulsory licensing should be accompanied by a set of sub-conditions based on the elements we developed from previous chapters. These requirements aim to prevent possible abuse of this provision and to minimize conflicts in international trade.

6.3.1. *Trigger threshold*

As discussed, the application of the PA should be based on uncertain risks which are *real* and *tangible* rather than hypothetical, minor, or trivial.[9] The PA is suggested to be invoked when the threat of harm passes the '*significant*' threshold.

TRIGGER THRESHOLD OF THE PRECAUTIONARY APPROACH IN 'PANDEMIC PHASE'

The imposition of public health measures involves significant costs, and policy-makers need to ensure that a cost-benefit option is made available regardless of limited resources in the event of a pandemic. According to the WHO, 'Because little may be known about the virulence and transmissibility of the next influenza pandemic virus until it has started spreading widely, judgments about the likely effectiveness and benefits of public health measures will often be difficult and may change over time.'[10] It is therefore necessary that an evidence-based approach following the WHO's guidance plays an essential role in the battle against global transient virus mutation. States can follow the WHO's recommendation at any specific pandemic phase and make their best decisions on health measures based on available pertinent evidence.[11]

However, if it is a prerequisite that a state can act to adopt a specific health measure only after scientific justification or full materialization of a potential disease outbreak, it may be too late to respond to the immediate threat. An evidence-based approach in international health protection may be central to public health strategies, but it has been identified as insufficient in order to cope with emergent and re-emergent public health risks.[12]

In times of rapid virus transmission, sufficient time to prepare and respond is the key to successful technical surveillance and stockpiling of vaccines and medicines. Therefore the PA is considered essential to risk management of a

The precautionary approach in compulsory licensing   175

public health emergency. The recommendation of stockpiling antiviral drugs sufficient for a state's population has been on the WHO's main agenda. Specifically, from Phase 3 of a pandemic alert period onwards, the major objective regarding antiviral drugs is to coordinate positioning of a possible global stockpile; from Phase 4 of a pandemic alert period, one of the national objectives is to assess and facilitate wider usage of antivirus and vaccines in later phases.[13] States are recommended to prepare sufficient stockpiles of antiviral drugs and vaccines as a precaution.

In order to keep alert to the evolution of new influenza virus strains and to build a surveillance network, the WHO has developed the website 'Global Outbreak Alert And Response Network' (GOARN) to keep track of virus activities globally.[14] Since 2005 guidance has been issued on preparedness for an influenza virus outbreak for states to follow.[15] A table of pandemic phases is published by the WHO which divides the pandemic phases into six stages (see Table 6.3.1). The table of pandemic phases is used as a tool for informing states of the updated threat of the virus. Each designation of phases is determined by the Director General of the WHO.[16]

Table 6.3.1 Trigger threshold of the PA in phase of pandemic alert

Phase	Probability of Pandemic	Description
1	Uncertain	No animal influenza virus reported to cause human infection
2		An animal influenza virus known to have caused human infection
3		An animal or human/animal influenza virus has caused sporadic cases or small clusters of disease in people, but no human-to-human transmission
4	Medium to high	**Human-to-human transmission** of an influenza virus able to sustain community-level outbreak
5	High to certain	The same virus has caused sustained community-level outbreaks in at least two countries in one WHO region
6	Pandemic in progress	In addition to the criteria defined in Phase 5, the same virus has caused sustained community-level outbreaks in at least one other country in another WHO region

Source: Adapted from 'WHO Pandemic Phase Descriptions and Main Actions by Phase', WHO (2009) Pandemic Influenza Preparedness and Response: A WHO Guidance Document, p. 27

176   *Recommendations*

The PA is applied under the stage of scientific uncertainty or insufficiency of scientific evidence when the risks to human life or health are identified as crossing the significant threshold. I suggest that the PA should be triggered when risks are uncertain, but a possibility of human-to-human transmission has been identified as increasing. Hence, the PA would be triggered between Phases 4 and 5 where a disease outbreak is not inevitable, but there is increased evidence of human-to-human transmission. At both Phases 4 and 5, the WHO and states should have started stockpiling sufficient medication for the population to combat the virus spread.[17]

It is noteworthy that the WHO also issued a 'Checklist for Influenza Pandemic Preparedness Planning' and recommended that states should devote time to preparing for an emergency in different pandemic phases.[18] The aim of this checklist is to equip states with sufficient capacity for virus surveillance and secure adequate medical treatment.[19] For example, one of the objectives of Phase 4 of the pandemic phase is to increase and deploy the vaccine supply.[20] It may thus be legitimate to say that the precautionary granting of a compulsory licence could be triggered from Phase 4 onwards.

BASED ON RISK ASSESSMENT OR AVAILABLE PERTINENT INFORMATION

According to the rationale of risk analysis, a scientific evaluation of the risk is suggested to be accompanied by the invocation of a precautionary grant (Annex A. 4 SPS Agreement; Article 15.2 CPB; Article 43.2 IHRs; WTO Appellate Body Report, *US – Continued Suspension (Hormones II)*, para. 530). If a full risk assessment cannot be produced due to time constraints or insufficiency of scientific evidence, relevant available information should also be taken into account. Thus, the implementation of the PA should start with a risk assessment or a valuation based on available pertinent information in order to identify the degree of scientific uncertainty at each stage.

In the circumstances of a public health emergency, the *provisional* granting of compulsory licensing can still be adopted prior to the completion of a full risk assessment, but it is expected to be subject to a limited duration and timeous review. If a full risk assessment cannot be carried out due to incomplete scientific evidence, then the decision should be triggered by available pertinent information from international organizations, for example, the recommendations from the WHO, as the objective suggestions from international organizations play a vital role when disputes arise.

If the time restraint is urgent and it is not possible to conduct an evaluation of risk, I also suggest that the state should officially announce a public health emergency to prove the said risks exist.[21] In most cases when states are reluctant to declare a national emergency due to other considerations, in order to increase transparency, I suggest that they can publish government statements about their objectives in adopting the measure of granting a compulsory licence.[22]

6.3.2. The action

The WHO also identified a government's leadership in the responsibility for national preparedness and response.[23] Governments have a duty and right to protect public health in an emergency. On the one hand, under the rationale of 'States' responsibility/Stewardship',[24] states have a *duty* to 'take *whatever steps are necessary* to ensure that everyone has access to health facilities, goods and services so that they can enjoy ... the highest attainable standard of physical and mental health' (para. 53 UN General Comment No. 14: The Right to the Highest Attainable Standard of Health, emphasis added).

On the other hand, states are also granted a margin of discretion within their sovereignty in determining the appropriate method of achieving the highest level of attainable health protection. Further, the UN General Comment sets out states' rights and obligations in the realization of people's right to health in the following paragraph:

> The most appropriate feasible measures to implement the right to health will vary significantly from one State to another. Every State has a *margin of discretion* in assessing which measures are most suitable to meet its specific circumstances.
>
> (Para. 53 UN General Comment No. 14, emphasis added)

In other words, under the rationale of international law, states have the responsibility to protect the public interest of health as well as to enjoy their autonomy in the determination of adopting health measures. This also has resonance with the Doha Declaration which has reaffirmed that 'Each Member has the right to grant compulsory licences and the freedom to determine the grounds upon which such licences are granted' (Para. 5(b)).[25]

(1) States' precautionary entitlements of compulsory licensing

Once the threat of harm is identified as *significant*, states enjoy the *conditional rights* to grant a compulsory licence in order to achieve an ALOP. In order to avoid abuse of this mechanism, the compulsory licensing grant is recommended to be examined by the necessity test in the WTO/TRIPS context.

(2) The necessity test

The interpretation of the necessity test in the WTO exists in the necessity provisions in different WTO agreements (Kapterian 2010: 89). Considering the necessity test in the GATT 1947, the Appellate Body adopted the three-step necessity test to examine if the health measure is necessary in the public health exception provision by examining whether the goal of the measure falls within the protection of human health; examining if the measure constitutes discrimination to international trade; and considering the weighing and

178 *Recommendations*

balancing test of the interests furthered by the challenged measure.[26] Comparatively, the necessity test in the SPS Agreement has slightly different phrasing: Members need to ensure that their SPS measure is applied *only to the extent necessary* to protect human, animal or plant life and health (Article 2.2). Members also need to ensure that such measures are *not more trade-restrictive* than required to achieve their appropriate level of SPS protection, taking into account technical and economic feasibility (Article 5.6).[27]

In addition, the WTO Appellate Body noted that the more important the protected interests are, the more easily a measure designed as enforcement instrument would be accepted as necessary (*Korea – Measures Affecting Imports of Fresh, Chilled and Frozen Beef, Korea – Beef*, para. 162).[28] It stated that the value of 'the preservation of human life and health' is 'vital and important in the highest degree' (*EC – Asbestos*, para. 172),[29] and it also indicated that in situations where risk of irreversible damage to human life and health are concerned (*EC – Hormones*, para. 124),[30] the threshold to apply the PA will be more relaxed. This suggests that the necessity test in issues dealing with life-threatening or life-terminating situations does not follow the typical necessity test in GATT 1947.

Further, scholars contend the necessity test in TRIPS has an important and different implication from the typical necessity test outside the TRIPS context (Correa 2002b: 16–17; Carvalho 2005). Consequently, considering its legal status as a conditional right in the WTO, which is similar to the provisional SPS measures, I suggest that the necessity test of a compulsory licence dealing with a public health emergency does not follow the typical necessity test in GATT 1947, but follows the requirement of an SPS measure for being 'not more trade-restrictive than required', which would need to be examined through the least restrictive measure (LRM) test in order to prove the necessity of the said grant.

LEAST RESTRICTIVE TO INTERNATIONAL TRADE

Given that compulsory licensing and SPS measures share the legal status of Members' conditional rights in the WTO,[31] we can interpret the necessity of a compulsory licence in view of the necessity test in the SPS Agreement. A Member's SPS measure is deemed necessary until the complainant proves otherwise through the LRM test (Kapterian 2010: 89). This is to say that the adopted health measure should be least trade-restrictive, and no other alternative measure exists to achieve the ALOP (footnote 3 of Article 5.6 SPS Agreement). Passing the LRM test, a compulsory licence would thus be deemed necessary until the complaining party proves otherwise.

Accordingly, in order to examine if the compulsory licence is the LRM, the complaining party needs to prove a *reasonable available alternative* measure existed. Such reasonable available alternative measure must: (1) achieve an ALOP, (2) be significantly less restrictive to trade, and (3) be technically and economically feasible.

The precautionary approach in compulsory licensing   179

In summary, we need to remember that the value of human life or health is of vital interest to the highest degree, and that the necessity test is more relaxed when human health or safety is a concern. A compulsory licence is deemed *necessary* unless the complaining party proves a reasonable available alternative existed.

6.3.3. Duty to review

The granting of a precautionary compulsory licence is an expedient action that is only justifiable when the scientific evidence about a risk remains unclear or insufficient. It is suggested that, at the time of adoption, it should be specified as to how often the measure should be subject to review (see *Japan – Varietals*[32] and *EC – Hormones* II[33]).

(1) The grant should be provisional

The precautionary measure should not be adopted once and for all, and the provisional approach reflects the nature of precautionary measures. Its function is similar to the issuing of preliminary injunctions in environmental cases, which could be issued before a full environmental impact assessment is completed in order to prevent further irreparable damage (*Southern Bluefin Tuna* Case;[34] Article 5.7 SPS Agreement[35]).

De Sadeleer notes that: 'Precaution is seen as a temporary measure pending further scientific information' (De Sadeleer 2008: 110). Sandin also contends that 'the time factor' is associated with the duty to review which plays an important role in the PA (Sandin 2006: 175). He argues that 'precaution is warranted only when information about the possible threat is lacking', and that information changes over time. The time factor is vital in the preparedness for a public health emergency due to the special characteristics of transient mutation of a virus in a pandemic.

(2) Transient mutation of a virus

Speed and time play a dominant role when humans compete with the unpredictable mutation of a novel influenza virus strain.[36] The mutation of the influenza virus is the core challenge to the containment of a pandemic. The influenza virus has been difficult to control due to its multitude of virus make-up.[37] The evolution and potential damage of the new type of virus strain is unpredictable, and there may be a significant period of time when it will be necessary to stay on guard and prepare for the next outbreak.[38] One flu virus can easily swap genetic information with another, and changes in their genetic make-up would make them more deadly.[39]

Hence, 'the time factor' of a potential disease outbreak should be taken into account in risk management. Further, provisional public health measures should be subject to review with updated scientific justifications within a reasonable period of time.

180   *Recommendations*

(3) Ongoing duty of monitor and review

A precautionary measure should be provisional; by the same token, it requires constant review to reassure that the measure is up to date and remains legitimate and proportionate. Under the circumstances of scientific uncertainty of a health threat, the precautionary granting of compulsory licensing devised for a higher level of protection is thus required for timeous review (Article 5.7 SPS; Article 43 IHRs; Scott 2009: 123; Appellate Body Report, *Japan – Measures Affecting Agricultural Products (Japan – Agricultural Products II)*, para. 93).[40] The International Court of Justice (ICJ) *Gabcikovo–Nagymaros* case demonstrates the importance of subsequent monitoring of the ongoing risks for ensuring the adopted measure is proportionate and effective.[41] A provisional SPS measure is subject to a review within a reasonable period of time; an additional public health measure in the IHRs should be reviewed within three months. However, the duty of review in the Cartagena Protocol on Biosafety (CPB)[42] appears to be less demanding as it does not designate a specific time span for review and is only subject to the exporter's request. The WTO Appellate Body also confirmed that the temporal issue should proceed on a case-by-case basis which includes the consideration of the difficulty in obtaining the additional information and the characteristics of the measure. It may be interpreted that the duty to review can be imposed according to the characteristics of the health risk and the government's policy objectives. Sunstein's notion on the *Information Disclosure Precautionary Approach* (IDPA) puts emphasis on the disclosure and distribution of knowledge of the risk before the specification of public policies (Sunstein 2005: 118).[43] The Commission for the European Union also acknowledges the principle of 'examination of scientific developments' which highlights the time factor and the development of scientific knowledge.[44] Consequently, a timeous review with the latest scientific evidence or scientific information is considered essential during a public health emergency.

Before the actual outbreak of a public health emergency, the cumulative scientific information can indicate the proper response at every pandemic phase. After the granting of a precautionary compulsory licence at pandemic Phases 4 to 5, the WHO and states shall still review and update information at each pandemic phase.[45]

According to TRIPS, the duration of the compulsory licensing should be limited, and it should be subject to judicial review or other independent review by a 'distinct higher authority' within the Member State (Article 31(c)(i) TRIPS). Consequently, for a transparent and systematic application, it is suggested that the precautionary grant should be subject to review along with the latest knowledge and development on the new virus strain, and a scientific evaluation should be carried out at pandemic Phases 4 and 5 in order to identify the degree of scientific uncertainty and to reassure the legitimacy of the grant. It would subsequently become an ordinary grant once the risks have been proved certain; on the contrary, it would need to be revoked or terminated if the threat of harm was proved to be below the *significant* threshold (see Figure 6.3.3).

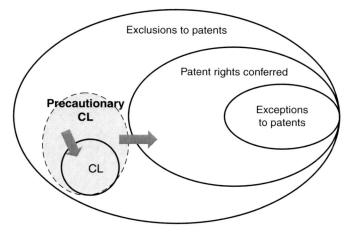

Figure 6.3.3 Review of a precautionary compulsory licence

6.3.4. *Other non-scientific factors*

The value of the PA is that it leaves a margin of safety and provides a channel for present and future generations to get involved with the decision-making of risk policies. It recognizes the limitations of science, and incorporates other non-scientific factors in risk management, such as public opinions as supporting evidence in the regulation of risks. One of the objectives of risk management is also to engage the lay public in order to increase transparency in the decision-making process. A WHO draft stated that: 'By involving a wide range of stakeholders in the process, the Precautionary Framework requires clarification of stakeholder interests as well as transparency in the way decisions are made.'[46] The public engagement in policy-making also reflects the value of respect and democracy in contemporary society. It empowers the lay public to make a collective informed decision on their vital interests of health and security.

However, given the limited time of a precautionary compulsory licence, it is noteworthy that the grant needs to take non-scientific factors into consideration in different social contexts. This would include respect for patients as the main consumers of pharmaceuticals and civilians' special social and cultural preferences.

(1) Patients as the main consumers of pharmaceuticals

The WTO Appellate Body highlighted that consumers' tastes and habits are 'very likely to be shaped by the health risks associated with a product which is known to be highly carcinogenic' (*EC – Asbestos*, para. 122).[47] Thus the health effects of a product play an important role in distinguishing the

182   *Recommendations*

likeness of products. In addition, based on the above like-product analysis, health risks associated with a given product would influence consumer behaviour. It is particularly noted by the Appellate Body that: 'If the risks posed by a particular product are sufficiently great, the ultimate consumer may simply cease to buy this product' (*EC – Asbestos*, para. 122).

The Appellate Body seems to subsume the health-effect factor within the physical property and consumers' perception and behaviour criteria in the 'likeness' analysis (Bernasconi-Osterwalder *et al.* 2006: 13). In the consideration of the health effect and consumers' perception of the precautionary granting of a compulsory licence, we would first need to take patients' perspectives into account in policy-making.

Patients are a unique group of consumers who are much more vulnerable and sensitive to pharmaceutical products than other customers of certain products. Pharmaceuticals are indispensable, and most of the time irreplaceable to patients unless they choose to give up their fight for health/life. The consumers of pharmaceuticals are the *patients inflicted by certain diseases*, who are apparently distinctive from other ordinary groups of customers on the market. It is self-explanatory that patients' perspectives need to be taken into account in the transaction of pharmaceuticals through the interpretation of international trade rules.

In other words, the transaction of pharmaceuticals cannot be seen as an ordinary carefree pleasure of open-market shopping behaviour; patients need to be diagnosed first to get prescriptions from professional health care providers before having access to drugs. After receiving the prescriptions, unless patients pursue alternative therapies, they have no other options but to survive on these prescriptions in order to maintain fundamental well-being. The nature of a defined market, this threshold to access, and the characteristic of indispensability can also be regarded as unique physical properties of pharmaceutical products. This also indicates the given drug's predominant position in the market, through which it enjoys exclusive patent protection for over 20 years and, during that time, it enjoys complete monopoly and does not share *a competitive relationship* with other generic drugs.

Considering the vulnerable position of patients and the non-competitiveness of patented drugs on the market, governments should be able to distinguish the 'unlikeness' of pharmaceutical patents from other patents. In this context, a precautionary track for compulsory licensing of pharmaceutical patents would not amount to discrimination in international trade.

(2) Civilians' social and cultural preferences

Risk assessment can be used as a means to assess health risks as well as to provide a form of reasoning in a regulatory system, but as Gostin notes: 'policy in the real world is confounded by scientific uncertainties, human values, and political compromises' (Gostin 2002: 127–30, 139). It is thus difficult to fully understand the risk posed to the community's health. He

The precautionary approach in compulsory licensing 183

also notes that scientists understand risk according to probabilistic assessment, but the lay public's understanding of risk 'includes personal, social, and cultural values' (Gostin 2002: 128).

Consequently, the public's view arises to complement the limitations and possible blind spot in science. As Breyer questions whether the risk policy tends to regulate low risks, but fails to regulate more serious health threats (Gostin 2002: 143), there may be gaps among the risks identified by scientists and the real existing threats to human health. Besides, Sunstein's argument of 'deliberative democracy' in the process of risk management also implies that citizens are not merely consumers; the regulatory choices should respect and be made after citizens' preferences and values (Sunstein 2005: 158).

Indeed, risks have their unique cultural implications that are deeply rooted in specific social, historical and geographical contexts. A WHO Report has stated that: 'once people frame a risk issue, it is very difficult to change their mind; therefore, technical risk assessments are largely irrelevant to people'.[48] Perceptions of risks vary from region to region, and variations should be allowed to reflect the diversity in different cultural contexts. Such variations would play an important role in deliberation when disputes arise in international trade.

In addition, Button observes that: 'Many cultures have particular practices that may seem irrational to the outsider' (Button 2004: 107–8). Due to different cultural backgrounds, some cultures are better prepared to overlook some risks, and some are more cautious in response to other risks due to inherent vulnerabilities. Various factors of civilians' social and cultural preferences would include individual state public policies in national IP and social welfare systems, the provision of health care and national health insurance.

In summary, due to special social and cultural backgrounds, states may need to adopt a broader margin of safety based on their preferred policies of risk management in IP within the flexibilities of TRIPS. Moreover, it is specifically argued by Correa that 'a country devastated by an epidemic may consider that adopting measures to combat it may be a matter of *"ordre public"*' (Correa 2007: 288). Developing countries may exercise domestic sovereignty and conditional rights in the WTO system to trim/limit certain IP protection in their legal system in order to safeguard their essential security interest in public health (Carvalho 2005: 151). This view also has resonance with the Doha debate which expresses that states enjoy the entitlements to determine the grounds to issue a compulsory licence in a health emergency.[49] Consequently, in disease-stricken areas such as South East Asian and South Sahara African countries, a state's particular geographical or political situation under an acute trans-border disease transmission may constitute a legitimate cause of the precautionary granting of compulsory licensing.

While the unknown risks are not acute, for example, where public health risks are posed by biotechnologies or nanotechnologies, government could provide channels for public participation to express their concerns and

184 *Recommendations*

perspectives towards the unknown risks (Articles 6, 7, 8 Aarhus Convention; Bruce 2007).

It is noteworthy that the WHO features the role of public engagement in pandemic preparedness. The following measures are suggested during Phases 1 to 3: building relations with journalists and other communications channels to familiarize them with related issues; developing communication strategies to inform and educate the public; initiating public health education campaigns on individual-level infection control measures; and increasing public awareness of measures to contain the spread of the pandemic.[50] At Phase 4, it is recommended that countries should gather feedback from the public, vulnerable and at-risk groups on attitudes towards the health measures and barriers affecting their willingness to comply. However, during the rapid virus transmission phase (Phases 5 to 6), there may not be sufficient time to engage the public in achieving a decisional communication.

(3) Non-scientific factor after a dispute has arisen

AMICUS BRIEFS IN WTO DISPUTE SETTLEMENT

Public participation in compulsory licensing in a public health emergency could also come at a rather late stage after a licence has been issued and a dispute has arisen. WTO Members have a legal right to participate as parties or third parties in a certain dispute through the submission of amicus briefs in the Dispute Settlement System (DSS). An amicus brief is a written document, submitted by WTO Members and non-Members including businesses, civil society groups and individuals as an interested non-party of the dispute. It can be a document or simply a letter to the DSB. This provides the only approach for non-governmental organizations to have a say in a particular dispute in the world trade forum. Further, both WTO Members and non-Members could submit *amicus curiae* (friend of the court) *briefs* to the DSS on the dispute over a compulsory licence.

The system of *amicus briefs* in the WTO DSS process would serve as a means to engage public opinion on the interpretation of the trade rules of IP; however, the WTO DSS has discretionary power whether or not to accept this information (Bernasconi-Osterwalder *et al.* 2006: 317–19; WTO Appellate Body Report, *United States – Imposition of Countervailing Duties on Certain Hot-Rolled Lead and Bismuth Carbon Steel Products Originating in the United Kingdom (US – Lead and Bismuth Carbon Steel)*, paras. 40–41).[51]

The WTO Panel also has the discretionary power to seek information and technical advice from any individual or body which it deems appropriate (Article 13 Understanding on Rules and Procedures Governing the Settlement of Disputes, Annex 2 (DSU)). The communication with the Members for information is also addressed in the working procedures of the Appellate Body (Article 17.9 DSU). It is further provided in the Working Procedures for Appellate Review that:

The precautionary approach in compulsory licensing 185

In the interests of fairness and orderly procedure in the conduct of an appeal, where a procedural question arises that is not covered by these Rules, a division may adopt an appropriate procedure for the purposes of that appeal only, provided that it is not inconsistent with the DSU, the other covered agreements and these Rules.

(Rule 16(1) Working Procedures for Appellate Review, WTO, WT/AB/WP/5, 4 January 2005)

Hence, the Appellate Body is also free to choose 'whether or not to accept and consider any information [in an amicus brief] that is pertinent and useful in an appeal' (Bernasconi-Osterwalder *et al.* 2006: 317–62).[52] When a dispute arises over the legitimacy of compulsory licensing of a particular drug in a public health emergency, non-state actors could also submit their amicus briefs as an interested non-party of the dispute. It can be anticipated that not only civil society but also non-state actors such as the WHO, the WIPO, the World Medical Association and Médicins Sans Frontières would have a say in promoting access to medicines in such disputes. In summary, the system of amicus briefs only plays a supplementary role in the interpretation of compulsory licensing, which is aimed at increasing transparency in the dispute settlement process of a grant, but the Panel and Appellate Body have the final discretionary power to accept and consider amicus briefs attached to a party or third party's submission (Bernasconi-Osterwalder *et al.* 2006: 323).

In short, it is suggested that the incorporation of non-scientific factors in the granting of a precautionary compulsory licence under a public health emergency be carried out prior to the full outbreak of a pandemic. After a full-fledged outbreak, governments may not have sufficient time to gather public perceptions of evidence due to time constraints. However, policy-makers should bear in mind that the different transaction model implies that drugs have a very distinct feature from other products on the market; the non-competitiveness of a patented drug could also be a legitimate factor in granting differential treatment in the interpretation of IP rules. In addition, civilians' special social, geographical and cultural preferences should be taken into account in the decision-making process relating to the application for a precautionary compulsory licence, preferably prior to the full outbreak of a pandemic. Lastly, the public can still submit their perceptions to the WTO DSS after a dispute has arisen over the legitimacy of a compulsory licence.

6.4. Conclusion

This chapter has demonstrated that the PA can be accommodated into compulsory licensing within the current flexibilities in TRIPS. It is argued that in an extreme situation, the precautionary granting of compulsory

186 *Recommendations*

licensing can offer a *margin of safety* to promote public health protection by means of provisional limitation to IP. IP policy-makers may choose to 'trim' the exclusive patent protection in extreme situations such as a public health emergency.

This chapter also argues that, based upon the rationale of risk management and the PA, health technologies associated with significant risk to human life or health may receive differential treatment in the IP regime. Such ethical differentiation of granting an expedient track of compulsory licensing of health technologies would not constitute discrimination and could be justified on the grounds of the harmonization of risk management in WTO law.

The elements of the PA in compulsory licensing can be summarized as follows.

- The trigger threshold: the invocation of a precautionary compulsory licence should occur between Phases 4 to 5 of the WHO's pandemic phases when the risk has passed the 'significant' threshold, and should be based on risk assessment or available pertinent information.
- The granting of a precautionary compulsory licence as a precautionary action: the precautionary granting of a compulsory licence is a state's conditional right in WTO, but it still has to be least restrictive to international trade. In other words, it should be used as a last resort; there should be no other available alternatives to relieve a state's burden of disease.
- Duty to review: the adopting state bears the ongoing duty to monitor the risk and review the grant. The grant should be abolished after the risk has been identified as non-significant.
- Other non-scientific factors: the role of public engagement in a public health emergency is limited due to time constraints, thus communication with the general public with regard to the scope of pharmaceutical patents should be carried out prior to the outbreak of a pandemic. Governments should bear in mind that differential treatment of a patented drug may be legitimate due to its non-competitiveness in the market. Civil society can still submit their opinions to the WTO DSS after a dispute has arisen.

Finally, given that the precautionary grant of a compulsory licence is within the domain of conditional rights of WTO Members, the burden of proof would be reversed to the complaining party to prove that the public health emergency does not exist in the invoking state and the grant is not an LRM. The precautionary grant of a compulsory licence should be presumed legitimate unless the complaining party proves otherwise.

Notes

1 *Doha Declaration on the TRIPS Agreement and Public Health* (Doha Declaration), adopted by the fourth Ministerial Conference of the World Trade Organization in Doha, Qatar, on 14 November 2001. WT/MIN(01)/DEC/2 of 20 November 2001. See Section 5.3.2 (2).
2 See Section 3.2.1.
3 WHO (2009) 'Pandemic Influenza Preparedness and Response: A WHO Guidance Document, Global Influenza Programme', p.17. http://www.who.int/influenza/resources/documents/pandemic_guidance_04_2009/en See Section 4.1.1 (1).
4 WHO (2011) 'Pandemic Influenza Preparedness Framework for the Sharing of Influenza Viruses and Access to Vaccines and Other Benefits', p. 18. http://www.who.int/influenza/resources/pip_framework/en/
5 Bill and Melinda Gates Foundation (2009) 'Options for the Design and Financing of an H5N1 Vaccine Stockpile: Key Findings and Study Methodology', p. 3. http://www.who.int/influenza/preparedness/pandemic/H5N1_Stockpile_Design_Feb2009.pdf
6 Above, note 5, p. 4.
7 See Section 5.3.2 (2).
8 See Section 2.1.1.
9 See Section 3.3.1 (1).
10 WHO (2007) 'Ethical Consideration in Developing Public Health Response to Pandemic Influenza', p. 3.
11 See above, note 3, p. 28.
12 UK Nuffield Council (2007) *Nuffield Council on Bioethics, Public Health: Ethical Issues*, p. 33.
13 See above, note 3, p. 38.
14 Global Outbreak and Response Network (GOARN), WHO, available at: http://www.who.int/csr/outbreaknetwork/en/
15 WHO (2005) 'Global Influenza Preparedness Plan', WHO/CDS/CSR/GIP/2005.5.
16 See above, note 3, p. 24.
17 See note 15 above. For example, the WHO needs to review and update recommendations for pandemic vaccine use strategies with partners; states need to review and assess vaccine use strategy following the recommendations.
18 WHO (2005) 'WHO Checklist for Influenza Pandemic Preparedness Planning', Epidemic Alert and Response, Department of Communicable Disease, Surveillance and Response, Global Influenza Programme, WHO/CDS/CSR/GIP/2005.4.
19 See above, note 15. WHO Global Influenza Preparedness Plan – the Role of the WHO and Recommendations for National Measures Before and During Pandemics, March 2005.
20 See above, note 15, p. 27.
21 For example, the WHO recommended that African states should declare HIV/AIDS 'a national emergency' in 1999.
22 Such considerations were taken into account in *Canada – Certain Measures Concerning Periodicals* for the purpose of showing that imported split-run and domestic non-split-run magazines were substitutable. WT/DS31/AB/R, AB-1997-2, 30 June 1997.
23 See above, note 3, pp.16–17.

188 *Recommendations*

24 See Section 3.2.1.

25 See above, note 1.

26 See Section 4.3.1 (1).

27 See Section 4.3.2 (4).

28 *Korea – Measures Affecting Imports of Fresh, Chilled and Frozen Beef (Korea – Beef)*, WT/DS169/AB/R, adopted 10 January 2001.

29 *European Communities – Measures Affecting Asbestos and Asbestos-Containing Products (EC – Asbestos)*, WT/DS135/AB/R, adopted 12 March 2001.

30 *European Communities – Measures Concerning Meat and Meat Products (EC – Hormones)*, WT/DS26/AB/R, adopted 16 January1998.

31 See Chapter 5, Section 5.4.

32 *Japan – Measures Affecting Agricultural Products (Japan – Varietals)*, WT/DS76/AB/R, adopted on 19 March 1999. See Chapter 4, Section 4.3.2 (3).

33 *United States – Continued Suspension of Obligations in the EC – Hormones Dispute (Hormones II)*, WT/DS320/AB/R, adopted 16 October 2008. See Chapter 4, Section 4.3.2 (3).

34 ITLOS Nos. 3 and 4. See Chapter 3, Section 3.2.2 (2).

35 For example, the United Nations Convention on the Law of the Sea (UNCLOS) recognized the adoption of provisional measures as an employment of the precautionary approach, and the WTO SPS Agreement also articulates that 'a Member may *provisionally* adopt SPS measures on the basis of available pertinent information' (emphasis added).

36 In order to secure the timeous supply of the vaccine and antivirus once the disease occurs, the WHO works on keeping track of the latest information on viruses and aims to have a better grasp of the virus through close monitoring and assessment of the threat globally. For example, the WHO has developed an 'Influenza virus tracking system' following the Convention of the 'Intergovernmental meeting on Pandemic Influenza Preparedness: Sharing of influenza viruses and access to vaccine[s] and other benefits', 21–23 November 2007. The tracking system is an interim electronic system for WHO Members, which offers the latest indications of the H5N1 virus and relevant information on vaccines. The Influenza Virus Tracking System, WHO, http://www.who.int/fluvirus_tracker

37 The terms H5N1, H1N1 and so on refer to a virus's ability to enter and leave host cells. H and N are the virus' surface proteins haemagglutinin and neuraminidase. Each H and N is quite distinct, and immunity to one strain is not carried to another. See: 'The Predictable Pandemic', *New Scientist*, 2 May 2009, p. 6; 'Pandemic's Progress: We Saw it Coming', *New Statesman*, 4 May 2009, pp.14–15.

38 The duty to review within a reasonable period of time becomes essential when facing an unpredictable and transient health threat, such as in health measures which aim to contain a rapid virus outbreak in the IHRs and the SPS Agreement.

39 'More Than 2 Billion People Worldwide Could Get it. Thousands of Schools May Shut down. And Millions Will Need to Be Vaccinated – Twice: Inside the Fight against a Flu Pandemic', *Time*, 24 August 2009, pp.15–19.

40 *Japan – Measures Affecting Agricultural Products (Japan – Agricultural Products II)*, WT/DS76/AB/R, adopted on 19 March 1999.

41 ICJ Report 7, see Chapter 3, Section 3.2.2 (1).

42 See Section 4.2.

43 See Section 3.3.2.

The precautionary approach in compulsory licensing   189

44 Communication from the Commission on the Precautionary Principle, Commission of the European Communities (EC Communication), Brussels, 2 February 2000. The EC Communication on the precautionary principle addresses the importance of advancement on scientific findings by expressing that health measures need to be 'modified or abolished by a particular deadline, in the light of new scientific findings'. It is also noted that: 'However, this is not always linked to the time factor, but to the development of scientific knowledge.'

45 For example, the WHO needs to review and update recommendations for pandemic vaccine use strategies with partners; states need to review and assess vaccine use strategy following the recommendations. See: WHO/CDS/CSR/GIP/2005.5, above, note 15.

46 WHO (2003) 'Risk Management Framework for Uncertain Risks' and 'Precautionary Framework for Public Health Protection', 2 May. Available at: http://www.who.int/peh-emf/meetings/archive/Precaution_Draft_2May.pdf

47 *European Communities – Measures Affecting Asbestos and Asbestos-Containing Products (EC – Asbestos)*, WT/DS135/AB/R.

48 WHO (2001) 'Precautionary Policies and Health Protection: Principles and Applications', Report on a WHO Workshop, Rome, Italy, 28–29 May, EUR/02/5027100, p.10.

49 See above, note 1.

50 See above, note 3, p. 35.

51 WTO Appellate Body Report, *United States – Imposition of Countervailing Duties on Certain Hot-Rolled Lead and Bismuth Carbon Steel Products Originating in the United Kingdom (US – Lead and Bismuth Carbon Steel)*, WT/DS138/AB/R, adopted 10 May 2000.

52 Appellate Body Report, *United States – Imposition of Countervailing Duties on Certain Hot-Rolled Lead and Bismuth Carbon Steel Products Originating in the United Kingdom (US –Lead and Bismuth Carbon Steel)*, WT/DS138/AB/R, adopted 10 May 2000, para. 39. Cases relevant to amicus briefs include *EC – Hormones*, paras. 155–6; *US – Shrimp/Turtle I*, paras. 7–10, 79–91; *Japan – Varietals*, paras. 118–31; *Australia – Salmon*, paras. 7.8–7.9; *EC – Asbestos*, paras. 6.1–6.4, 8.12–8.14, 50–57.

7 Conclusion

The precautionary approach as a means to differentiate health technologies in intellectual property

7.1. Overview

This book has developed a means for adopting a precautionary approach (PA) to encourage states in taking advantage of the flexibilities of compulsory licensing in the Agreement on Trade-Related Aspects of Intellectual Property Rights (TRIPS) to promote access to medicines in a public health emergency.

7.2. Problem and solution

This book began with a discussion of the dissatisfaction with the compulsory licensing provision between the tension of international health and international trade, specifically in the context of IP.[1] Compulsory licensing indeed has a positive impact on the moderation of public and private interests in IP protection, yet it has been effectively dormant in many countries and the unsatisfactory implementation of the condition of 'national emergency or other circumstances of extreme urgency' has been identified due to the inherent limitations of the WTO rules and the international political settings. Compulsory licensing has not played its full part as a tool for meeting the general public's needs in circumstances of a public health emergency. Though the Doha Declaration in 2001 reaffirmed states' right to grant a compulsory licence,[2] developing countries barely resort to this mechanism due to possible trade retaliation from developed countries. This book therefore adopts the PA and the structure of risk analysis as a means for helping states embody the flexibilities of IP in the Doha Declaration.

Since the Doha Declaration, the world has experienced a series of pandemic attacks which forces us to contemplate the significance of the PA and risk management in a risk society. This also implies that risk management based on the rationale of the PA has a role to play at the interface between international health and IP. This book, therefore, proposes to incorporate the structure of risk analysis, specifically risk management, into the IP regime in order to accommodate a sufficient margin of safety in a risk society. Particularly, the PA has thus been adopted to supplement the gap in scientific evidence and to serve as a safety valve in compulsory licensing in preparedness for a public health emergency.

The WHO has also suggested that states take full advantage of the flexibilities in the TRIPS Agreement in order to promote access to medicines, yet empirical studies show that states are still hesitant to grant a compulsory licence based on the condition of 'national emergency or other circumstances of extreme urgency'. They prefer to use other tracks such as 'anti-competitiveness' and 'public non-commercial use' to avoid conflicts in international trade. Hence, this book has attempted to redefine the condition of 'national emergency or other circumstances of extreme urgency' through the lens of precaution and risk management, and to reaffirm states' precautionary entitlements to grant a compulsory licence as part of a preparedness plan following the WHO's recommendation in a public health emergency. Instead of pursuing stronger legal arguments, this book focuses on a PA analysis which would bolster the political and/or moral basis for compulsory licensing in a public health emergency. This mechanism will then serve as a foundation to boost states' confidence in granting a compulsory licence in a public health emergency.

7.3. Approach adopted

In pursuing this solution, I started with the review of the PA from the perspective of 'State responsibility' in international law and, particularly, I also found that the 'State stewardship' model of public health policy-making has been developed at the domestic level.[3] With respect to these, I have also looked at the international level in the context of the different legal instruments available to examine the current practice of the PA. By means of a philosophical review of the PA, I have also developed a *moderate* model of this approach in the domain of the research.[4]

This book has reviewed the PA employed in international public health and international trade. It was noted that the PA has been widely practiced in the realm of human health and safety. International legal instruments have adopted the PA and the structure of risk analysis to safeguard human health and safety; yet I also found regimes conflict and inconsistencies in relation to the PA in different legal regimes,[5] particularly in the WTO regime, and that the legal status of the PA has been an issue of debate. This is even more ambiguous in TRIPS. Thus this book has focused on the extent to which the PA could be incorporated into the IP regime in relation to human health and security with an emphasis on the compulsory licensing provision.

In developing this solution, this book has analysed the legal status of the PA in different WTO instruments, especially in the General Agreement on Tariffs and Trade (GATT 1947),[6] the Agreement on the Application of Sanitary and Phytosanitary Measures (SPS Agreement),[7] and the Agreement on Technical Barriers to Trade (TBT Agreement).[8]

192 *Recommendations*

I have also explored the possible interpretation of compulsory licensing regarding 'national emergency and other circumstances of extreme urgency' by means of the lens of precautionary entitlements in the WTO regime. I have also proposed a comparative study of exemptions in the WTO obligations, which also have resonance with exemptions to the TRIPS obligations in terms of legal status.[9]

This approach has also been examined to reaffirm states' *precautionary entitlement* to grant a compulsory licence through the interpretation of existing international instruments. It aims to act as an underpinning to states' act of compulsory licensing when states adopt the precautionary granting of a compulsory licence following the conditions developed in Chapter 6.

7.4. Proposals and arguments developed

First, this book noted that states enjoy the precautionary entitlement to take measures to achieve their appropriate level of public health protection.[10] *Second*, I developed a *moderate and prescriptive* version of the PA delineating the trigger threshold of significant risk of harm, uncertainty, and action along with other non-scientific factors for future application in the context of my research. I argued that this model of the PA could be recast into various risks with minor alterations of the sub-conditions depending on different characteristics of each given risk.[11]

I also noted that states have *precautionary rights and duties* in international law to safeguard public health in the examination of the legal instruments of the International Health Regulations (IHRs), the Codex Alimentarius, and the Cartagena Protocol on Biosafety.[12] Following the examination of instruments in relation to the PA in the WTO, it was noted that the PA in the SPS Agreement enjoys a higher legal status, namely as an excluding provision/a conditional right in the WTO legal hierarchy, than that of the exception provisions in GATT.[13] *Third*, I therefore argue that WTO Members enjoy precautionary entitlements in exercising their conditional rights in achieving an appropriate level of public health protection (ALOP).

I have also borrowed the WTO legal hierarchy to illustrate exemptions to IP in TRIPS.[14] Considering the legal status of compulsory licensing, I have looked into the interpretation of the Doha Declaration and the principles and goals of TRIPS.[15] *Fourth*, therefore, it was argued that compulsory licensing, like the provisional SPS measures, enjoys a higher legal status as an excluding provision, which can be deemed as a conditional right of WTO Members.[16] Then I argue that a compulsory licence granted under specific conditions would be considered compliant with Members' obligations to TRIPS unless a complaining Member proves otherwise.

This book has also examined whether the adoption of the PA in compulsory licensing would constitute discrimination in TRIPS. It was then stressed that the risk factor could legitimize differential treatment in WTO law.[17]

Fifth, I have therefore argued that the risk factor could legitimize differential treatment in the adoption of the PA in compulsory licensing of a pharmaceutical patent with regard to taking an expedient trigger to invoke 'national emergency or other circumstances of extreme urgency'.[18] *Finally,* I also took compulsory licensing in pandemic preparedness as an example to examine the precautionary model I developed in the previous chapters. Following a risk assessment or an objective evaluation of a pandemic based on the WHO's recommendations, I have concluded that, under certain conditions, states can invoke compulsory licensing in a pandemic preparedness plan to exercise their precautionary entitlements in TRIPS in order to achieve an ALOP.[19]

7.5. Some challenges and responses

7.5.1. *A better approach than the Doha Declaration?*

The Doha Declaration indeed sought to relieve the disease burden of developing countries by means of providing a signpost in the access to medicines debates, yet due to political restraints in international settings, this declaration nevertheless fails to fully realize the goal it promised. Most developing countries are still deterred from seeking the flexibilities in TRIPS fearing that trade retaliation would follow. This book has thus proposed a means for embodying the flexibilities in the Doha Declaration specifically in relation to its interpretation of 'national emergency or other circumstances of extreme urgency' in compulsory licensing.

This book has also equipped states with a model to embody their *precautionary entitlements* in order to claim their conditional rights to compulsory licensing in a public health emergency. However, it is beyond the scope of this book to address the political reasons underlying a state's decision to grant a compulsory licence. This book only provides a policy tool for states to realize their *conditional rights* in the WTO/TRIPS regime. It would ultimately depend on individual states' policy-making in IP and risk management, taking all factors into consideration, to decide if this approach would be best adopted in a preparedness plan for a public health emergency.

7.5.2. *Non-scientific factors?*

This book has suggested that states trigger the precautionary granting of a compulsory licence with a scientific risk assessment or scientific information, yet other non-scientific factors in their IP/risk policy making exist. For example, a state's particular values and social make-up, political and geographic context may cause the said state to also base its decision upon civilians' social and cultural preferences. Particularly in a pharmaceutical market, given that patients are the sole/main consumers of a patented drug, patients' rights and needs would need to be taken into serious account in order to reflect a state's rights and obligations in the realization of people's right to health.

194 *Recommendations*

Unlike other unknown risks deriving from new technologies, which may be regulated alongside with public engagement, due to time constraints, an acute public health emergency technically could only afford proper public engagement prior to the actual outbreak of a pandemic, namely during pandemic Phases 1 to 4.[20] In addition, public engagement could also come at a rather late stage in the form of amicus briefs to the WTO Dispute Settlement System (DSS) after a dispute is filed. It is fair to say that governments would still need to take comments from civil society, particular those from patients' perspectives, into consideration in their IP/risk policy making. It may also be further explored whether 'anticipatory engagement', which is employed for the governance of emerging technologies,[21] is possible in a public health emergency.

7.5.3. Data exclusivity?

As discussed in Chapter 1,[22] the application of confidentiality to pharmaceutical test data provides a trade secrets obstacle to access in addition to the patents obstacle. The data exclusivity provision (Article 39.3 TRIPS) could de facto limit the use of compulsory licensing by preventing generic pharmaceutical companies from relying on the originator's clinical data when applying to register a generic version during the period of data exclusivity (Wakely 2011b: 758). It then begs the question as to whether the PA would also provide a ground for tempering data exclusivity post compulsory licensing.

The inbuilt flexibility for compulsory licensing to temper patent protection is not reflected under the data exclusivity provision in TRIPS. There is thus a quest for the interpretation of an implicit exception to override the obstacle for access to medicines. Commentators argue that the data exclusivity provision in TRIPS only requires protection against unfair commercial use, but not an obligation to provide trade secrets protection, and thus there should be implicit permission to disclose such data for the need of public interest (Correa 2002a; Yamane 2011: 471; Carvalho 2005: 389, 394; Wadlow 2008: 355, 370).

The above argument illustrates that the regulation of data exclusivity involves strong 'public interest' consideration. One option to temper data exclusivity is compulsory licensing of the test data; another would be to consider a waiver of Article 39.3 to avoid repeating clinical trials for the same data. Carvalho holds that though Article 39.3 is silent as to an explicit exception for data exclusivity, compulsory licensing of test data is possible under the TRIPS umbrella (Carvalho 2005: 397); however, it would nevertheless be ineffective and causing delay. Thus a waiver of the data exclusivity regime would be an intuitive corollary of the PA to compulsory licensing in order to achieve a systematic and coherent interpretation of the legal text. The PA should be equally applicable to compulsory licensing and to data exclusivity in order to swiftly address domestic stockpiling needs for drugs.

7.6. Beyond this book

This work primarily focuses on the extent to which the precautionary approach could be crystallized in the IP regime. There are discussions on the ways in which innovation could be spurred beyond the IP regime, as discussed in the first chapter when the Health Impact Fund (HIF) is evaluated, as well as scholarly attempts to explore possibilities in stimulating innovation beyond the patent system.[23]

For fostering an organic and adaptive IP system in order to timeously strike a balance between trade and health, this book has argued for an expedient trigger threshold of compulsory licensing when dealing with a preparedness plan for an acute public health emergency. In order to examine if a different trigger threshold of the said compulsory licence would constitute discrimination in TRIPS, this book has also explored the legitimate differentiation of health technologies from other technologies. I have adapted the 'like-product' analysis from the WTO DSS as a threshold device into the discussion of the differentiation of pharmaceutical technologies. Regarding the compulsory licensing of acute-disease drugs, new questions will arise in interpreting the legitimate differentiation of health technologies.

For example, I have argued that differentiation should be made when health technologies are *strongly* associated with *significant* risks to human life and health. Yet, the next question moves to the identification and interpretation of the concept of '*strongly* associated with *significant* risks to human life and health'. Again, this should be based on scientific evidence or pertinent scientific information, which is carried out by convincing organizations, to increase transparency and objectivity.

Our discussion in the context of TRIPS and the Doha Declaration has concluded that this proposal may be found to be consistent with the obligations of a state under the TRIPS/WTO framework. If a WTO Member makes a complaint to the WTO DSS with regard to a compulsory licence, the complaining state needs to prove that the public health emergency did not exist in the invoking state as well as that the granting of a compulsory licence was not a least restrictive measure (LRM). The invoking party may submit their objective risk assessment or relevant information/recommendations from the WHO regarding the public health emergency to defend their cause.

In addition to compulsory licensing, this book could serve as a foundation to further explore the extent to which the PA would be better accommodated in the IP regime; for example, other exception and excluding provisions in TRIPS in order to enhance access to essential medicines. It can be anticipated that the employment of the PA in the IP regime would serve to promote a balance in the rights and obligations of patent holders, and legitimize a safety factor in the trade world. Hopefully, we would then be equipped to distinguish technologies which are associated with public interest and security that have fundamentally different implications for society from other technologies in IP (Abbott 2005: 77).

196   *Recommendations*

Finally, moving beyond our discussion of health technologies, the contribution of this book could also be explored in relation to other technologies associated with the reduction or elimination of risks to the environment or technologies which aim to redress climate change and other environmental concerns. This would then require more detailed investigation into the 'significant implications' of environmental technologies and the strength of the link between the said technology and the risk.

7.7. Closing thought

This book has developed a solution based on the PA in order to revisit public health emergency in TRIPS when national policy-makers are in a position to resort to the granting of a compulsory licence in an acute emergency situation. Throughout, this book has drawn upon philosophical and legal implications of the PA, as well as used existing international legal instruments with regard to health and security to illustrate that the PA and the rationale of risk management could be incorporated into the IP regime in order to take full advantage of the TRIPS flexibilities.

The final message is straightforward: a safety factor based on the PA is strongly recommended to be accommodated into the compulsory licensing mechanism. This book has reviewed the rationale of this approach, the objectives and the principles, as well as exemptions to obligations in the TRIPS Agreement. Hence, it has concluded that the granting of a compulsory licence in a public health emergency falls within the domain of *conditional rights* in the WTO framework; compulsory licensing is deemed consistent with a state's obligations under TRIPS unless a complaining Member proves otherwise. A model of the PA has been developed which is fit for purpose in its chosen realm of application and which could serve to ensure that two worlds – trade and health – need not collide.

Notes

1 See Section 1.2.
2 See Section 1.2.3.
3 See Section 3.2.1.
4 See Section 3.3.3.
5 See Section 4.4.2.
6 See Section 4.3.1.
7 See Section 4.3.2.
8 See section 4.3.3.
9 See Section 5.3.2.
10 See Sections 2.1.2 (1), 3.2.3 (1), 4.3.2 (1).
11 See Section 3.5.
12 See Chapter 4.
13 See Section 4.3.2.

14 See Section 5.3.2.
15 See Section 5.3.2 (2).
16 Ibid.
17 See Chapter 2 and Chapter 6.
18 See Section 6.3.
19 Ibid.
20 See Section 6.3.4.
21 See Philbrick, M. and Barandiaran, J. (2009) 'The National Citizens' Technology Forum: Lessons for the Future' 36(5) *Science and Public Policy* 335; Barben, D., Fisher, E., Selin, C., Guston, D.H. (2008) 'Anticipatory Governance of Nanotechnology: Foresight, Engagement, and Integration' in Hackett, E.J., Amsterdamska, O., Lynch, M.E. and Wajcman, J. (eds) *The Handbook of Science and Technology Studies*, Cambridge, MA: MIT Press; Guston, D.H. (2010) 'The Anticipatory Governance of Emerging Technologies' 19(6) *Journal of the Korean Vacuum Society* 432.
22 See Section 1.2.4.
23 Suthersanen, U., Dutfield, G. and Chow, K.B. (eds) (2007) *Innovation without Patents: Harnessing the Creative Spirit in a Diverse World*, Cheltenham: Edward Elgar.

Bibliography

Table of cases and legislation

(All websites last accessed June 2013)

Cases

Decisions of the bodies of the WTO DSS and associated documents

Australia – Measures Affecting the Importation of Salmon, WT/DS18/AB/R, adopted 20 October 1998

Brazil – Measures Affecting Patent Protection. Request for the establishment of a Panel by the United States, WT/DS199/1, 2001

Brazil – Measures Affecting Imports of Retreaded Tyres, WT/DS332/R WT/DS332/AB/R, adopted 3 December 2007

Canada – Certain Measures Concerning Periodicals, WT/DS31/AB/R, AB-1997-2, 30 June 1997

Canada – Patent Protection of Pharmaceutical Products, WT/DS114/R, adopted 17 March 2000

European Communities – Report for the Importation, Sale and Distribution of Bananas, WT/DS27/AB/R, adopted 25 September 1997

European Communities – Measures Concerning Meat and Meat Products, WT/DS26/AB/R, adopted 16 January1998

European Communities – Measures Affecting Asbestos and Asbestos-Containing Products, WT/DS135/AB/R, adopted 12 March 2001

European Communities – Measures Affecting the Approval and Marketing of Biotech Products, WT/DS291/R, WT/DS292/R, WT/DS293/R, adopted 29 February 2006

European Community – Trade Description of Sardines, WT/DS231/R, adopted 23 October 2002

European Union and a Member State – Seizure of Generic Drugs in Transit, Request for Consultation by India and Brazil, WT/DS408/1; WT/DS409/1, adopted 19 May 2010

India – Patent Protection for Pharmaceutical and Agricultural Chemical Products, WT/DS50/AB/R, adopted 16 January 1998

Japan – Measures Affecting Agricultural Products, WT/DS76/AB/R, adopted on 19 March 1999

Bibliography 199

Japan – Taxes on Alcoholic Beverages, WT/DS8/AB/R, WT/DS10/AB/R, WT/DS11/AB/R, adopted 1 November 1996

Korea – Measures Affecting Imports of Fresh, Chilled and Frozen Beef, WT/DS169/AB/R, adopted 10 January 2001

Philippines – Taxes on Distilled Spirits, WT/DS396/AB/R, WT/DS403/AB/R, adopted 21 December 2011

Spain – Tariff Treatment of Unroasted Coffee, L/5135, adopted 11 June 1981, BISD 28S/102

Thailand – Restrictions on Importation of and Internal Taxes on Cigarettes, 7 November 1990, BISD 37S/200

United States – Prohibition of Imports of Tuna and Tuna Products from Canada, adopted 22 February 1982, BISD 29S/91 611

United States – Import Prohibition of Certain Shrimp and Shrimp Products, WT/DS58/AB/R, adopted 6 November 1998

United States – Standards for Reformulated and Conventional Gasoline, WT/DS2/AB/R, adopted 20 May 1996

United States – Imposition of Countervailing Duties on Certain Hot-Rolled Lead and Bismuth Carbon Steel Products Originating in the United Kingdom, WT/DS138/AB/R, adopted 10 May 2000

United States – Continued Suspension of Obligations in the EC – Hormones Dispute, WT/DS320/AB/R, adopted 16 October 2008

United States – Measures Concerning the Protection and Sale of Clove Cigarettes, WT/DS406/AB/R, adopted 24 April 2012

United States – Measures Concerning the Importation, Marketing and Sale of Tuna and Tuna Products, WT/DS381/AB/R, adopted 13 June 2012

Decisions of international courts

Nicaragua v. United States of America, International Court of Justice, 1986

Gabcikovo–Nagymaros Case, ICJ Report 7, 1997, paras. 105–114

Southern Bluefin Tuna Case, International Tribunal for the Law of the Sea, Nos. 3 and 4, 1999

MOX Plant Case (Ireland v. United Kingdom), International Tribunal for the Law of the Sea, Nos. 10 and 15, 2001

Decisions of bodies of the European Economic Community, European Community and European Union

Alpharma Inc. v. Council of the EU (2002), Case T-70/99, Judgment of the Court of First Instance (Third Chamber), 11 September 2002

Monsanto Agricoltura Italia and Others, Case C-236/01, Judgment of 2003

ECJ Case C–236/01, Monsanto Agricoltura Italia SpA and Others v. Presidenza del Consiglio dei Ministri and Others ('Monsanto'), ECR 2003 I–08105, adopted 9 September 2003

Pfizer Animal Health v. Council of the EU (2002), Case T-13/39 and C-329/99, Judgment of the Court of First Instance (Third Chamber), 11 September 2002.

Commission of the European Communities v. Kingdom of Denmark, Case C-192/01, Judgment of 23 September 2003

200 *Bibliography*

Commission of the European Communities v. French Republic, Case C-24/00, Judgment of 5 February 2004

Press Release No 71/02, Judgments of the Court of First Instance in Cases T-13/99 and T-70/99, Press and Information Division, the Court of Justice of the European Communities, 11 September 2002

Decisions of India

Compulsory Licence Application No. 1 of 2011

Novartis AG v. Union of India and Others, Supreme Court of India, Civil Appeal Nos. 2706-2716 of 2013

Decisions of South Africa

High Court of South Africa, Pharmaceutical Manufacturers' Association of South Africa *et al.* v. President of the Republic of South Africa, Case No 4183/98, 1998

Legislation

Primary, secondary and regulatory output

UNITED KINGDOM

Tranquillisers Report, HC 197, 1973

Patents Act 1977

HM Government, A Better Quality of Life: A Strategy for Sustainable Development for the United Kingdom, 1999

Civil Contingencies Act 2004

Gowers Review of Intellectual Property, HMSO, 2006

Public Health Legislation in Scotland: A Consultation, Scottish Executive, 2006

Nuffield Council on Bioethics, 'Public Health: Ethical Issues', 2007.

National Institute for Health and Clinical Excellence (NICE), 'Social Value Judgements: Principles for the Development of NICE Guidance', 2nd edn, 2008.

National Institute for Health and Clinical Excellence (NICE), 'Methods for the Development of NICE Public Health Guidance', 2nd edn, 2009.

EUROPEAN COMMUNITY/EUROPEAN UNION

Directive 67/548 on the Approximation of the Laws, Regulations, and Administrative Provisions of the Member States Relating to the Classification, Packaging, and Labelling of Dangerous Substances

Directive 79/409 Relative to the Conservation of Wild Birds

Directive 79/831 amending for the sixth time Directive 67/548/EEC on the approximation of the laws, regulations and administrative provisions relating to the classification, packaging and labelling of dangerous substances

Directive 80/778 relating to the quality of water intended for human consumption

Directive 81/602 concerning the prohibition of certain substances having a hormonal action and of any substances having a thyrostatic action

Bibliography 201

Directive 88/146 prohibiting the use in livestock farming of certain substances having a hormonal action

Directive 88/299 on trade in animals treated with certain substances having a hormonal action and their meat, as referred to in Article 7 of Directive 88/146/EEC

Directive 90/219 on the Contained Use of Genetically Modified Micro-Organisms

Directive 90/220 on the Deliberate Release into the Environment of Genetically Modified Organisms

Directive 91/271 Urban Waste Water Directive

Directive 92/43 Concerning the Conservation of Natural Habitats and Wild Fauna and Flora

Directive 96/61 on Integrated Pollution Prevention and Control (IPPC)

Directive 98/81 on the Contained Use of Genetically Modified Micro-Organisms

Directive 2001/18 on the Deliberate Release into the Environment of Genetically Modified Organisms and Repealing

Council Decision 80/372 Concerning CFCs in the Environment

Regulation 2821/98 forbade the use of several antibiotics in animal feed

Regulation 1829/2003 on Genetically Modified Food and Feed

UNITED STATES

35 USC Section 200

The Proposed Act of 35 USC Section 158

Cuban Liberty and Democratic Solidarity (Libertad) Act of 1996 (Helms–Burton Act)

Leahy-Smith America Invents Act 35 USC Sections 321; 311

REPUBLIC OF SOUTH AFRICA

Constitution of the Republic of South Africa, No. 108 of 1996

South African Medicines and Related Substances Control Amendment Act 1997, Republic of South Africa Government Gazette No. 18505, Act No. 90, 1997, 12 December 1997

BELGIUM

Patent Law of 28 March 1984, as amended on 28 January 1997

BRAZIL

Constitution of the Federal Republic of Brazil (Constituição da República Federativa do Brasil)

Brazil's Intellectual Property Law

CANADA

Canada Patent Act Section 55.2

FRANCE

Intellectual Property Code

202 *Bibliography*

TAIWAN

Taiwan Intellectual Property Office (TIPO) Rule No. 09418601140, 8 December 2006.

INDIA

Constitution of India
Patents Act of 1970

Treaties, Declarations And Resolutions

UNITED NATIONS

Convention on the Law of Treaties, Vienna, 1155 UNTS 331, 1969

Resolution 29/332, 29 United Nations General Assembly Official Records (UNGAOR), Supp31, 1974

United Nations Convention on the Law of the Sea, 1982

World Charter for Nature, UN General Assembly Resolution 37/7, Annex B. no. 1, 28 October 1982

Convention for the Protection of the Ozone Layer, Vienna, 1985

Convention on Early Notification of a Nuclear Accident, Vienna, 1986

Protocol on Substances that Deplete the Ozone Layer, Montreal, 1987

Convention on the Regulation of Antarctic Mineral Resource Activities, Wellington, 1988

UN General Assembly Resolution 43/53 on Protection of Global Climate for Present and Future Generations of Mankind, 1988

UN Environment Programme Governing Council Decision 15/27 on the Precautionary Approach to Marine Pollution, Including Waste-Dumping at Sea, 1989

UN General Assembly Resolution 44/225 on Large-Scale Pelagic Driftnet Fishing and its Impact on the Living Marine Resources of the World's Oceans and Seas, 1989

Convention on the Control of Transboundary Movements of Hazardous Wastes and their Disposal, Basel, 1989

Declaration of the Third International Conference on the Protection of the North Sea, The Hague, 1990

UN Environment Programme Governing Council Decision SS II/4 on a Comprehensive Approach to Hazardous Waste, 1990

Convention on Environmental Impact Assessment in a Transboundary Context, 1991

UN General Assembly Resolution 46/215 on Large-Scale Pelagic Driftnet Fishing and its Impact on the Living Marine Resources of the World's Oceans and Seas, 1991

Declaration on the UN Conference on Environment and Development, Rio de Janeiro, UN Doc.A/CONF.151/26, Vol. I, Annex I, 1992

Agenda 21, UN Doc. A/CONF.151/26/REV.1 (Vol. I), Adopted 14 June 1992, Rio de Janeiro

United Nations Convention on Biological Diversity, Nairobi, 1992

UN Environment Programme Governing Council Decision 18/32 on Persistent Organic Pollutants, 1995

Bibliography   203

UN Environment Programme Governing Council Decision 19/13 C on Persistent Organic Pollutants, 1997

UN General Assembly Resolutions S/19-2 (Programme for the Further Implementation of Agenda 21), 1997

UNECE Convention on Access to Information, Public Participation in Decision-Making and Access to Justice in Environmental Matters, Arhus, Denmark, 25 June 1998

General Comment No. 14: the Right to the Highest Attainable Standard of Health (Article 12 of the International Covenant on Economic, Social and Cultural Rights), adopted by the Committee on Economic, Social and Cultural Rights on 11 May 2000, E/C.12/2000/4, 11 August 2000

Cartagena Protocol on Biosafety to the Convention on Biological Diversity, Montreal, 2000

Convention on Persistent Organic Pollutants, Stockholm, 2001

General Assembly Resolution 59/25, 2004

United Nations Human Rights Council Resolution, Promotion and Protection of All Human Rights, Civil, Political, Economic, Social and Cultural Rights, including the Right to Development, A/HRC/23/L.10/Rev.1, 11 June 2013

UNITED NATIONS INTERNATIONAL LAW COMMISSION (ILC)

Report of the 61st conference of the ILA Committee of the Enforcement of Human Rights Law, Paris, 1984

The commentary to the 1994 International Law Commission Draft Articles on the Law of the Non-Navigational Uses of international Watercourses, the commentary to Article 3 paras. 13–15 and the commentary to Article 4, para. 7, 1994

Draft Articles on State Responsibility, ICJ Report 7, 1997

Commentary on Article 1 of the Draft Articles on Harm Prevention, 2001

Commentary to Article 2(a) of the Draft Articles on Harm Prevention, 2001

EUROPEAN UNION/EUROPEAN COMMUNITY

Treaty on European Union (Maastricht Treaty) 1992

Treaty on the European Union, as amended by the Maastricht Treaty, 7 February 1992

Consolidated Version of the Treaty Establishing the European Community (EC Treaty), Official Journal of the European Union C 321 E/2, 29 December 2006

Consolidated Versions of the Treaty on European Union and of the Treaty Establishing the European Community (consolidated text) OJC 321E of 29 December 2006

Treaty of Lisbon 2007/COJ 306 17 December 2007

Consolidated Version of the Treaty on European Union, C 115/15, 9 May 2008

Consolidated Versions of the Treaty on European Union and the Treaty on the Functioning of the European Union (TFEU), March 2010

European Council (1997) Green Paper on the General Principles of Food Law in the European Union and its Communication on Consumer Health and Food Safety

European Council (1997) Regulation 258/97 on novel foods and novel food ingredients

European Parliament (1998) Resolution on the Green Paper on the General Principles of Food Law in the European Union

204   Bibliography

European Council (2000) Communication from the European Commission on the Precautionary Principle, Communication COM 1, Brussels.

European Council (2000) Resolution on the Precautionary Principle, SN 400/00 ADD 1 20 EN Annex III, Nice, adopted 9 December.

European Council (2001) European Environmental Agency Report, Late Lessons from Early Warnings: the Precautionary Principle 1896–2000, Environmental Issue Report No. 22, EEA, Copenhagen

GATT

GATT (1949) Corrigendum to the Summary Record of the Twenty-second Meeting, Contracting Parties Third Session, General Agreement on Tariffs and Trade, GATT/CP.3/SR.22, Corr.1, 20 June

GATT (1975) L/4250, 17 November

GATT (1982) Decision Concerning Article XXI of the General Agreement, Decision of 30 November 1982, General Agreement on Tariffs and Trade, L/5426, 2 December

International human rights and related instruments

International Covenant on Civil and Political Rights 1966 999 UNTS 171 and Optional Protocol 999 UNTS 302

International Covenant on Economic, Social and Cultural Rights 1966 003 UNTS 3

United Nations Economic and Social Council Siracusa Principles on Limitations and Derogations from Provisions in the ICCPR UN Doc. E/CN.4/1985/4, Annex (1985)

United Nations Commission on Human Rights Resolution 2004/26: Access to Medication in the Context of Pandemics: Such as HIV/AIDS, Tuberculosis, and Malaria, 2004

World Health Organization

WHO (1946) WHO Constitution

WHO (1987) Environmental Health Criteria document No. 70, Principles for the Safety Assessment of Food Additives and Containments in Food, Geneva

WHO (1998) International Programme on Chemical Safety (IPCS), Environmental Health Criteria 203 – Chrysotile Asbestos

WHO (1999) Globalization and Access to Drugs, 2nd edn

WHO (1999) Guidelines for Treatment of Dengue Haemorrhagic Fever in Small Hospitals (ix)

WHO (2001) 'Globalisation and Health: Results and Options', 79 Bull. 834–84

WHO (2001) Global Health Security: Epidemic Alert and Response, 21 May

WHO (2001) 'Precautionary Policies and Health Protection: Principles and Applications', Report on a WHO Workshop, Rome, Italy, 28–29 May, EUR/02/5027100

WHO (2002) The World Health Report 2002 – Reducing Risks, Promoting Healthy Life

WHO (2002) 'Implications of the Doha Declaration on the TRIPS Agreement and Public Health', Correa, C.M., WHO/EDM/PAR/2002.3

WHO (2003) 'Access to Essential Medicines: a Global Necessity', 32 *Essential Drugs Monitor*

WHO (2003) 'Access to Essential Medicines as a Human Right', 33 *Essential Drugs Monitor*

WHO (2003) Annual Report of the Monitoring, Surveillance Network for Resistance to Antibiotics

WHO (2003) 'Risk Management Framework for Uncertain Risks' and the 'Precautionary Framework for Public Health Protection' of the draft, 2 May

WHO (2004) 'The Precautionary Principle: Protecting Public Health, the Environment and the Future of Our Children', Martuzzi, M. and Tickner, J.A. (eds).

WHO (2004) World Health Organization Fourth Ministerial Declaration on Environment and Health, EUR/04/5046267/6, Budapest, Hungary 23–25 June

WHO (2005) 'Access to Medicines, Intellectual Property Protection: Impact on Public Health', WHO Drug Information Vol. 19, No. 3

WHO (2005) 'WHO Checklist for Influenza Pandemic Preparedness Planning, Epidemic Alert and Response', Department of Communicable Disease, Surveillance and Response, Global Influenza Programme, WHO/CDS/CSR/GIP/2005.4

WHO (2005) 'WHO Global Influenza Preparedness Plan: The Role of WHO and Recommendations for National Measures before and during Pandemics', Department of Communicable Disease, Surveillance and Response, Global Influenza Programme, WHO/CDS/CSR/GIP/2005.5

WHO (2005) 'Dealing with Uncertainty: Setting the Agenda for the 5th Ministerial Conference on Environment and Health, 2009', Copenhagen, Denmark, 15–16 December, EUR/06/5067987

WHO (2005) Revision of the International Health Regulations (IHRs)

WHO (2005) 'The Use of Flexibilities in TRIPS by Developing Countries: Can They Promote Access to Medicines?', World Health Organization Commission on Intellectual Property Rights, Innovation and Public Health ('CIPIH') Study 4C

WHO (2006) Final Report Commission on Intellectual Property Rights, Innovation and Public Health

WHO (2006) 'WHO Rapid Advice Guidelines on Pharmacological Management of Humans Infected with Avian Influenza A (H5N1) Virus', WHO/PSM/PAR/2006.6

WHO (2006) 'Elements of a Global Strategy and Plan of Action: Progress to Date in the Intergovernmental Working Group, Intergovernmental Working Group on Public Health, Innovation and Intellectual Property', Agenda item 2.3, A/PHI/IGWG/1/5, 8 December

WHO (2007) 'Ethical Considerations in Developing a Public Health Response to Pandemic Influenza', WHO/CDS/EPR/GIP/2007.2

WHO (2007) Issues Paper – Invest in Health, Build a Safer Future

WHO (2008) 'The Use of Flexibilities in TRIPS by Developing Countries: Can They Promote Access to Medicines?' WHO Medicines Strategy 2008–2013, Draft 8, 13 June

WHO (2009) 'Pandemic Influenza Preparedness and Response: A WHO Guidance Document', Global Influenza Programme

WHO (2011) 'Pandemic Influenza Preparedness Framework for the Sharing of Influenza Viruses and Access to Vaccines and Other Benefits', available at: http://apps.who.int/gb/pip/

206 *Bibliography*

WHO (2013) 'Pandemic Influenza Risk Management WHO Interim Guidance', WHO/HSE/HEA/HSP/2013.3

WHO/AFRO Press Releases (1999) 'African Countries Urged to Declare HIV/AIDS A National Emergency', 24 June 1999

World Health Assembly (1999) Resolution 52.19, 'Revised Drug Strategy', 24 May

World Health Assembly (2002) Resolution 55.14, 'Ensuring Accessibility of Essential Medicines', 18 May

World Health Assembly (2004) Resolution 57.14, 'Scaling up Treatment and Care within a Coordinated and Comprehensive Response to HIV/AIDS', 22 May

World Health Assembly (2005) Resolution 58.3, 'Revision of the International Health Regulations', 23 May

World Health Assembly (2006) 'Public Health, Innovation, Essential Health Research and Intellectual Property Rights: Towards a Global Strategy and Plan of Action', WHA59.24, 27 May

World Health Assembly (2007) 'Pandemic Influenza Preparedness: Sharing of Influenza Viruses and Access to Vaccines and Other Benefits', WHA 60.28, 23 May

World Health Assembly (2007) Fifth Report of Committee B A60/64, 24 May

World Medical Association

World Medical Association (2000) Declaration of Helsinki: Ethical Principles for Medical Research Involving Human Subjects, revised edn, Edinburgh, 52 World Medical Association General Assembly, October

World Trade Organization

Agreement establishing the World Trade Organization 1994 (WTO Agreement) incorporating General Agreement on Tariffs and Trade 1994 incorporating the General Agreement on Tariffs and Trade 1947, Marrakesh Agreement Establishing the World Trade Organization, Annex 1A

Dispute Settlement Understanding ('DSU'), Annex 2 to the WTO Agreement

Agreement on Trade-Related Aspects of Intellectual Property Rights, Marrakesh Agreement Establishing the World Trade Organization, Annex 1C

Agreement on the Application of Sanitary and Phytosanitary Measures, Marrakesh Agreement Establishing the World Trade Organization, Annex 1A: Multilateral Agreements on Trade in Goods

Agreement on Technical Barriers to Trade, Marrakesh Agreement Establishing the World Trade Organization, Annex 1A: Multilateral Agreements on Trade in Goods

Doha Declaration on the TRIPS Agreement and Public Health, adopted by the fourth Ministerial Conference of the World Trade Organization in Doha, Qatar, on 14 November 2001. WT/MIN(01)/DEC/2 of 20 November 2001

WTO (1997) Communication from the Chairman of the Panel, United States – The Cuban Liberty and Democratic Solidarity Act, WT/DS38/5

WTO (2002) Communication from the European Communities and Their Members to the TRIPS Council Relating to Paragraph 6 of the Doha Declaration on the TRIPS Agreement and Public Health, Brussels, 20 June

Bibliography   207

WTO (2005) Rule 16(1) Working Procedures for Appellate Review, World Trade Organization, WT/AB/WP/5, 4 January

WTO (1996) Trade Policy Reviews: Second Press Release and Chairperson's Conclusions, United States: November 1996, PRESS/TPRB/49, 12 November.

WTO (2003) WTO General Council Decision of 30 August 2003, Implementation of Paragraph 6 of the Doha Declaration on the TRIPS Agreement and Public Health, Doc. WT/L/540 and Corr.1, 1 September

WTO (2005) WTO General Council Decision of 6 December 2005, Amendment of the TRIPS Agreement, WT/L/641, 8 December, with attachment 'Protocol Amending the TRIPS Agreement' (with Annex setting out Article 31 bis)

WTO (2007) Rwanda, Notification Under Paragraph 2(a) of the Decision of 30 August 2003 on the Implementation of Paragraph 6 of the Doha Declaration on the TRIPS Agreement and Public Health, Circulated 17 July 2007, WTO Council for TRIPS, IP/N/9/RWA/1, 19 July

WTO, WHO, WIPO (2013) 'Promoting Access to Medical Technologies and Innovation: Intersections between Public Health, Intellectual Property and Trade'

Miscellaneous (in chronological order)

Codex Alimentarius (1989) Guidelines for Simple Evaluation of Food Additive Intake, CAC/GL 03-1989

Codex Alimentarius (2012) Glossary of Terms and Definitions (Residues of Veterinary Drugs in Foods), CAC/MISC 2-2012

Codex Alimentarius (2013) Codex Alimentarius Commission 21st Procedural Manual, Joint FAO/WHO Food Standards Programme, FAO, Rome

FAO (1994) The Precautionary Approach to Fisheries with Reference to Straddling Fish Stocks and Highly Migratory Stocks, UN Doc A/CONF.164/INF/8

FAO/WHO (1995) Report of the Joint FAO/WHO Expert Consultation, Application of Risk Analysis to Food Standards Issues, Geneva, Switzerland, 13–17 March, WHO/FNU/FOS/95.3

The Intergovernmental Agreement on the Environment (IGAE) (1992) signed in May 1992 by all heads of government in Australia

Wingspread Statement on the Precautionary Principle (1998) Wingspread, Wisconsin.

Secondary materials: articles, books and reports

Abbott, F.M. (2005) 'Toward a New Era of Objective Assessment in the Field of TRIPS and Variable Geometry for the Preservation of Multilateralism' 8(1) *Journal of International Economic Law* 77.

Abbott, F.M. (2002) 'The Doha Declaration on the Trips Agreement and Public Health: Lighting A Dark Corner at the WTO' 5(2) *Journal of International Economic Law* 469.

Abbott, F.M. (2011) Intellectual Property and Public Health: Meeting the Challenge of Sustainability, Global Health Programme Working Paper No. 7/2011, 15 November 2011.

Abbott, F.M. and Reichman, J.H. (2007) 'The Doha Round's Public Health Legacy: Strategies for the Production and Diffusion of Patented Medicines under the Amended TRIPS Provisions' 10 *Journal of international Economic Law* 921.

208 Bibliography

Aginam, O. (2006) 'Between Life and Profit: Global Governance and the Trilogy of Human Rights, Public Health and Pharmaceutical Patents' 31 *North Carolina Journal of International Law and Commercial Regulations* 901.

Alsegard, E. (2004) 'Global Pharmaceutical Patents after the Doha Declaration – What Lies in the Future' 1(1) *SCRIPT-ed*.

Amollo, R. (2009) 'Revisiting the TRIPS Regime: Rwanda-Canadian ARV Drug Deal "Tests" the WTO General Council Decision', 17(2) *African Journal of International and Comparative Law* 240–69.

Ansari, N. (2002) 'International Patent Rights in a Post-Doha World' 11 *WTR Currents: International Trade Law Journal* 57.

APEC (2003) 'Economic Impact of SARS on Tourism in Seven Selected APEC Member Economies', Asia-Pacific Economic Cooperation ('APEC'), 22nd Tourism Working Group Meeting, 2003/TWG22/016.

Attaran, A. (2002) 'The Doha Declaration on the TRIPS Agreement and Public Health, Access to Pharmaceuticals, and Options under WTO Law' 12 *Fordham Intellectual Property, Media and Entertainment Law Journal* 859.

Baetens, F. (2007) 'Safety until Proven Harmful? Risk Regulation in Situations of Scientific Uncertainty: The GMO Case' 66(2) *Cambridge Law Journal* 276.

Baggott, R. (2000) *Public Health: Policy and Politics*, Basingstoke: Palgrave Macmillan.

Baker, B.K. (2004) 'Arthritic Flexibilities for Accessing Medicines: Analysis of WTO Action Regarding Paragraph 6 of the Doha Declaration on the TRIPS Agreement and Public Health' 14 *Indiana International and Comparative Law Review* 613.

Barben, D., Fisher, E., Selin, C., Guston, D.H. (2008) ' Anticipatory Governance of Nanotechnology: Foresight, Engagement, and Integration' in Hackett, E.J., Amsterdamska, O., Lynch, M.E. and Wajcman, J. (eds) *The Handbook of Science and Technology Studies*, Cambridge, MA: MIT Press.

Barton, C. (1998) 'The Status of the Precautionary Principle in Australia: Its Emergence in Legislation and as a Common Law Doctrine' 22 *Harvard Environmental Law Review* 517.

Bentley, L. and Sherman, B. (2008) *Intellectual Property Law*, 3rd edn, New York: Oxford University Press.

Bermann, G.A. and Mavroidis, P.C. (2006) *Trade and Human Health and Safety*, New York: Cambridge University Press.

Bernasconi-Osterwalder, N., Magraw, D., Oliva, M.J., Tuerk, E. and Orellana, M. (eds) (2006) *Environment and Trade: A Guide to WTO Jurisprudence*, London: Earthscan.

Bill and Melinda Gates Foundation (2009) *Options for the Design and Financing of an H5N1 Vaccines Stockpile: Key Findings and Study Methodology*.

Birnie, P., Boyle, A. and Redgwell, C. (2009) *International Law and the Environment*, 3rd edn, New York: Oxford University Press.

Bloche, M. (2002) 'WTO Deference to National Health Policy: Toward an Interpretive Principle' *Journal of International Economic Law* 825–48.

Bloche. M.G. and Jungman, E.R. (2003) 'Health Policy and the WTO' 31 *Journal of Law, Medicine and Ethics* 529–45.

Bohanes, J. (2002) 'Risk Regulation in WTO Law: A Procedure-Based Approach to the Precautionary Principle' 40 *Columbia Journal of Transnational Law* 323.

Boutillon, S. (2002) 'The Precautionary Principle: Development of an International Standard' 23 *Michigan Journal of International Law* 429.

Bibliography 209

Bronckers, M. and Quick, R. (eds) (2000) *New Directions in International Economic Law*, The Hague: Kluwer Law International.

Brown, A. (2008) 'The Interface between Intellectual Property, Competition and Human Rights: Overview of Field And Proposed Contribution to Knowledge' in Pattanaik, M.K. (ed.) *Human Rights and Intellectual Property*, India: The Icfai University Press.

Brown, A.E.L. (2012) *Intellectual Property, Human Rights and Competition: Access to Essential Innovation and Technology*, Cheltenham: Edward Elgar.

Brownlie, I. (2003) *Principle of Public International Law*, 6th edn, Oxford: Clarendon Press.

Brownsword, R. (2004) 'Regulating Human Genetics: New Dilemma for A New Millennium' 12(14) *Medical Law Review*.

Brownsword, R. (2008) 'So What Does the World Need Now?' in Brownsword, R. and Yeung, K. (eds) *Regulating Technologies: Legal Futures, Regulatory Frames and Technological Fixes*, Portland, Oregon: Hart Publishing.

Bruce, A. (2007) 'The Public domain: Ideology vs. Interest' in Waelde, C. and MacQueen, H. *Intellectual Property: The Many Faces of the Public Domain*, Cheltenham: Edward Elgar.

Button, C. (2004) *The Power to Protect: Trade, Health and Uncertainty in the WTO*, Portland, Oregon: Hart Publishing.

Cameron, E. (2004) 'Patents and Public Health: Principle, Politics and Paradox' 1(4) *SCRIPT-ed*.

Cameron, J. (1999) 'The Precautionary Principle: Core Meaning, Constitutional Framework and Procedures for Implementation' in Harding, R. and Fisher, E. (eds) *Perspectives on the Precautionary Principle*, Sydney: The Federal Press, Ch. 2.

Cann, W.A. Jr. (2001) 'Creating Standards and Accountability for the Use of the WTO Security Exception: Reducing the Role of Power-Based Relations and Establishing a New Balance between Sovereignty and Multilateralism' 26 *Yale Journal of International Law*.

Carvalho, N.P. (2005) *The TRIPS Regime of Patent Rights*, 2nd edn, The Hague: Kluwer Law International.

Chang, S.W. (2007) 'WTO for Trade and Development Post Doha' 10(3) *Journal of International Economic Law* 553.

Charnovitz, S., Bartels, L., Howse, R., Bradley, J., Pauwelyn, J. and Regan, D. (2004) 'The Appellate Body's GSP Decision' 3(2) *World Trade Review* 257.

Chaves, G.C. (2007) 'Case Study on the Use of TRIPS Flexibilities in Brazil' (presentation given at the Global Forum for Health Research Conference, Comparative Program on Health and Society Satellite Session – Access to Medicines, Human Rights and Trade Rules: Comparative and International Perspectives, Beijing, 29 October 2007, on file with the author).

Cheyne, I. (2006a) 'The Precautionary Principle in the EC and WTO Law: Searching for a Common Understanding' 8(4) *Environmental Law Review* 257–77.

Cheyne, I. (2006b) 'Risk and Precaution in World Trade Organization Law' 40(5) *Journal of World Trade* 837–64.

Cheyne, I. (2007) 'Gateways to the Precautionary Principle in WTO Law' 19 *Journal of Environmental Law* 155.

Cheyne, I. (2009) 'Proportionality, Proximity and Environmental Labelling in WTO Law' 12 *Journal of International Environmental Law* 927.

210 Bibliography

Chowdhury, S.R. (1989) *Rule of Law in a State of Emergency: The Paris Minimum Standards of Human Rights Norms in a State of Emergency*, New York: St Martin's Press.

Christoforou, T. (2003) 'The Precautionary Principle in European Community Law and Science' in Tickner, J.A. (ed.) *Precaution, Environmental Science and Preventive Public Policy*, Washington DC: Island Press.

Coleman, L.O. (2002) 'The European Union: An Appropriate Model for a Precautionary Approach?' Winter, 25 *Seattle University Law Review* 609.

Concise Oxford English Dictionary, 11th edn, UK: Oxford University Press.

Condon, B.J. (2006) *Environmental Sovereignty and the WTO: Trade Sanctions and International Law*, New York: Transnational Publishers.

Cornish, W. and Llewelyn, D. (2007) *Intellectual Property: Patents, Copyright, Trade Marks and Allied Rights*, 6th edn, London: Sweet & Maxwell.

Correa, C.M. (2002a) 'Protection of Data Submitted for the Registration of Pharmaceuticals: Implementing the Standards of the TRIPS Agreement', South Centre in collaboration with the Department of Essential Drugs and Medicines Policy of the World Health Organization.

Correa, C.M. (2002b) 'Implications of the Doha Declaration on the TRIPS Agreement and Public Health' *Health Economics and Drugs*, EDM Series No. 12, pp. 16–17.

Correa, C.M. (2007) *Trade Related Aspects of Intellectual Property Rights: A Commentary on the TRIPS Agreement*, New York: Oxford University Press.

Correa, C.M. (2009) 'A Model Law for the Protection of Undisclosed Data' in Meléndez-Ortiz, R. and Roffe, P. (eds) *Intellectual Property and Sustainable Development: Development Agendas in a Changing World*, Cheltenham: Edward Elgar.

Correa, C.M. and Matthews, D. (2011) *The Doha Declaration Ten Years on and Its Impact on Access to Medicines and the Right to Health*, New York: United Nations Development Programme.

Cottier, T. (1998) 'The Relationship between World Trade Organisation Law, National and Regional Law' 1(1) *Journal of International Economic Law* 83.

Covelli, N. (2003) 'The Health Regulation of Biotech Foods under the WTO Agreements' 6(4) *Journal of International Economic Law* 773.

Covelli, N. and Hohots, V. (2003) 'The Health Regulation of Biotech Foods under the WTO Agreements' 6(4) *Journal of International Economic Law* 773–95.

Crawford, J. (1999) 'Revisiting the Draft Articles on State Responsibility' 10(2) *European Journal of International Law* 436.

Crawford, J. (2008) *Brownlie's Principles of Public International Law*, 8th edn, Oxford: Oxford University Press.

Cullet, P. (2003a) 'Patents and Health in Developing Countries' in Hatchard, J. and Perry, A. (eds) *Law and Development: Facing Complexity in the 21st Century*. London: Cavendish, pp. 78–98.

Cullet, P. (2003b) 'Patents and Medicines: the Relationship between TRIPS and the Human Right to Health' *International Affairs* 79(1): 139–60.

De Sadeleer, N. (2008) *Environmental Principles: From Political Slogans to Legal Rules*, New York: Oxford University Press.

Diebold, N.F. (2008) 'The Morals and Order Exceptions in WTO Law: Balancing the Toothless Tiger and the Undermining Mole' 11(1) *Journal of International Economic Law* 43.

Drahos, P. (2001) 'Bilateralism in Intellectual Property', London: Oxfam.

Bibliography 211

Droge, S., Trabold, H., Biermann, F., Bohm, F. and Brohm, R. (2004) 'National Climate Change Policies and WTO Law: A Case Study of Germany's New Policies' *World Trade Review* 161.

Du, M. (2010) 'Autonomy in Setting Appropriate Level of Protection under the WTO Law: Rhetoric or Reality?' 13(4) *Journal of International Economic Law* 1077–1102.

Dunoff, J.L. (2006) 'Lotus Eaters: Reflections on the *Varietal* Dispute, the SPS Agreement and WTO dispute resolution' in Bermann, G.A. and Mavroidis, P.C. (eds) *Trade and Human Health and Safety*, Columbia Studies in WTO Law and Policy, New York: Cambridge University Press.

Epps, T. (2008) *International Trade and Health Protection: A Critical Assessment of the WTO's SPS Agreement*, Cheltenham: Edward Elgar.

Fergusson, I.F. (2003) 'The WTO, Intellectual Property Rights, and the Access to Medicines Controversy', CRS Report for Congress.

Fidler, D.P. (2000) *International Law and Public Health: Materials on and Analysis of Global Health Jurisprudence*, Transnational Publishers Inc.

Fidler, D.P. (2002) 'A Globalized Theory of Public Health Law' 30 *Journal of Law, Medicine and Ethics* 150.

Fidler, D.P. (2004a) 'Constitutional Outlines of Public Health's "New World Order"' 77 *Temple Law Review* 247.

Fidler, D.P. (2004b) 'Fighting the Axis of Illness: HIV/AIDS, Human Rights, and U.S. Foreign Policy' 17 *Harvard Human Rights Journal* 99.

Fidler, D.P. (2009) 'The Swine Flu Outbreak and International Law' 13(5) *ASIL Insights*.

Fisher, E., Jones, J. and von Schomberg, R. (eds) (2006) *Implementing the Precautionary Principle: Perspectives and Prospects*, Cheltenham: Edward Elgar.

Forrest, M. (2000) 'Using the Power of the World Health Organization: The International Health Regulations and the Future of International Health Law' 33 *Columbia Journal of Law and Social Problems* 153.

Frankel, S. (2005/2006) 'WTO Application of "the Customary Rules of Interpretation of Public International Law" to Intellectual Property' 46 *Virginia Journal of International Law* 365.

Freedman, C.D. (2000) 'Software and Computer-Related Business-Method Inventions: Must Europe Adopt American Patent Culture?' 8 *International Journal of Law and IT* 285.

Freestone, D. (1994) 'The Road from Rio: Environmental Law after the Earth Submit' 6 *Journal of Environmental Law* 211.

Freestone, D. (1999) 'International Fisheries Law since Rio: The Continued Rise of the Precautionary Principle' in Boyle, A. and Freestone, D. (eds) *International Law and Sustainable Development*, US: Oxford University Press.

Freestone, D. and Hey, E. (eds) (1995) *The Precautionary Principle and International Law*, The Hague: Kluwer Law International.

Gamharter, K. (2004) *Access to Affordable Medicines: Developing Responses under the TRIPS Agreement and EC Law*, Horn, Austria: Springer.

Gathii, J.T. (2006) 'How Necessity May Preclude State Responsibility for Compulsory Licensing under the TRIPS Agreement' 31 *North Carolina Journal of International Law and Commercial Regulation* 943.

Gee, D. and Stirling, A. (2003) 'Late Lessons from Early Warnings: Improving Science and Governance Under Uncertainty and Ignorance' in Tickner, J.A. (ed.)

212 *Bibliography*

Precaution, Environmental Science, and Preventive Public Policy, Washington DC: Island Press.

Gervais, D. (2003) *The TRIPS Agreement: Drafting History and Analysis*, 2nd edn, London: Sweet & Maxwell.

Gervais, D. (2005) 'Towards a New Core International Copyright Norm: The Reverse Three-Step Test' 9 *Marquette Intellectual Property Law Review* 1.

Gervais, D.J. (ed.) (2007) *Intellectual Property, Trade and Development: Strategies to Optimize Economic Development in a TRIPS-Plus Era*, New York: Oxford University Press.

Geuze, M. and Wager, H. (1999) 'WTO Dispute Settlement Practice Relating to the Trips Agreement' 2(2) *Journal of International Economic Law* 347.

Goh, G. (2006) 'Tipping the Apple Cart: the Limits of Science and Law in the SPS Agreement after Japan – Apples' 40(4) *Journal of World Trade* 655–86.

Goldstein, B. and Carruth, R.S. (2004) 'The Precautionary Principle and/or Risk Assessment in World Trade Organization Decisions: A Possible Role for Risk Perception' 24(2) *Risk Analysis* 491–9.

Gostin, L.O. (2000) *Public Health Law: Power, Duty, Restraint*, California University Press.

Gostin, L.O. (2001) 'Public Health, Ethics, and Human Rights: A Tribute to the Late Jonathan Mann' 29 *Journal of Law, Medicine and Ethics* 121.

Gostin, L.O. (ed.) (2002) *Public Health Law and Ethic: A Reader*, University of California Press.

Gostin, L.O. (2004) 'International Infectious Disease Law: Revision of the World Health Organization's International Health Regulations' 291(21) *JAMA* 2623.

Gostin, L.O. (2005) 'World Health Law: Toward A New Conception of Global Health Governance for the 21st Century' 5 *Yale Journal of Health Policy, Law and Ethics* 413.

Grando, M.T. (2006) 'Allocating the Burden of Proof in WTO Disputes: A Critical Analysis' 9(3) *Journal of International Economic Law* 615–56.

Green, A. and Epps, T. (2007) 'The WTO, Science, and the Environment: Moving Towards Consistency' 10(2) *Journal of International Economic Law* 285.

Grosche, A. (2006) 'Software Patents, Boon or Bane for Europe?' 14 *International Journal of Law and Information Technology* 257.

Gross, O. and Aolain, F.N. (2006) *Law in Time of Crisis: Emergency Power in Theory and Practice*, Cambridge: Cambridge University Press.

Gruskin, S. (2004) 'Is There A Government in the Cockpit: A Passenger's Perspective of Global Public Health: The Role of Human Rights' 77 *Temple Law Review* 313.

Guadamuz, A. (2006) 'The Software Patent Debate' 1(3) *Journal of Intellectual Property Law and Practice* 196–206.

Guston, D.H. (2010) 'The Anticipatory Governance of Emerging Technologies' 19(6) *Journal of the Korean Vacuum Society*.

Haigh, N. (1994) 'The Introduction of the Precautionary Principle into the UK' in O'Riordan, T. and Cameron, J. (eds) *Interpreting the Precautionary Principle*, London: Earthscan, pp. 229–51.

Hahn, M.J. (1991) 'Vital Interests and the Law of GATT: An Analysis of GATT's Security Exception' 12 *Michigan Journal of International Law* 558.

Harding, R. and Fisher, E. (1999) *Perspectives on the Precautionary Principle*, NSW, Australia: The Federation Press.

Harris, J. and Holm, S. (2002) 'Extending Human Lifespan and the Precautionary Paradox' 17(3) *Journal of Medicine and Philosophy* 355–68.

Bibliography   213

Helfer, L.R. (2004) 'Regime Shifting: The TRIPS Agreement and New Dynamics of International Intellectual Property Lawmaking' 29 *Yale Journal of International Law*.

Hestermeyer, H. (2007) *Human Rights and the WTO – the Case of Patents and Access to Medicines*, New York: Oxford University Press.

Ho'en, E. (2002) 'TRIPS, Pharmaceutical Patents, and Access to Essential Medicines: A Long way from Seattle to Doha' *Chicago Journal of International Law*.

Holer, J. and Elworthy, S. (1998) 'The BSE Crisis: A Study of the Precautionary Principle and the Politics of Science in Law' in Reece, H. (ed.) *Law and Science: Current Legal Issues* Volume 1, New York: Oxford University Press.

Hollies, A. and Pogge, T. (2008) 'The Health Impact Fund: Making New Medicines Accessible for All' in Pogge, T., Rimmer, M. and Rubenstein, K. (eds) *Incentives for Global Health*, Cambridge: Cambridge University Press.

Horng, D-C. (2005) 'The Research Regarding the National Security Exception in WTO' 17 *The Chinese (Taiwan) Yearbook of International Law and Affairs* 165–211.

Howarth, W. (2008) 'The Interpretation of 'Precaution' in the European Community Common Fisheries Policy' 20 *Journal of Environmental Law* 213.

Howse, R. (2000) 'The Canadian Generic Medicines Panel: A Dangerous Precedent in Dangerous Times' 3(4) *Journal of World Intellectual Property* 493–508.

Howse, R. (2002) 'The Appellate Body Rulings in the Shrimp/Turtle Case: A New Legal Baseline for the Trade and Environment Debate' 27 *Columbia Journal of Environmental Law* 491.

Hung, P. (2010) 'The Precautionary Approach under the Right to Health Dilemma' 24(1) *International Review of Law, Computers and Technology* 71–80.

Jackson, J.H. (1978) 'The Crumbling Institutions of the Liberal Trade System' 12 *Journal of World Trade Law* 93: 98–101.

Jackson, J.H. (1979) 'Governmental Disputes in International Trade Relations: A Proposal in the Context of the GATT' 13 *Journal of World Trade Law* 1: 3–4.

Jackson, J.H. (1997) *The World Trading System: Law and Policy of International Economic Relations*, 2nd edition, Cambridge, MA: MIT Press.

Jans, J. (2003) 'EU Environmental Policy and the Civil Society' in Jans, J. (ed.) *The European Convention and the Future of European Environmental Law*, Europa Law Publishing.

Johns, F. (2008) 'The Risks of International Law' 21(4) *Leiden Journal of International Law* 783–6.

Jones, J. and Bronitt, S. (2006) 'The Burden and Standard of Proof in Environmental Regulation: the Precautionary Principle in an Australian Administrative Context' in Fisher, E., Jones, J. and von Schomberg, R. (eds) *Implementing the Precautionary Principle: Perspectives and Prospects*, Cheltenham, UK: Edward Elgar Publishing.

Kapterian, G. (2010) 'A Critique of the WTO Jurisprudence on "Necessity"' 59(1) *International and Comparative Law Quarterly* 89.

Kelly, C.R. (2006) 'Power, Linkage and Accommodation: The WTO as an International Actor and Its Influence on Other Actors and Regimes' 24 *Berkeley Journal of International Law* 79.

Kennedy, M. (2010) 'When Will the Protocol Amending the TRIPS Agreement Enter into Force?' 13(2) *Journal of International Economic Law* 459–73.

Khor, M. (2009) 'Patents, Compulsory Licences and Access to Medicines: Some Recent Experiences', Third World Network.

214 *Bibliography*

Killoran, A., White, P., Millward, L. and Fischer, A. (2009) 'NICE Update: NICE Public Health Guidance' 31(3) *Journal of Public Health* 451–2.

Kimball, A.M. (2006) *Risky Trade: Infectious Disease in the Era of Global Trade*, UK: Ashgate Publishing.

Kolitch, S. (2006) 'The Environmental and Public Health Impacts of U.S. Patent Law: Making the Case for Incorporating a Precautionary Principle' 36(1) *Environmental Law* 221–56.

Kong, Q. (2002) 'Can the WTO Dispute Settlement Mechanism Resolve Trade Disputes between China and Taiwan?' 5 *Journal of International Economic Law* 747.

Kopelman, L.M., Resnick, D. and Weed, D.L. (2004) 'What is the Role of the Precautionary Principle in the Philosophy of Medicine and Bioethics?' 29(3) *Journal of Medicine and Philosophy* 255–8.

Kriebel, D. and Tickner, J. (2001) 'Reenergizing Public Health through Precaution' 91(9) *American Journal of Public Health* 1351.

Kriebel, D., Tickner, J., Epstein, P., Lemons, J., Levins, R., Loechler, E.L., Quinn, M., Rudel, R., Schettler, T. and Stoto, M. (2001) 'The Precautionary Principle in Environmental Science' 109(9) *Environmental Health Perspectives* 871.

Krikorian, G. (2009) 'The Politics of Patents: Conditions of Implementation of Public Health Policy in Thailand' in Haunss, S. and Shadlen, K.C. (eds) *Politics of Intellectual Property: Contestation Over the Ownership, Use, and Control of Knowledge and Information*, UK: Edward Elgar Publishing.

Laurie, G.T. (1996) 'Biotechnology and Intellectual Property: A Marriage of Inconvenience?' in McLean, S. (ed.) *Contemporary Issues in Law, Medicine and Ethics*, Chapter 12.

Laurie, G. (2004) 'Patenting Stem Cells of Human Origin' *European Intellectual Property Review* 59–66.

Laurie, G. and Hunter K. (2009) 'Mapping, Assessing and Improving Legal Preparedness for Pandemic Flu in the United Kingdom' 10(2) *Medical Law International* 101–37.

Leith, P. (2004) 'Software Patents', JISC Briefing Paper.

Leith, P. (2007) *Software and Patents in Europe*, New York: Cambridge University Press.

Lester, S., Mercurios, B. and Davies, A. (2012) *World Trade Law: Text, Materials and Commentary*, 2nd edn, Oxford: Hart Publishing.

Li, P.H. (2013) 'Rights and Responsibilities in Patents: A Precautionary Patent Framework in WTO Law' 9 *European Intellectual Property Review*.

Liddell, K. (2010) 'The Health Impact Fund: A Critique' in Pogge, T., Rimmer, M. and Rubenstein, K. (eds) *Incentives for Global Public Health: Patent Law and Access to Essential Medicines*, New York: Cambridge University Press.

Lin, T-Y (2010) 'The Forgotten Role of WHO/IHR in Trade Response to 2009 A/H1N1 Influenza Outbreak' 44(3) *Journal of World Trade* 515–43.

Lindsay, P. (2003) 'The Ambiguity of GATT Article XXI: Subtle Success or Rampant Failure?' 52 *Duke Law Journal* 1277.

Love, J. (2007a) 'Measures to Enhance Access to Medical Technologies, and New Methods of Stimulating Medical R & D' 40 *UC Davis Law Review* 679.

Love, J. (2007b) 'Recent Examples of the Use of Compulsory Licenses on Patents', KEI Research Note 2, 8 March.

Love, J. and Hubbard, T. (2007) 'The Big Idea: Prizes to Stimulate R & D for New Medicines' 82 *Chicago-Kent Law Review* 1519.

Bibliography 215

Mack, E. (2006) 'The World Health Organization's New International Health Regulations: Incursion on State Sovereignty and Ill-fated Response to Global Health Issues' 7 *Chicago Journal of International Law* 365.

Mackenzie, R. and Eggers, B. (2000) 'The Cartagena Protocol on Biosafety' *Journal of International Economic Law* 525–43.

MacMaolain, C. (2003) 'Using the Precautionary Principle to Protect Human Health: Pfizer v Council' 28(5) *European Law Review* 723–34.

McNelis, N. (2000) 'EU Communication on the Precautionary Principle' *Journal of International Economic Law* 545–51.

MacQueen, H.L. (2008) 'Towards Utopia or Irreconcilable Tensions? Thoughts on Intellectual Property, Human Rights and Competition Law' in Pattanaik, M.K. (ed.) *Human Rights and Intellectual Property*, India: The Icfai University Press.

MacQueen, H., Waelde, C., Laurie, G. and Brown, A. (2010) *Contemporary Intellectual Property: Law and Policy*, 2nd edn, New York: Oxford University Press.

McRae, D.M. (2000) 'GATT Article XX and the WTO Appellate Body' in Bronckers, M. and Quick, R. (eds) *New Directions in International Economic Law*, The Hague: Kluwer Law International.

Malbon, J. and Lawson C. (eds) (2008) *Interpreting and Implementing the TRIPS Agreement: Is it fair?*, Cheltenham, UK: Edward Elgar.

Marceau, G. and Trachtman, J.P. (2002) 'The Technical Barriers to Trade Agreement, the Sanitary and Phytosanitary Measures Agreement, and the General Agreement on Tariffs and Trade: A Map of the World Trade Organization Law of Domestic Regulation of Goods' 36(5) *Journal of World Trade* 811–81.

Marceau, G. and Trachtman, J. (2006) 'A Map of the World Trade Organization Law of Domestic Regulation of Goods' in Bermann, J. and Mavroidis, P. (eds) *Trade and Human Health and Safety*, New York: Cambridge University Press.

Martuzzi, M. (2007) 'The Precautionary Principle: In Action for Public Health' 64 *Occupational and Environmental Medicine* 569–670.

Mascher, S. (1997) 'Taking a "Precautionary Approach": Fisheries Management in New Zealand' 14 *European Public Law Journal* 70–79.

Maskus, K.E. and Reichman, J.M. (2004) 'The Globalisation of Private Knowledge Goods and the Privatisation of Global Public Goods' 7(2) *Journal of International Economic Law* 279.

Matthews, D. (2006) 'From the August 30, 2003 WTO Decision to the December 6, 2005 Agreement on an Amendment to TRIPS: Improving Access to Medicines in Developing Countries?' 2 *Intellectual Property Quarterly* 91–130.

Matthews, D. (2011) *Intellectual Property, Human Rights and Development: The Role of NGOs and Social Movements*, Gloucester: Edward Elgar Publishing.

Mehta, Michael D. (2001) 'Public Perceptions of Genetically Engineered Foods: Playing God or Trusting Science' 12 *Risk: Health, Safety and Environment* 205.

Meier, B.M. (2006) 'Employing Health Rights for Global Justice: the Promise of Public Health in Response to the Insalubrious Ramifications of Globalization' 39 *Cornell International Law Journal* 711.

Meier, B.M. (2007) 'Advancing Health Rights in a Globalized World: Responding to Globalization through a Collective Human Right to Public Health' 35 *Journal of Law, Medicine and Ethics* 545.

Meier, B.M. and Mori. L.M. (2005) 'The Highest Attainable Standard: Advancing A Collective Human Right to Public Health' 37 *Columbia Human Rights Law Review* 101.

216   Bibliography

Mercurio, B. (2006) 'Resolving the Public Health Crisis in the Developing World: Problems and Barriers of Access to Essential Medicines' 5 *Northwestern University Journal of International Human Rights* 1.

Milano, T.J. (2006) 'Understanding And Applying International Infectious Disease Law: U.N. Regulations During An H5N1Avian Flu Epidemic' 6 *Chicago-Kent Journal of International and Comparative Law* 26.

Mitchell, A.D. (2007) 'The Legal Basis for Using Principles in WTO Disputes' 10(4) *Journal of International Economic Law* 795.

Morris, J. (ed.) (2000) *Rethinking Risk and the Precautionary Principle*, Oxford: Butterworth-Heinemann.

Motaal, D.A. (2005) 'Is the WTO Anti-Precaution?' 39(3) *Journal of World Trade* 483–501.

Movsesian, M.L. (1999) 'Sovereignty, Compliance, and the World Trade Organization: Lessons from the History of Supreme Court Review' 20 *Michigan Journal of International Law* 775, 791–5.

Murphy, K.A. (2009) 'The Precautionary Principle in Patent Law: A View from Canada' 12(6) *The Journal of World Intellectual Property* 649–89.

Myers, N.J. and Raffensperger, C. (eds) (2006) *Precautionary Tools for Reshaping Environmental Policy*, Cambridge, Massachusetts: The MIT Press.

Nanda, N. and Lodha, R. (2002) 'Making Essential Medicines Affordable to the Poor' 20 *Wisconsin International Law Journal* 581.

Neumann, J. and Turk, E. (2003) 'Necessity Revisited: Proportionality in World Trade Organization Law after Korea – Beef, EC – Asbestos and EC – Sardines' 37(1) *Journal of World Trade* 199–233.

Ng, E.S.-K. (2010) 'The Impact of the Bilateral US–Singapore Free Trade Agreement on Singapore's Post-TRIPs Patent Regime in the Pharmaceutical Context' 16(5) *International Trade Law and Regulation* 121–8.

Nucara, A. (2003) 'Precautionary Principle and GMOs: Protection or Protectionism?' 9(2) *International Trade Law and Regulation* 47–53.

Oesch, M. (2003) 'Standards of Review in WTO Dispute Resolution' 6(3) *Journal of International Economic Law* 635.

Opderbeck, D.W. (2005) 'Patent, Essential Medicines, and the Innovation Game' 58 *Vanderbilt Law Review* 501.

O'Riordan, T. and Cameron, J. (eds) (1994) *Interpreting the Precautionary Principle*, London: Routledge.

Orrego Vicuña, F. (1999) *The Changing International Law of High Seas Fisheries*, Cambridge: Cambridge University Press.

Outterson, K. (2008) 'Should Access to Medicines and TRIPS Flexibilities be Limited to Specific Diseases?' 34 *American Journal of Law and Medicine* 279.

Overwalle, G.V. (2007) 'Reshaping Bio-patents: Measures to Restore Trust in the Patent System' in Somsen, H. (ed.) *The Regulatory Challenge of Biotechnology: Human Genetics, Food and Patents*, Cheltenham: Edward Elgar.

Park, J. (2005) 'Has Patentable Subject Matter Been Expanded? – A Comparative Study on Software Patent Practices in the European Patent Office, the United States Patent and Trademark Office and the Japanese Patent Office' 13 *International Journal of Law and Information Technology* 336.

Pearce, N. (2004) 'Public Health and the Precautionary Principle' in Martuzzi, M. and Tickner, J. (eds) *The Precautionary Principle: Protecting Public Health, the Environment and the Future of Our Children*, Copenhagen: WHO.

Peel, J. (2006) 'A GMO by Any Other Name ... Might Be an SPS Risk!: Implications of Expanding the Scope of the WTO Sanitary and Phytosanitary Measures Agreement' 17(5) *European Journal of International Law* 1009–31.

Pellerano, M.B. and Montague, P. (2006) 'Democratic Tools: Communities and Precaution' in Myers, N.J. and Raffensperger, C. (eds) *Precautionary Tools for Reshaping Environmental Policy*, Cambridge, MA: The MIT Press.

Perez, O. (2007) 'Anomalies at the Precautionary Kingdom: Reflections on the GMO Panel's Decision', 6(2) *World Trade Review* 265–80.

Perrez, F.X. (2003) 'The World Summit on Sustainable Development: Environment, Precaution and Trade – A Potential for Success and/or Failure' 12 *Review of European and International Environmental Law* 12.

Perrez, F.X. (2008) 'Risk Regulation, Precaution and Trade' in Wuger, D. and Cottier, T. (eds) (2008) *Genetic Engineering and the World Trade System: World Trade Forum*, New York: Cambridge University Press.

Petersen, A., Anderson, A., Wilkinson, C. and Allan, S. (2007) 'Nanotechnologies, Risk and Society' 9(2) *Health, Risk and Society* 117–24.

Petersmann, E.-U. (1997) *The GATT/WTO Dispute Settlement System: International Law, International Organization and Dispute Settlement*, London: Kluwer Law International.

Peterson, M. (2006) 'The Precautionary Principle Is Incoherent' 26(3) *Risk Analysis* 595.

Philbrick, M. and Barandiaran, J. (2009) 'The national Citizens' Technology Forum: Lessons for the Future' 36(5) *Science and Public Policy*.

Pogge, T. (2010) 'The Health Impact Fund: Better Pharmaceutical Innovations at Much Lower Prices' in Pogge, T., Rimmer, M. and Rubenstein, K. (eds) *Incentives for Global Public Health: Patent Law and Access to Essential Medicines*, New York: Cambridge University Press.

Porter, G., Denning, C., Plomer, A., Sinden, J. and Torremans, P. (2006) 'The Patentability of Human Embryonic Stem Cells in Europe' 24 *Nature Biotechnology* 653–5.

Priess, H.-J. and Pitschas, C. (2000) 'Protection of Public Health and the Role of the Precautionary Principle under WTO Law: A Trojan Horse before Geneva's Wall' 24 *Fordham International Law Journal* 519.

Raffensperger, C. and Tickner, J. (eds) (1999) *Protecting Public Health and the Environment: Implementing the Precautionary Principle*, Washington DC: Island Press.

Raustiala, K. (2003) 'Rethinking the Sovereignty Debate in International Economic Law' 6(4) *Journal of International Economic Law* 842.

Rodrigues, E.B. Jr (2012) *The General Exception Clauses of the TRIPS Agreement: Promoting Sustainable Development*, Cambridge: Cambridge University Press.

Rodrigues, E.B. Jr. and Murphy, B. (2006) 'Brazil's Prior Consent Law: A Dialogue between Brazil and the United States over where the TRIPS Agreement Currently Sets the Balance between the Protection of Pharmaceutical Patents and Access to Medicines' 16 *Albany Law Journal of Science and Technology* 423.

Rowlandson, M. (2010) 'The Ordre Public and Morality Exception and its Impact on the Patentability of Human Embryonic Stem Cells' 32(2) *European Intellectual Property Review* 67.

Ruessmann, L.A. (2002) 'Putting the Precautionary Principle in Its Place: Parameters for the Proper Application of a Precautionary Approach and the Implications for Developing Countries in Light of the Doha WTO Ministerial' 17 *American University International Law Review* 905.

218 Bibliography

Salmon, N. (2005) 'What's "novel" about it? Substantial equivalence, precaution and consumer protection 1997–2004' 7(2) *Environmental Law Review* 138–49.

Sampat, B.N., Shadlen, K.C. and Amin, T.M. (2012) 'Challenges to India's Pharmaceutical Patent Laws' 337 *Science* 414.

Sandin, P. (1999) 'Dimensions of the Precautionary Principle' 5(5) *Human and Ecological Risk Assessment* 889–907.

Sandin, P. (2004) 'Better Safe than Sorry: Applying Philosophical Methods to the Debates on Risk and the Precautionary Principle' Doctoral Thesis in Philosophy, Royal Institute of Technology, Stockholm.

Sandin, P. (2005) 'Naturalness and De Minimis Risk' 27(2) *Environmental Ethics* 191–200.

Sandin, P. (2006) 'A Paradox out of Context: Harris and Holm on the Precautionary Principle' 15(2) *Cambridge Quarterly of Health Care Ethics* 175–83.

Sands, P. (2003) *Principles of International Environmental Law*, 2nd edn, Cambridge: Cambridge University Press.

Sapsin, J.W., Gostin, L.O., Vernick, J.S., Burris, S., Teret, S.P. (2004) 'SARS and International Legal Preparedness Symposium on SARS, Public Health, and Global Governance' 77 *Temple Law Review* 155: 158–60.

Savoie, B. (2007) 'Thailand's Test: Compulsory Licensing in an Era of Epidemiologic Transition' 48 *Virginia Journal of International Law* 211.

Scherer, F.M. and Watal, J. (2002) 'Post-TRIPS Options for Access to Patented Medicines in Developing Nations' 5(4) *Journal of International Economic Law* 913–39.

Scott, J. (2009) *The WTO Agreement on Sanitary and Phytosanitary Measures: A Commentary*, New York: Oxford University Press.

Segger, M.-C. and Gehring, M.W. (2003a) 'Precaution, Health and the World Trade Organization: Moving toward Sustainable Development' 29 *Queen's Law Journal* 133.

Segger, M.-C. and Gehring, M.W. (2003b) 'The WTO and Precaution: Sustainable Development Implications of the WTO Asbestos Dispute' 15 *Journal of Environmental Law* 289.

Sell, S.K. (2002) 'Post-TRIPS Developments: The Tension between Commercial and Social Agendas in the Context of Intellectual Property' 14 *Florida Journal of International Law* 193.

Sell, S.K. (2003) *Private Power, Public Law: The Globalization of Intellectual Property Rights*, Cambridge: Cambridge University Press.

Sell, S.K. (2004) 'The Quest for Global Governance in Intellectual Property and Public Health: Structural, Discursive, and Institutional Dimensions' 77 *Temple Law Review* 363.

Sen, A. (2013) 'WTO Unimpressed with Patent Violation Charges against India' *The Hindu Business Line*, 26 April.

Sherman, P.B. (2004) 'Pandemics and Panaceas: The World Trade Organization's Efforts to Balance Pharmaceutical Patents and Access to AIDS Drugs' 41 *American Business Law Journal* 353.

Somsen, H. (ed.) (2007) *The Regulatory Challenge of Biotechnology: Human Genetics, Food and Patents*, Cheltenham: Edward Elgar.

Somsen, H. (2008) 'Cloning Trojan Horses' in Brownsword, R. and Yeung, K. (eds) *Regulating Technologies: Legal Futures, Regulatory Frames and Technological Fixes*, Portland: Hart Publishing.

Stiglitz, J. (2003) *Globalization and Its Discontents*, New York: W.W. Norton & Company.

Bibliography 219

Stiglitz, J.E. and Jayadev, A. (2013) 'India's Patently Wise Decision' *Project Syndicate*, 8 April 2013.

Stirling, A. (1999) On Science and Precaution in the Management of Technological Risk, Final Report of a project for the EC Forward Studies Unit under the auspices of the ESTO Network.

Streinz, R. (1998) 'The Precautionary Principle in Food Law' 8 *European Food Law Review* 413.

Streinz, R. (2009) 'Risks Decisions in Cases of Persisting Scientific Uncertainty: The Precautionary Principle in European Food Law' in Woodman, G.R. and Klippel, D. (eds) *Risk and the Law*, New York: Routledge-Cavendish.

Sun, Haochen (2004) 'The Road to Doha and Beyond: Some reflections on the TRIPS Agreement and Public Health' 15 *European Journal Of International Law* 123.

Sunstein, C. (2005) *Laws of Fear: Beyond the Precautionary Principle*, Cambridge: Cambridge University Press.

Sunstein, C. (2009) 'Trimming' 122 *Harvard Law Review* 1049.

Sunstein, C.R. (2010) 'Irreversibility' 9 *Law, Probability and Risk* 227–45.

Suthersanen, U., Dutfield, G. and Chow, K.B. (eds) (2007) *Innovation without Patents: Harnessing the Creative Spirit in a Diverse World*, Cheltenham: Edward Elgar.

Tait, J. (2001) 'More Faust than Frankenstein: The European Debate about the Precautionary Principle and Risk Regulation for Genetically Modified Crops' 4(2) *Journal of Risk Research* 175–89.

Taubman, A. (2008a) 'Unfair Competition and the Financing of Public-Knowledge Goods: The Problem of Test Data Protection' 3(9) *Journal of Intellectual Property Law and Practice* 591.

Taubman, A. (2008b) 'Rethinking TRIPS: "Adequate Compensation" for non-voluntary Patent Licensing' *Journal of International Economic Law* 927.

Taubman, A. (2011) *A Practical Guide to Working with TRIPS*, New York: Oxford University Press.

Taylor, R. (2009) 'In Practice: Legal Update: Hard Choice over Software' 3 *Law Society Gazette*.

Teegarden, H. (2004) *Patents Throughout the World*, USA: Clark Boardman Callaghan, West Group.

Thailand, the Ministry of Public Health and the National Health Security Office (2007) 'Facts and Evidences on the 10 Burning Issues Related to the Government Use of Patents on Three Patented Essential Drugs in Thailand', Document to Support Strengthening of Social Wisdom on the Issue of Drug Patents, ISBN 978-974-94591-5-7.

Tickner, J.A. (ed.) (2003) *Precaution, Environmental Science and Preventive Public Policy*, Washington DC: Island Press.

Tickner, J. and Kriebel, D. (2006) 'The Role of Science and Precaution in Environmental and Public Health Policy' in Fisher, E., Jones, J. and von Schomberg, R. (eds) *Implementing the Precautionary Principle: Perspectives and Prospects*, Cheltenham: Edward Elgar.

Tinker, C. (1996a) 'State Responsibility and the Precautionary Principle' in Freestone, D. and Hey, E. (eds) *The Precautionary Principle and International Law: The Challenge of Implementation*, The Hague, Kluwer Law International.

Tinker, C. (1996b) 'State Responsibility for Biological Diversity Conservation under International Law' in Freestone, D. and Hey, E. (eds) *The Precautionary Principle and International Law: The Challenge of Implementation*, The Hague: Kluwer Law International.

220 Bibliography

Torremans, P. (ed.) (2008) *Intellectual Property and Human Rights: Enhanced Edition of Copy Right and Human Rights*, The Hague: Kluwer Law International.

Transatlantic Consumer Dialogue (2000) Recommendations on Health Care and Intellectual Property, Doc. No. Health-4-00, Early Working of Patents and Research Exceptions, February 2000. Available at: http://tacd.org/index.php?option=com_docman&task=cat_view&gid=76&Itemid=40

Trouwborst, A. (2002) *Evolution and Status of the Precautionary Principle in International Law*, International Environmental Law and Policy Series, The Hague: Kluwer Law International.

Trouwborst, A. (2006) *Precautionary Rights and Duties of States*, Leiden: Martinus Nijhoff Publishers.

Tsang, K.W.T. (2005) 'H5N1 Influenza Pandemic: Contingency Plans' 366 *Lancet* 553–4.

UNCTAD-ICTSD (2005) *UNCTAD-ICTSD Resource Book on TRIPS and Development*, Cambridge: Cambridge University Press.

Van den Bossche, P. (2008) *The Law and Policy of the World Trade Organization – Text, Cases and Materials*, 2nd edn, New York: Cambridge University Press.

VanderZwaag, D. (1994) *CEPA and the Precautionary Principle/Approach*. Hull, Quebec: Minister of Supply and Services

Verkerk, R. (2009) 'Codex Alimentarius: Focus on True Threats, not Disinformation' 77 *Caduceus* 24.

Von Tigerstrom, B. (2005) 'The Revised International Health Regulations and Restraint of National Health Measures' 13 *Health Law Journal* 35–76.

Wadlow, C. (2008) 'Regulatory data protection under TRIPs Article 39(3) and article 10 bis of the Paris Convention: is there a doctor in the house?' *Intellectual Property Quarterly*.

Waelde, C. and MacQueen, H. (eds) (2007) *Intellectual Property: The Many Faces of the Public Domain*, Cheltenham: Edward Elgar.

Wakely, J. (2011a) 'Compulsory Licensing under TRIPs: An Effective Tool to Increase Access to Medicines in Developing and Least Developed Countries' 33(5) *European Intellectual Property Review* 299–309.

Wakely, J. (2011b) 'The Impact of External Factors on the Effectiveness of Compulsory Licensing as a Means of Increasing Access to Medicines in Developing Countries' 33(12) *European Intellectual Property Review* 756–70.

Walker, E.M. (2007) 'The HIV/AIDS Pandemic and Human Rights: A Continuum Approach' 19 *Florida Journal of International Law* 335.

Weed, D. (2004) 'Precaution, Prevention, and Public Health Ethics' 29(3) *Journal of Medicine and Philosophy* 313–32.

Weinberg, J. (2005) 'The Impact of Globalisation on Emerging Infectious Disease' in Lee, K. and Collin, J. (eds) *Global Change and Health*, London School of Hygiene and Tropical Medicines, Open University Press 56–9

Welsh, R. and Ervin, D.E. (2006) 'Precaution as an Approach to Technology Development: The Case of Transgenic Crops' 31(2) *Science, Technology and Human Values* 153–72.

Whiteside, K.H. (2006) *Precautionary Politics: Principle and Practice in Confronting Environmental Risk*, Cambridge, MA: MIT Press.

Wiener, J. and Rogers, M. (2002) 'Comparing Precaution in the United States and Europe' 5 *Journal of Risk Research* 317, 320–21.

Winham, G. (2003) 'International Regime Conflict in Trade and Environment: The Biosafety Protocol and the WTO' 2(2) *World Trade Review* 131.

Winter, G. (2003) 'The GATT and Environmental Protection: Problems of Construction' 15 *Journal of Environmental Law* 113.

Woodman, G.R. and Klippel, D. (eds) (2009) *Risk and the Law*, New York: Routledge-Cavendish.

Writing Committee of the World Health Organization (WHO) Consultation on Human Influenza A/H5 (2005) 'Avian Influenza A (H5N1) Infection in Humans 353 *New England Journal of Medicine* 1374–85.

Wuger, D. and Cottier, T. (eds) (2008) *Genetic Engineering and the World Trade System: World Trade Forum*, New York: Cambridge University Press.

Yamane, H. (2011) *Interpreting TRIPS: Globalisation of Intellectual Property Rights and Access to Medicines*, Oxford: Hart Publishing.

Young, M.A. (2007) 'The WTO's Use of Relevant Rules of International Law: An Analysis of the Biotech Case' 56(4) *International and Comparative Law Quarterly* 907–30.

Yuan, K.Y. (2009) 'The Public Health and Clinical Perspective of Emerging Infectious Diseases: From Avian to Swine Flu' 41st Asia-Pacific Academic Consortium for Public Health ('APACPH') Conference, 3 December 2009, Taipei, Taiwan.

Index

Entries in italic refer to tables or figures.

Aarhus Convention (2003) 73
Abbott, F.C. 13, 38
Abbott Laboratories 162
acceptability: right to health 7
Acceptable Daily Intake (ADI) 98
acceptable level of risk 74
access to information 73
access to medicines: anti-competitive
  approach 15; Bolar exception 147; Brazil
  152; compulsory licensing 14; essential
  8, 10, 11, 23–4, 154; overprotection as
  an obstruction to 13; a PA and enhanced
  3; political reality and power asymmetry
  18; right to 8; tension between IP and 17
accessibility: right to health 7
action: as key element of the PA 65, *see
  also* precautionary action
Action Programme on Essential Drugs
  (WHO) 7
Action Programmes on the Environment
  (1973 to 1992) 56
additional conservatism 171
additional health measures 89, 90, 93, 94–6
additional safety factor 98–9, 152
Advanced Informed Agreement (AIA) 101
advisory committees (NICE) 52
affirmative defence 17, *105*, 131, *132*,
  133, 149
Agenda 21 (Rio Declaration) 73
Agreement on the Application of Sanitary
  and Phytosanitary Measures *see* SPS
  Agreement
Agreement on Technical Barriers to Trade
  see TBT Agreement
agricultural products: varietal testing
  requirement 121–2
AIDS *see* HIV/AIDS

air pollution legislation: and emergence of
  PA 51
Alpharma Inc. 59
Alpharma Inc v. the Council of the EU
  60–1, 69, 70
alternative assessment 89
ambiguity: of GATT XXI 118
amicus briefs 184–5
animal feed: antibiotics in 59–60, 69
Annex 2 (IHRs) 92
Annex III (CPB) 102
anthrax threat 160
Anti-Catastrophe Principle 64, 71–4,
  77, 149
anti-competitiveness 14–15
antibiotics: in animal feed 59–60, 69
anticipated harm 64, 66, 71, 82
anticipatory action 51
antiretroviral drugs 8
antiviral drugs 91, 161, 164, 175
anuencia previa 152–3
ANVISA 152–3
Aolain, F.N. 148
Appellate Body (WTO): *Australia –
  Salmon* 69; *Canada – Pharmaceutical
  Patents* 34, 35; cautious approach 13–14,
  134; conditional rights *105*; discretion to
  accept amicus briefs 185; *EC – Asbestos*
  35, 107, 125; *EC – Hormones* 124;
  EC – Biotech 125, 126; *EC – Hormones*
  69, 79, 123; *EC – Sardines* 129; *Japan –
  Varietals* 121–2; *Philippines – Taxes on
  Distilled Spirits* 35–6; SPS measures as
  a temporary safety valve 132; *US – Tuna*
  130; *US – Cloves* 129; *US – Gasoline* 109;
  "weighing and balancing" process 109,
  110, 112

applied-ethics approach 50, 63
appreciable harm 66
approach: use of term 80, 81, 82
appropriate/acceptable level of protection
(ALOP): adoption of additional health
measures 95; compulsory licensing 165,
172; determining 61, 74, 90, 106–8;
right to achieve/establish 37, 57–8, 110;
right to determine 40, 60, 93, 157, 158,
172; SPS Agreement 106–7, 119–20,
133; TBT Agreement 127, 133
Argentina 125, 138
argumentative PA 64–5, 65, 76
Article 1 (CPB) 102
Article 2 (SPS) 126
Article 2.1 (TBT) 128
Article 2.2 (SPS) 125
Article 3(b) (Indian Patents Act) 150
Article 3.1 (SPS) 123
Article 3.3 (SPS) 106, 119, 123
Article 5 (SPS) 123
Article 5.1 (SPS) 123, 125
Article 5.7 (SPS) 106, 119, 122, 123, 132
Article 6 (Codex Stan 94) 129
Article 7 (EC Basic Regulation) 56–7
Article 7 (TRIPS) 13, 14, 157
Article 8 (TRIPS) 13, 14, 157
Article 8.1 (TRIPS) 158
Article 10.6 (CPB) 102
Article 11.8 (CPB) 102
Article 12 (ICESCR) 7
Article 12(1) (ICESCR) 7
Article 12.2(c) (ICESCR) 7
Article 15.1(c) (ICESCR) 6
Article 17(d) (IHRs) 91
Article 23 (Cartagena Protocol) 73
Article 25(1) (UDHR) 7
Article 27 (TRIPS) 16, 34
Article 27 (UDHR) 6
Article 27(2) (TRIPS) 40
Article 27(3) (TRIPS) 40
Article 27.1 (TRIPS) 33, 34, 36
Article 27.2 (TRIPS) 150
Article 28 (TRIPS) 16
Article 28.1 (TRIPS) 148
Article 30 (TRIPS) 34, 147, 148
Article 31 (TRIPS) 154, 155–6, 165
Article 31(b) (TRIPS) 162
Article 31(f) (TRIPS) 20
Article 31f (TRIPS) 159
Article 31(h) (TRIPS) 20
Article 33 (TRIPS) 148
Article 38(1)(c) (*Statute of the ICJ*) 79
Article 39.3 (TRIPS) 21–2

Article 68 (IPL, Brazil) 16
Article 73 (TRIPS) 149
Article 114 (TFEU) 58
Article 191 (TFEU) 58
Article 191.2 (TFEU) 75
Article III: 4 (GATT) 35
Article X: 3 (TRIPS) 20
Article XIX (GATT) 115
Article XX(b) (GATT) 108, 109, 111, 112,
118, 127, 158
Article XX(g) (GATT) 109
Article XXI (GATT) 116–18, 148, 149
Article XXI(b) (GATT) 113–14
asbestos case (EC) 35, 38, 107, 108, 109,
110–11, 125
Asia 19, 24
Australia 19, 48, 55–6, 67, 70
Australia – Salmon 69
autonomous rights 120, 123, 127, 150,
157, 158, 165
availability: right to health 7
avian flu 24, 160–1

Bayer Inc. 160
Bayh-Dole Act 15
Belgium 154
beta crystalline form: imatinib mesylate
150, 151
bias: due to globalized patent regime 22
bilateral trade agreements 10
bioavailability 151
biodiversity 75, 101
biosafety: protocol *see* Cartagena Protocol
on Biosafety
Biosafety Clearing-House 101
biotechnology(ies) 100–3, 128, *see also*
EC – Biotech
bioterrorism 40
bird flu *see* avian flu
Birnie, P. 51, 55, 79–80
Bloche, M.G. 9, 159
Bolar exception 147
bovine spongiform encephalopathy (BSE)
crisis 56, 78, 107
Brazil 8, 9, 15–16, 17, 152–3
Brazil – Retreaded Tyres 111–12
Bronitt, S. 76
Brown, A.E.L. 38–9
Brownsword, R. 52, 64
burden of proof 140; allocation of 78,
99, 116; ALOP 123, 158; and the
application of the PP 59; Cartagena
Protocol 137–8; *EC – Sardines* 129;
IHRs 137; public health emergency 149;

224 *Index*

reversal of 71, 76, 105, 106, 132; SPS
Agreement 127
Button, C. 107, 183

Canada 19, 20, 24, 110–11, 124, 125, 147,
160, 162
Canada – Pharmaceutical Patents 34, 35,
37, 38, 108, 147–8
cancer drugs 17, 162–4
carcinogenicity 35
Cartagena Protocol on Biosafety 73,
100–3; Articles *see* Articles; duty of
review in 180; the PA in 51; versus SPS
Agreement 137–8
Carvalho, N.P. 14, 157, 158
cause and effect 69, 75
cautious approach 13–14, 134, 157
cell fusion 100
certain risks 68
Chapeau 112
Charnovitz, S. 105, 165
Checklist for Influenza Pandemic
Preparedness Planning (WHO) 176
chronic diseases: compulsory licensing 162
cigarettes 109–10, 129
ciprofloxacin 160, 162
citizens' preferences 182–3
climate change 6, 23, 51, 53, 54, 128
clinical data 21, 22
clopidogrel 162
clove cigarettes 129
Codex Alimentarius 51, 56, 60, 73–4, 89,
96–100, 138
Codex Stan 94 129
collaboration 9, 91
command dimension: of the PA 65
Commissaire du Gouvernement Légal
(France) 37
Commission On Intellectual Property
Rights, Innovation and Public Health
(CIPIH) 10, 11, 19
Commissions on Human Rights Resolution
(UN) 10
Committee on Economic, Social and
Cultural Rights (CESCR) 6, 7
Committee on the Revision of Patent Laws
(1957-59) 8
commonsense: PP as a statement of 50
*Communication on the Precautionary
Principle* (EC) 56, 58–9, 69, 98
Community institutions: and
the PP 59–60, 61
compensation rules 71
compensatory regime: data protection 21

competition 13, 22, 38, 130, 147, 151
competitiveness: in "like-product" analysis
35–6
complexity: uncertainty due to 68
compulsory labels 128
compulsory licensing/licences 14, 40,
41–2; as an autonomous right 165;
as an exclusion to IP 164–5; as an
exemption from TRIPS obligations 13;
as a conditional right 133, 158, 171–3;
conditions for granting 14–17; data
exclusivity 21; as a diplomatic threatening
tool 164; discretion in 114; Doha
Declaration 19, 41, 155, 157, 165, 172,
190; in emergency situations 19, 174–85;
government resentment 22; interpretation
of 13, 14; invocation of 81; legal status
17; limited number of countries taking
advantage of 17; margin of safety 172,
185–6; most significant barrier to using
19; notification system for triggering
159; pharmaceuticals and the differential
treatment of adopting the PA 173–4;
post-grant exemptions 36; precautionary
entitlements 177–9, 183; redefinition of,
through the PA 171–3; state hesitation in
granting 191; as tool to limit IP protection
154–6; trade retaliation in response to 18;
trend of 160–4; trigger threshold 17, 19,
159, 172, 174–6
conditional rights (excluding rules) 104,
105; compulsory licensing as 133, 158,
171–3; distinction between exception
rules and 106; higher level of health
protection as a 119, 123, 134; the PA
as 131–2; version of PA *134*, *see also*
health exclusions
Conference of the Parties to the
Convention on Biodiversity (2000) 100
confined within definite limits 148
consistency 52, 58, 59, 122
Consolidated Versions of the Treaty on
European Union 57
constitutions: and the right to health 8–9
constructive PA 89
consultation 71
Consultative Mechanism 16
Contracting Parties 117
"contrary to public health" 153
Convention on Biological Diversity (UN) 75
*Convention on Straddling and Highly
Migratory Fish Stocks* (1995) 80
cooperation: on research on impacts of
LMOs 102

Index 225

Correa, C.M. 17, 21, 149, 150, 158
cost-benefit analysis 52, 59, 64, 78, 89, 140
cost-effectiveness 23, 54, 81
costs: of environmental harm 49
counterfeiting 22
Court of First Instance (CFI) 56, 59–60
Crown use: and compulsory licensing (UK) 16
Cuba 37–8, 115
cultural preferences 182–3
cultural traditions: desired level of protection 107
cumulative scientific information 180
customary international law 57, 79, 80

damage *see* potential harm/damage; serious or irreversible harm/damage
data exclusivity 21–2, 194
De Sadeleer, N. 68, 179
Dealing with Uncertainty Report (WHO) 89
decision-making: in compulsory licensing 19; PA as integral part of 49, 51; participatory 71, 72, 73, 181; WTO provisions 11
defensive bargaining tool: compulsory licensing as 18
deliberative democracy 64, 78, 97, 135, 183
Department of Health (Taiwan) 161
Department of Health (UK) 81
developed countries 18, 154
developing countries 12, 14, 18, 22, 32, 153, 183
differential pricing 163
differential treatment: adopting the PA in compulsory licensing of pharmaceutical patents 173–4; legitimacy of 13, 32–7, 39
diplomacy 18, 113, 114, 115, 116, 164
direct data protection 21
Directive 2001/18/EC 58, 125
Director General of the WHO 91
discretion: over use of term "contrary to public health" 153, *see also* member discretion; state discretion
discrimination 33, 34–5, 120, 173–4, *see also* non-discrimination
disease(s): compulsory licensing of chronic 162; containment 90; emergence of newly discovered infectious 23; globalized patent regime and neglect of 22, *see also individual diseases*; virus surveillance; virus transmission
dispute resolution: compulsory licensing 17
Dispute Settlement Body (DSB) 12, 16, 106, 110, 115, 124, 147, 149

Dispute Settlement System (DSS) 9, 96, 104, 157, 184–5
disputed measures: examination of 112
distinct higher authority 180
distributive justice 64, 78
Doha Declaration 10, 17, 193; compulsory licensing 19, 41, 155, 165, 172, 190; flexibilities in TRIPS 17, 20, 155–6; and public health 40, 156–60
"dolphin-safe" labelling schemes 130
drugs *see* medicines
duty: of information disclosure 72, 78; scientific assessment and monitoring 55, *see also* states' rights and duties
duty to review 70, 78, 140, 179–80

early warnings: late lessons from 136
early working exception 147
Ebola 91
economic benefits: willingness to take risks 24
economic development: at price of pandemic outbreaks 24
economic factors: in determining ALOP 120
economic instruments: use of 71
economic perspective: the PA from an 64
economic welfare 114
Efavirenz 17
effective conservation 55, 70
efficacy: test of 151
Emergency Committee (WHO) 91
emergency risk management for health (ERMH) 24
enabling precaution 49
enforcement 12, 13, 22, 76, 137, 153, 157, 178
environmental awareness 73
environmental deterioration 24, 53
environmental education 73
environmental impact assessment 54–5
environmental law 50, 56, 58, 62, 63
environmental policy 47, 49, 50, 53, 54
environmental protection 32, 47, 48, 56, 58
environmental regulations 49, 137
environmental risks 51, 54
environmental treaties 50, 56, 62, 138
epistemological uncertainty 68
essential medicines 7, 8, 10, 11, 23–4, 154
essential security interests 114, 116, 149
essential technologies 38
ethical debates: inclusion of pharmaceuticals in the IP regime 164
ethical differentiation: health technologies 32–40, 135

226 *Index*

European Commission (EC): *Communication on the Precautionary Principle* 56, 58–9, 69, 98; examination of scientific developments 180; reference to *World Charter for Nature* 54; on scientific uncertainty 68

European Community (EC): Directive 2001/18 58, 125; *EC – Asbestos* 35, 38, 107, 108, 109, 110–11, 125; *EC – Biotech* 76, 108, 124–6, 133, 135, 136, 138; *EC – Continued Suspension (Hormones II)* 108, 124; *EC – Hormones* 69, 79, 108, 123, 124, 133; *EC – Sardines* 128–9; Regulation 258/97 125

European Council Resolution on the Precautionary Principle 59, 78

European Court of Human Rights 149

European Court of Justice (ECJ) 49, 56, 61, 69, 70, 71

European Environment Agency (EEA) 48, 89, 136

European Patent Convention (EPC) 154

European Patent Office (EPO) 150, 154

European Union (EU): *Brazil - Retreaded Tyres* 111–12; consideration of the PA in structure of risk analysis 98; free trade and complaints against 9; Helms-Burton Act 115–16; and the PP 56–61; public health protection 37

evidence-based approach 47, 174

examination: of disputed measures 112; of scientific developments 59, 180

exception(s): interpretation of, TRIPS 148; to patent rights 34

exception rules/provisions 104, 105; distinction between excluding rules and 106; interpretation of 106; version of PA *134*, *see also* health exception; security exception

excess marketing 22

excluding provisions *see* conditional rights

exemptions: from WTO obligations 104, 105–6, 130–4

experimental-use exceptions 147

exporters: notification under the AIA 101

extreme urgency *see* national emergency

fairness 52

fear 107

Federal Food, Drug and Cosmetic Act (FFDCA) 129

"field of technology": banning of discrimination in 33; differentiation

based on 36; public interests and exceptions to patent rights 34

flexibilities in TRIPS 146; access to essential medicines 10; Doha Declaration 17, 20, 156–7; pharmaceutical products and limit on use of 21; restraint against exercising 12; taking advantage of 153, 191

flexibility: of GATT XXI 118

Food and Agriculture Organization (FAO) 60, 96, 97

food labelling 100

food law 56

food and medicine: compulsory licensing 16

food products: scientific evidence for banning 135–6

food safety 56, 59–60, 96–100

food standards 96

footwear: import restrictions 114–15

forecaring/foresight principle 51

four-if formula 64, 65

Fourth Ministerial Declaration on Environment and Health (WHO) 88

France 37, 40, 110, 154, 164

free trade 9, 81, 104; enforcement 12; as goal of economic globalization 32; moderate precaution 88; non-discrimination in 33–4, 122; possibility of virus transmission 11; reconciliation of health protection and 93; tension between health and global 11, 134; to promote human health 9; and unknown risks 12

Free Trade Agreements (FTAs) 20–1

Freestone, D. 49, 62, 75

future generations: precaution as a giving voice to 49

Gabcikovo–Nagymaros case 54–5, 67, 180

GATT: Articles *see* Articles; "like product" analysis 35; the PA in 108–18, 130–1; philosophy of 32–3

General Assembly (UN) 53, 54

General Comments (UN): (No. 14) 7, 177; (No. 17) 6

General Principles of Food Law in the European Union (1997) 56

general public health measures 93, *94*

generic drugs 21, 147, 182

genetically modified organisms (GMOs) 58, 73, 100, 125, *see also EC – Biotech*

geographical situations: compulsory licensing 183

Germany 51, 78, 164

Gervais, D. 14

global collaboration/cooperation 9, 90
global governance 9
global market access 33, 104
Global Outbreak Alert and Response
   Network (GOARN) 91, 175
global quota system: for shoes, Sweden
   114, 115
global virus surveillance network 89–96,
   161, 172
globalization 3, 24, 32, 40, 90, 134–5
Globalization and Access to Drugs (WHO)
   10
globalized patent regime 22
*Goals and Principles of Environmental
   Impact Assessment* 54
Gostin, L.O. 182
government leadership: in preparedness
   and response and 177
Government Pharmaceutical Organization
   (Thailand) 162
Gowers Review of Intellectual Property 14
Grando, M.T. 105
grave harm 67
Gross, O. 148

H1N1 9, 24, 91
H5N1 17, 24, 161
Hahn, M.J. 116–17
Hatch-Waxman Act (1984) 154
health: MDGs and improvement of 8; as a
   sub-species of *ordre public* 150; tension
   between global free trade and 11, 134,
   see also public health; right to health
health crises: as national emergencies 157
health effects: role in distinguishing
   likeness of products 181–2
health exception (GATT) 108–9; definition
   of necessary 131; precautionary
   measures under 109–12; purpose of
   109; rules and principles of the PA in
   112–13; weak PA 130
health exception (TRIPS) 147–8
health exclusions: patent protection 40;
   TRIPS 149–65
Health Impact Fund (HIF) 22–3
health impacts: legitimate differentiation
   of technologies 36; serious 92
health measures: as an autonomous right
   150; as a conditional right 134; least
   restrictive to trade 91; necessity test 177;
   public interest and adoption of 13, *see
   also* additional health measures
health policy: evidence-based approach
   47; margin of safety 49; precautionary

approach 49; public engagement 73;
   risk assessment as basis for 123; state
   sovereignty 93
health protection: and adoption of the
   PA 61; as a de facto interpretive
   principle 159; differentiation of health
   technologies 36; evidence-based
   approach 174; highest priority given to
   37; measures *see* health measures; the PA
   as integral to decision-making process in
   49, 51; sporadic application of PA 137;
   State responsibility 37, 52; WHO 9, 93;
   WTO member autonomy 12, *see also*
   appropriate/acceptable level of protection
health regulation: influence of the PA 63;
   State stewardship model 52, *see also*
   International Health Regulations
health risks: cautious approach 157;
   differential treatment of products
   36; elimination of trade barriers 12;
   globalization 24, 40; health technologies
   associated with 39–40; "like-product"
   analysis 35, 37–9; of products, and
   consumer behaviour 182; waste tyre
   accumulation 111
health technologies: ethical differentiation
   32–40, 135
Helms-Burton Act (1996) 115–16
Hey, E. 49, 62, 75
hierarchy of risks 68
high prices (drugs) 8, 22
high probability of a serious harm 64, 71, 78
higher level of health protection 37, 57, 93,
   95, 119, 120, 123, 134, 177, 180
higher-than-normal safety factor 98
HIV/AIDS: access to essential drugs
   23–4; compulsory licensing 15, 16, 17;
   free delivery of antiretroviral drugs 8;
   hesitation in declaring a public emergency
   19; PA approach to contaminated blood
   37; pricing and IP protection of drugs 10;
   as target of MDGs 8
Howse, R. 33–4
human rights 6–7, 38, 149
Hungary 54, 67
Hunter, K. 81
hypothetical approach: to risk 69

imatinib mesylate: beta crystalline form
   150, 151
import bans 91, 109, 110, 111–12, 121, 123
import decisions 101, 102
import restrictions: footwear, Sweden 114–15
importers 101, 102–3

228 *Index*

in vitro nucleic acid techniques 100
independent review: of compulsory
  licensing 180
India 8, 9, 17, 150, 162–4
India – Pharmaceutical Patents 37, 108
indispensability: of pharmaceuticals 182
individual choice 52
Industrial Property Law (Brazil) 153
infectious diseases 23
influenza 24, 176, 179, *see also* avian flu;
  swine flu
information: access to 73; exchange/
  sharing 74, 101; right to 67, 78;
  uncertainty due to lack of 68
information disclosure: burden of 82; duty
  of 72, 78; recognition of need for 137
Information Disclosure Precautionary
  Approach (IDPA) 64, 71, 72, 82, 92, 99,
  117, 127, 130, 140, 153, 159–60
Information Disclosure Precautionary
  Principle (IDPP) 180
injustice: of patent monopoly system 22
innovation: Indian IP regime as stifling
  151; and patent protection 164;
  technological 13, 38, 147
insignificant risks 66
intelligibility 63
intergenerational equity 49
Intergovernmental Agreement on the
  Environment (1992) 48
International Chamber of Commerce 70
International Court of Justice (ICJ) 53,
  54–5, 180
International Covenant on Economic,
  Social and Cultural Rights (ICESCR)
  6, 7, 37
international environmental treaties 50,
  56, 62
International Health Regulations (IHRs):
  the PA in 51, 89–96; State responsibility
  172; versus SPS Agreement 137
international law 65; customary 57, 79,
  80; environmental 50, 58, 62, 63;
  fragmentation of risk regulation in 23–5;
  interpretation of 157; the PA in 53, 64,
  70, 79; State responsibility 52, 172, *see
  also* Cartagena Protocol on Biosafety;
  World Health Organization; World Trade
  Organization
International Law Commission (ILC) 66, 67
international policy 62
international political atmosphere: and
  moderation of strong PA 118
international standards 130, 133, 135

international trade: PA as a tool for
  protectionism 66
International Tribunal of the Law of the
  Sea (ITLOS) 54, 55, 70
interpretation: of compulsory licensing 13,
  14; of exception rules 106; of GATT
  XXI 116–17; national security interests
  149; of public international law 157; of
  treaties 13; of TRIPS 13–14
investigation teams (WHO) 91
IP: an holistic approach to 41–2; autonomy
  in the limitation of 34; CIPIH report on
  10; as a human right 6–7; interpretation
  and understanding of, through global
  health 11; medicines beyond 22–3;
  role and function of 13; TRIPS and
  objectives of 13
IP protection: discretion in limiting 183;
  field of technology 33; social and
  economic welfare 157–8; technological
  innovation 13; trimming *see* trimming;
  TRIPS 146
IP regime: access to medicines 3, 17;
  inclusion of pharmaceutical products in
  164; the PA and risk analysis as a safety
  valve in 24–5
IPRs: agreement on trade-related *see*
  TRIPS; as an incentive to product
  development 10; on need for a broader
  perspective 14; pharmaceutical patents
  20–1; right to health 6–7, 24
Ireland 69
irreversible harm *see* serious or irreversible
  harm/damage
it considers necessary 114, 116, 131
Italy 164

Jackson, J. 18
Japan – Varietals 121–2, 124, 133
Jayadev, A. 151
Joint Expert Committee on Food Additives
  (JECFA) 98
Jones, J. 76
judicial review 116, 117, 156, 180
Jungman, E.R. 9
justifiable differential treatment 36, 38, 41

Kimball, A.M. 24
knowledge diffusion 147
Kriebel, D. 49, 51, 62

labelling 100, 128–30, 133
lack of scientific certainty 48, 63, 69, 75,
  101, 102

Index 229

lack of scientific evidence 100, 176
Laing J 80
Lamy, P. 163
last mile problem 22
last resort 76, 117, 131
late lessons: from early warnings 136
Laurie, G. 81
Leahy-Smith America Invents Act 154
least inconsistent 112
least restrictive measure (LRM) test 178–9
least restrictive to trade 57, 71, 91, 92, 95, 99, 112, 126, 140
legal hierarchy: of exemptions from WTO obligations 105–6, 130–4; of the precautionary approach in TRIPS *159*
legal instruments: PA appearance in 51
legal status: compulsory licensing 17; of the PA 78–82
legitimacy: compulsory licences 41–2; of the PA 67
legitimate differentiation 13, 32–7, 39, 135
less favourable treatment 110, 128, 129
liability 71
life-saving pharmaceutical products: public interest and 14
"like-product" analysis 32–7; GMOs 125, 136; health risks 37–9, 182; as a threshold device 39
likeness: of pharmaceutical patents and other patents 153
limited: interpretation of 148
limited exceptions 108, 147
limited interpreted 131
Lin, T-Y. 9
living modified organisms (LMOs) 51, 100, 101, 102
living standards 7, 32
loss of life: as trigger for compulsory licensing 42
low probability of a serious harm 71, 78

Maastricht Treaty 58
magnitude of harm 72, 77
Major Groups: in United System 73
"march-in" rights 15
margin of appreciation: in adoption of PA measures 90, 133; compulsory licensing 19; exercising precautionary entitlements 114; national security 116, 149; safety factor as, in patent protection 25
margin of safety: in ADI 98; compulsory licensing 172, 185–6; employment of 71; the PA as 104; in policy-making 49; public engagement and 74; risk

management 72, 149, 183; risk regulation 135
marine environment: the PA in 50, 54
Mascher, S. 80
Matthews, D. 17
measurable harm 66
meat/meat products *see EC – Hormones*
medicine/drugs: access to *see* access to medicines; beyond IP 22–3; compulsory licensing 16, 164; prices/pricing *see* prices/pricing; stockpiling 17, 42, 91, 160, 161, 162, 175; test of efficacy 151, *see also* essential medicines; generic drugs
Médicins Sans Frontières 185
member autonomy (WTO): in the limitation of IP 34; public health protection 12; to invoke GATT XXI 117
member discretion (EC): in determining ALOP 61
member discretion (WTO): adoption of health measures 112; in determining *ordre public* 150; in determining security 113; in risk management 116
menthol cigarettes 129
Mexican tuna 130
Millennium Development Goals (MDGs) 8
minority opinion 107
minority scientific evidence 69
mitigating action 75
Model Essential Drugs List (WHO) 11
moderate PA 74, 76, *77*, 81, 82–3, 88, 93, 95, 99, 127, 140, 160
monitoring: duty of 55, 180
Monopolies Commission Report 16
monopoly 22, 151, 182
morality 146, 150
mortality rate: flu (H5N1) 161
Most-Favoured-Nation (MFN) treatment 11, 33
Motaal, D.A. 69
MOX Plant case 69
multilateral environmental agreements (MEAs) 100, *see also* Cartagena Protocol on Biosafety

national emergency: accommodation of PA into the identification of 32; compulsory licensing 15, 156, 164; concept of 161; ethical differentiation 135; provisional limitation of patent protection 172; redefining through precaution and risk management 191; right to determine what constitutes 157; TRIPS interpretation 19

230 *Index*

National Health Vigilance Agency *see* ANVISA
National Institute for Health and Care Excellence 47
National Institute for Health and Clinical Excellence (NICE) 47, 52, 59
National Institute for Intellectual Property (INPI) 152, 153
national security 113, 115, 116, 148, 149, 150
national treatment (NT) principle 11, 33, 39, 110
necessary: definition in exception rules 131
necessity 122
necessity test 109, 112–13, 126, 128, 158, 177–8
Netherlands 9
New Zealand 55–6, 67, 70
Nexavar 162–4
"no toxic effect" level 98
"no-observed effect" level 98
non-discrimination 9, 11, 33–4, 40, 59, 122, 128, 135
non-economic values 12, 104
non-governmental organizations (NGOs) 9, 48, 162, 184, 185
non-product-related standards 128
non-scientific factors 64, 107, 161, 181–5, 193–4
non-scientific values 52
non-tariff barriers 11, 33, 104
notifiable diseases 90–1
notification: of PHEIC 90; states' duties 92–3; triggering compulsory licensing 159; under the AIA 101
Novartis case 150–1
Nuffield Council on Bioethics 47, 52, 80
nutrition: right to 8

obligations *see* states' rights and obligations
"one-size-fits-all" approach 14, 34, 116
ongoing duty of monitoring and review 180
ontological uncertainty 68
ordre public 40, 150
Oseltamivir (Tamiflu) 161, 162
over-regulation: risk of 71
ozone depletion 51, 53

pandemic alert 161, 174–6, 180
pandemic preparedness 17, 32, 42, 176, 177, 179, 184
pandemics: containment 172; global demand for vaccines 172; as price of economic development 24, *see also* influenza; SARS

Paris Minimum Standards of Human Rights Norms in a State of Emergency 19
participatory decision-making 71, 72, 73, 181
patent laws: Brazil 152; Britain 16; data protection 22; differentiation based on field of technology 36; France 40; inclusion of the PA 150; India 8; US 154, *see also individual acts*
patent protection: and innovation 164; pharmaceuticals 9–10, 11, 12–13, 36, 37, 164; provisional limitation in national emergency 172; public health exclusions 40; risk analysis and the PA in 24–5; TRIPS 6; US 15
patent rights: exceptions to 34, 146, 147, 158; legal hierarchy of the PA, TRIPS *159*; limiting *see* trimming; as territorial 14
patentability 146; ANVISA 152, 153; exclusions 21, 40; Novartis case 150–1
Patents Acts: Canada 147–8; India 150, 163; UK 16, 39
patents/system: compulsory licensing 18; problems due to globalized regime 22; proposal to reform 23; unfairness of 22, *see also* pharmaceutical patents
patients: as main consumers of pharmaceuticals 181–2
Perez, O. 75
Perrez, F.X. 62–3, 80
Peru 128, 129
Pfizer Animal Health v. Council of the EU 59–60, 69
pharmaceutical industry 15, 38
pharmaceutical patents: ANVISA 152, 153; challenge to, US 154; differential treatment of adopting the PA in compulsory licensing of 173–4; IPRs, United States 20–1; protection 9–10, 11, 12–13, 36, 37, 164; US challenge to 154
pharmaceutical policies: and essential medicines 11
pharmaceutical products: inclusion in the IP regime 164; patients as main consumers of 181–2; public interest and life-saving 14; TRIPS-plus 21
Phase 3 (pandemic alert) 161, 175
Phase 4 (pandemic alert) 175, 176, 180
Phase 5 (pandemic alert) 176, 180
Philippines – Taxes on Distilled Spirits 35–6
physical properties: "like product" analysis 35
pig culling 91
plague 91
Plavix 162

Pogge, T. 22, 23
policy-making: public engagement 181
political component: in risk assessments 61
political objectives 60
political reality: access to medicines 18
political situations: compulsory licensing 183
pork imports: banning of foreign 91
positive right: compulsory licensing as 17
post-grant exemptions 36
post-grant measure 154–65
post-grant opposition 154
potential harm/damage 48, 50–1, 136, 179
power asymmetry: access to medicines 18
power-oriented diplomacy 18
pre-grant issues 36
pre-grant measure 150–3
pre-grant opposition 151
precaution: as contentious in relation
    to health exception provision 108;
    distinguished from prevention 50–1;
    enabling 49; legitimate differentiation of
    technologies 39; priority over scientific
    justification 47
precautionary action 64, 65, 69,
    70–1; based on risk assessment 150;
    compulsory licensing as a 155–6
precautionary approach 3; as an evolving
    principle 79; and compulsory licensing
    171–4; development of 47; distinction
    between PP and 79–82; formulations
    47–9; inclusion in patent laws 150; legal
    status and terminology 78–82; legitimate
    differential treatment of pharmaceutical
    technologies 32; as mandatory 65,
    70; models 63–4, 77; origins and
    applications 49–61; philosophical
    elements 62–78; redefinition of 139–40;
    regimes conflict and 136–8; research
    see research; as a safety valve in IP
    regime 24–5; as supplementing gap in
    scientific evidence 190; TRIPS 164–5;
    unknown risks and the adoption of 39; in
    the WHO 88–100; in the WTO 103–34
precautionary bans 71
precautionary entitlements 52, 66, 82, 134,
    193; compulsory licensing 177–9, 183;
    margin of appreciation in exercising
    114; in TRIPS 146–7, 172
precautionary measures: international
    references to 62
precautionary principle: criticism of 71;
    distinction between PA and 79–82;
    the EU and 56–61; in international
    law 79; international references to 62;

justification for public policy actions 48;
    lack of consensus on term 50; Sandin
    model 63; as statement of commonsense
    50, see also Communication on the
    Precautionary Principle
Precautionary Tripod 63, 65, 77
prescriptive PA 65, 70, 75, 76, 140;
    ANVISA as 153; compulsory licensing
    as 159; in risk management 138; in
    TRIPS 148; in the WHO 95, 98, 99; in
    the WTO 113, 117, 127, 130, 133
preservation of human life and health 178
prevention: precaution distinguished from
    50–1
preventive measures 60, 69
preventive principle 50
prices/pricing (drugs) 10, 23, 147, 163; high
    8, 22; reduction 8, 16, 18, 41, 160, 164
Principle 15 (Rio Declaration) 47–8, 65,
    66, 69, 102
principle: use of term 80, 81
prior consent mechanism: ANVISA 152–3
prior information 71
private interests 13, 16
private property: TRIPS and intact
    protection of 136
private rights: public interest and the
    taking of 14
product differentiation 128
product regulation 128
product standards 128
product-related standards 128
product/technology: legitimate
    differentiation 13; probability of serious
    harm and ban on 64, 71
products, process and production methods
    (PPMs) 128
Prohibitory Precautionary Approach (PPA)
    64, 71
proportionality 52, 59, 63, 70, 71, 76
proportionality test 109, 110, 112
propriety rights: data protection 21
protected interests: and acceptance of
    health measures 178
protectionism 11, 62, 66, 76, 114, 116
protective measures 59–60, 61, 62
provisional approach: compulsory
    licensing 179
provisional measures: adoption of 55–6,
    58; SPS 56, 76, 120–1, 132, 133
public emergency 19
public engagement/participation 72–4,
    89, 140; compulsory licensing 184;
    government provision of channels for

232 *Index*

183–4; pandemic preparedness 184; policy-making 181; public health emergency 78; risk communication as 97; risk management 72, 82, 181
public fear: desired level of protection 107
public health: comprehensive use of PA 137; concerns, and the implementation of TRIPS 10; Doha Declaration 156–60; ethics and the PA 50; globalization as a double-edged sword 24; importance of precaution in 47; laws, state's obligation regarding 7; NICE guidance 47; protection *see* health protection; relationship between TRIPS and 154; strategy, obligation to implement 7; as a trade concern 11
public health emergency: autonomous right to employ health measures 150; burden of proof 149; compulsory licensing 17, 174–85; declaration of, at domestic level 19; public engagement 78; right to health 11; risk management 41
public health emergency of international concern (PHEIC): compulsory licensing 14; declaration of a 91; definition 90; failure to declare 18–20; notification 90; scope 90–1; security exception 149; state sovereignty and autonomy 95; states' rights and duties under 91–3
Public Health, Innovation and Intellectual Property Rights (CIPIH) 10, 11, 19
public interest(s): adoption of health measures 13; compulsory licensing 17; ethical differentiation 135; exceptions to patent rights 34; morality 150; promoting balance between private interests and 13, 16; taking of private rights 14; technologies associated with 38
public non-commercial use: and compulsory licensing 15–17, 162
public policy: ethical differentiation 135
public risk 90

quality: right to health 7
quantitative risk assessment (QRA) 51, 69
quarantine 91, 93, 121

rapid virus transmission 174
reaction 49
real, grave and imminent peril 54, 55
reasonable available alternative measure 178
reasonable period of time 57, 122, 138, 156, 179, 180
regimes conflict: and the PA 136–7

Regulatory Exception (Canada Patents Act) 147–8
research: contributions 5–6; limitation 3–4; parameters 3; on risk and monitoring 71; structure 4–5
research and teaching exception 147
residual risks 68
response teams (WHO) 91
restrictive in scope, extent, amount 148
retaliation 12, 18, 41, 146, 163, 165, 190, 193
retreaded tyres 111–12
reversal of burden of proof 71, 76, 105, 106, 132
reverse engineering 16
review: importer's obligation to 102–3; necessity of 74; precaution as part of 63, *see also* duty to review
right(s): of states *see* states; to health 3, 6–25, 88, 152, 177; to information 67, 78; to life 8; to protect public health 133; to retaliate 12, *see also* autonomous right(s); conditional right(s)
Rio Declaration on Environment and Development 47–8, 66, 69, 72–3, 75, 102
risk(s): acceptable level of 74; burden of disclosing 72; as contentious in relation to health exception provision 108; environmental 51, 54; hypothetical approach 69; levels of 68; minimization, virus transmission 89; of over-regulation 71; willingness to take/accept 24, 107, *see also* unacceptable risk; uncertain risks; unknown risks; zero risk
risk analysis 24–5, 72, 89, 97–8, 99, 171, 190
risk assessment(s): adoption of protective measures 60, 62; and the AIA procedure 101; as basis for health policy 123; and the CPB 102; as determining unacceptable risk 60; importance of basing SPS measures on 124; level of unacceptable risk 67; and the PA 61, 81, 89, 99, 150; probabilistic 183; qualitative 69; quantitative 51, 69; scientific 52, 55, 61, 63, 125, 176; steps 97, 98; technical 183
risk communication 67, 72, 73–4, 97
risk management: avoidance of rigidity 135; deliberative democracy 183; ethical differentiation 135; of GMOs 125; labelling as 128; legitimate differentiation of technologies 39; margin of discrimination in 116; the PA and 47, 53, 89, 138, 174–5; precaution as part of 63; process 97, 98; provisional

Index   233

suspension of the exclusiveness of patent protection 154; public engagement 72, 82, 181; public health emergency 41; time factor in 179, *see also* emergency risk management for health

risk perception 72, 107

risk regulation: AIDS-contaminated blood 37; inclusion of public perception of risk 107; influence of PA 63; in international law 23–5; the PA and 47, 49; precaution-prevention distinction 50; as primary task in WTO legislation 12; risk communication in 73–4

risk society 25, 39, 190

Roche 161

Rodrigues, E.B. 148

rule-oriented diplomacy 18

Russia 91

Rwanda 20

safety: protection of human 9

safety factor: in ADI standard 98; adopting PA as 39; in TRIPS 3, *see also* margin of safety

safety net: the PA as 52, 72, 155

safety valve: the PA as 24–5, 49, 114, 116, 132, 191

Sandin, P. 63, 64, 65, 70, 77, 179

Sands, P. 62, 76

sardinops sagax 128–9

SARS 19, 24, 89, 91, 93, 161

scholarly approaches: on definition of the PA 82

scientific assessment 52, 55, 61, 63, 125, 176

scientific developments: examination of 59, 180

scientific evidence: adoption of additional health measures 95; PA as supplementing gap in 190; product bans and 135–6; subsequently proven harmful effects without 136, *see also* lack of scientific evidence

scientific justification 72, 122; adoption of health measures 165, 174; Cartagena Protocol 138; complaints about lack of, *EC – Biotech* 125; duty to review 179; in exception rules 131; higher level of health protection 120; precautionary actions 150; priority of precaution over 47; trade bans 109

scientific principles: and adoption of additional health measures 95

scientific uncertainty: adoption of additional health measures 95, 108;

Codex Alimentarius 99; duty to review 180; and the PA 50, 51, 52, 63, 89, 176; protective measures 60; provisional measures 55; SPS Agreement 119, 132; as triggering threshold 67–70, 75

Section 3(d) (Indian Patents Act) 151

Section 41 (UK Patents Act) 39

Section 55.2 (Canada Patents Act) 147–8

Section 907(a)(1)(A) (FFDCA) 129

security: and the PP 56

security exception (GATT) 108, 113; definition of necessary 131; precautionary measures under 114–16; purpose of 113–14; rules and principles of the PA under 116–18; strong PA 130

security exception (TRIPS) 148–9

sensitivity (human): as an additional safety factor 98

serious health impact 92

serious or irreversible harm/damage: implementation of the PA 54; obligation to avoid 52; the PA as mandatory 65; provisional SPS measures 120; state's right to act 64, 70; as a threshold 66–7, 75, 178; to the environment 48, 49, 52

shelter: right to 8

significant harm/damage: definition 66; state's right to act 64, 70; as a threshold 66, 67, 82; uncertain risks regarded as valid 135

significant risk(s): duty of notification 92; implementation of the PA 54, 65; product categorization 136

significant threshold: compulsory licensing and 172; unknown risk 140

Singapore 93

social preferences 107, 182–3

social services: right to 8

socio-economic considerations 13, 102, 116, 135, 157–8

Somsen, H. 49, 64

South Africa 8, 15, 17

South African Medicines and Related Substances Control Amendment Act 15

Southern Bluefin Tuna Case 55–6, 67, 70

Special 301 Priority Watch List 162

SPS Agreement 3, 118; ALOP 106–7, 119–20; applicability to GATT health exception 108, 110–11; burden of proof 76; Cartagena Protocol versus 137–8; case studies 121–6; compulsory licensing 160; food safety 96; IHRs versus 137; necessity test in 178; the PA in 51, 79, 126–7, 132–3; provisional

234 *Index*

measures 56, 120–1, 132, 133; purpose of 118

standards *see* food standards; international standards; living standards; technical standards

state(s): hesitation in granting compulsory licenses 191; precautionary entitlements *see* precautionary entitlements; rights and duties 52, 63–4, 65, 82, 91–3, 95, 114; rights and obligations 7, 52, 61, 64, 177

state autonomy 95, 157, 159

state discretion 114, 135, 149, 177, 183

state responsibility 37, 52–3, 64, 134, 172, 177

state sovereignty 36, 93, 95, 157, 171–2, 177, 183

State stewardship model 52, 134, 172, 177

Statute of the International Court of Justice 79

Stiglitz, J.E. 151

Stockpiling Exception (Canada Patents Act) 148

stockpiling medicines 17, 42, 91, 160, 161, 162, 175

Streinz, R. 56

strong PA 74, 75, 76, *77*, 118, 130, 153

substitutability: and likeness 36

Sunstein, C. 63, 64, 71–2, 75, 77, 78, 149, 155, 180, 183

Supplementary Protection Certificate (SPC) system 36

Sweden 164

Sweden – Import Restrictions on Certain Footwear 114–15

swine flu (H1N1) 9, 17, 24, 91

Switzerland 164

Taiwan 41, 160–1

Taiwan Intellectual Property Office (TIPO) 161

Tamiflu 161, 162

tangible harm 66

Taubman, A. 18, 19, 21, 155

TBT Agreement 3, 127; case studies 128–30; the PA in 133; technical regulations 127–8

technical advice 184

technical regulations (TBT) 127–8

technical risk assessments 183

technical standards 128

technical surveillance 174

technological collaboration 91

technological innovation 13, 38, 147

technology: enabling precaution 49; patent protection 5, *see also* biotechnology; field of technology; health technologies; product/technology

temporary ADI 98

temporary recommendations (WHO) 95

temporary safety valve: SPS provisional measures as 132

Thailand 15, 17, 19, 160, 162

Thailand – Cigarettes 109–10

therapeutic efficacy 151

they consider necessary 113, 114

threat of harm 65, 66

three-step test 148, 177

threshold (triggering): compulsory licensing 17, 19, 172, 174–6; irreversible damage to human life and health 178; "it considers necessary" standard 115–16; real, grave and imminent peril as 55; risk assessment 81; scientific uncertainty as 67–70; "serious or irreversible" harm as a 66–7; significant harm as 66, 82; to distinguish between strong and weak PA 75–6; unknown risk 140

Tickner, J. 49, 51

time factor: duty to review 179, 180

time restraints: and government announcements 176

Tinker, C. 74

toxicity 35

trade: agreements 10, 20–1; conflicts over GMO labelling 100; globalization 24; liberalism 24, 33, 104; liberalization 12, 115; retaliations 12, 18, 41, 146, 163, 165, 190, 193; sanctions 104, 162, 163; supremacy 134–6, *see also* free trade; international trade; least restrictive to trade

Trade-Related Aspects of Intellectual Property Rights *see* TRIPS

Transatlantic Consumer Dialogue 34

transboundary harm: significant 66

transboundary movements: of LMOs 101

transboundary waste dumping 53

transient mutation of a virus: duty to review 179

transparency 52, 63, 181

travel 24, 92

travel bans 91

Treaty on the Functioning of the European Union (TFEU) 57, 58, 73, 75

Treves J 80

triggering threshold *see* threshold

Index 235

trimming 71–2, 149; legitimacy under threat to national security 150, *see also* ANVISA; compulsory licensing
TRIPS 3, 6; amendment 20; Articles *see* Articles; compulsory licensing 14–17, 171–3, 180; consideration of public health concerns in implementing 10; failure to declare a PHEIC 18–20; flexibilities *see* flexibilities in; health exceptions 147–8; health exclusions 149–65; IP rights as not entailing unwarranted delays 153; necessity test 178; non-discrimination 33–4; objectives and principles 13–14; precautionary approach 164–5; precautionary entitlements 146–7; protection of pharmaceutical patents 9–10, 11, 12–13; protection of private property 136; safety factor in 3, *see also* Doha Declaration
TRIPS-plus 17–18, 21
Trouwborst, A. 52, 54, 62, 63–4, 65, 66, 70, 71, 77, 82
tuna 55–6, 67, 70, 130

UN: General Comments *see* General Comments; proliferation of the PA 53–6
UN Charter 7, 54, 89, 149
UN Commissions on Human Rights Resolution 10
UN Committee on Economic, Social and Cultural Rights (CESCR) 6, 7
UN Conference on Trade and Development and the International Centre for Trade and Sustainable Development (UNCTAD-ICTSD) 22
UN Convention on Biological Diversity 75
UN Convention on the Law of the Sea (UNCLOS) 55–6
UN International Covenant on Economic, Social and Cultural Rights (ICESCR) 6, 7, 37
UN Millennium Project 8
unacceptable risk 60, 66, 67
uncertain risks 68, 128, 135–6
uncertainty: analysis 89; burden of disclosing 72; and enabling precaution 49; models of the PA 65; WHO report 89, *see also* scientific uncertainty
undisclosed data: protection of 21
undue delay 125, 126, 133, 138, 153, 163
unfair commercial use: protection of undisclosed data 21
unfairness: of patent monopoly system 22

United Kingdom 16, 69
United States: challenge to pharmaceutical patents 154; compulsory licensing 15, 160, 162; *EC – Biotech* 125; *EC – Hormones* 124; Helms-Burton Act 115–16; and *Japan Varietals* 121–2; Patent law 154; pharmaceutical patents and IPRs 20–1; suit against Brazilian IPL 16; trade sanction against Thailand 162; Wingspread Conference 48
United System 73
Universal Declaration of Human Rights 6, 7
unknown risks: adoption of the PA 39; free trade and 12; globalization and increased 40; legitimacy of the PA 67; management of 72; public participation in expressing concerns 183–4; significant threshold 140
unlike products 33, 38, 128
"unreasonable and otherwise unmanageable risk" 66
Uruguay Round 118
US – Cloves 129
US – Gasoline 109, 110
US – Tuna 130

vaccines 17, 172, 174
values *see* non-economic values; non-scientific values
VanderZwaag, D. 74
variability: uncertainty due to 68
varietal testing requirement 121–2
Vicuña, O. 80
Vienna Convention on the Law of Treaties (VCLT) 13, 106
virus surveillance: global 89–96, 161, 172
virus transmission: autonomous right to employ health measures 150; as challenge to values and rights of states 23; free trade and possibility of 11; globalization and increased 40; international stockpiling of vaccines 17, 174; risk minimization 89
voluntary labels 128
voluntary licences 156, 172
Vorsorgeprinzip 51

Waiver Decision (2003) 20
wastefulness: due to globalized patent regime 22
weak PA 74, 75, 76, 77, 130, 148
weighing and balancing process 109, 110, 112

236 Index

willingness to accept risk 24, 107
Wingspread Conference 48, 75
World Charter for Nature (UN) 53–4
World Health Assembly (WHA) 10, 17
World Health Organization (WHO) 3,
10–11; Action Programme on Essential
Drugs 7; Checklist for Influenza
Pandemic Preparedness Planning 176;
Dealing with Uncertainty Report 89;
emergency risk management for
health 24; Globalization and Access
to Drugs 10; goal of 9, 88; GOARN
91, 175; government leadership in
preparedness and response 177;
institutional clash between WTO and
9–10; Model Essential Drugs List 11;
the PA in 88–100; on problem of PP
principle 50

World Intellectual Property Organization
(WIPO) 185
World Medical Association 185
World Trade Organization (WTO) 3;
Appellate Body *see* Appellate Body;
Articles *see* Articles; burden of proof
76; deference to national autonomy
159; dispute settlement *see* Dispute
Settlement Body; Dispute Settlement
System; institutional clash between
WHO and 9–10; members *see* member
autonomy; member discretion; the PA
in 103–34; principles and exemptions
9, 11–12, 104, 105–6, 130–4, *see also*
GATT; SPS Agreement; TRIPS
worst-case scenario 71

zero risk 37, 59, 69, 120